Mary J. Capito

Ashland School.

WORDS,
SOUNDS, &
THOUGHTS

OTHER CITATION PRESS BOOKS
BY DOROTHY HENNINGS

Smiles, Nods, and Pauses: Activities to Enrich Children's Communication Skills, 1974

Keep Earth Clean, Blue and Green: Environmental Activities for Young People (with George Hennings), 1976

WORDS, SOUNDS, & THOUGHTS

More Activities to Enrich Children's Communication Skills

DOROTHY GRANT HENNINGS

PROFESSOR OF EDUCATION
KEAN COLLEGE OF NEW JERSEY

Citation Press/Scholastic   New York   1977

Library of Congress Cataloging in Publication Data
Hennings Dorothy Grant.   Words, sounds, and thoughts.
Bibliography: p.   1.   Language arts (Elementary)   I.   Title.
   LB1576.H337   1977   372.6'044   76-57242
   ISBN 0-590-09616-8 (paper)   ISBN 0-590-07522-5 (hardcover)

Cover and book design by Kathleen F. Westray

1   2   3   4   5   81   80   79   78   77

FOR REPRINT PERMISSION, GRATEFUL ACKNOWLEDGEMENT IS MADE TO:

Argus Communications and Richard Lessor, copyright holders for "Happiness is like a butterfly."

Atheneum Publishers, Inc. for "Be My Non-Valentine" and "A Cliché" from IT DOESN'T ALWAYS HAVE TO RAIN by Eve Merriam, copyright © 1964 by Eve Merriam; and "Sound of Fire" from WHAT IS THAT SOUND! by Mary O'Neill, text copyright © 1966 by Mary O'Neill.

Ruth Belov Gross for "Rain" from THE LAUGH BOOK, text copyright © 1971 by Ruth Belov Gross.

Harper & Row, Publishers, Inc. for the excerpt from CHARLOTTE'S WEB by E. B. White, copyright, 1952, by E. B. White.

King Features for Henry by John Liney, © King Features Syndicate, Inc. 1974.

Alfred A. Knopf, Inc. for "Dreams" from THE DREAMKEEPER & OTHER POEMS by Langston Hughes, copyright 1932 by Alfred A. Knopf, Inc. and renewed 1960 by Langston Hughes.

Macmillan Publishing Co., Inc. for "Two Old Crows" from COLLECTED POEMS by Vachel Lindsay, copyright 1917 by Macmillan Publishing Co., Inc. Renewed 1945 by Elizabeth C. Lindsay.

Rand McNally & Co. for the excerpts from WOULD YOU PUT YOUR MONEY IN A SAND BANK? by Harold Longman, copyright 1968 Harold S. Longman.

Random House, Inc. for the excerpt from PLAY ON WORDS by Alice and Martin Provenson, copyright © 1972 by Alice and Martin Provenson. Saturday Review Press/E.P. Dutton & Co. for "Blow Up" from STREET POEMS by Robert Froman, copyright © 1971 by Robert Froman.

· To my husband George, ·
who always helps

·

CONTENTS

Words are the bridges we build
To reach each other.

"THE WRITTEN WORD," MARY O'NEILL

BEFORE BEGINNING

his book is a source—

a source of activities in which youngsters process and produce language as they think about things around them.

This book is a means—

a means through which teachers can bring students into contact with the myriad ways verbal language is used.

This book is a beginning—

a beginning on which teachers can base their own original activities to enrich children's communication skills.

This book is a plea—

a plea to make language learning relevant and pleasurable for young people in schools, whether English be their first or second language.

A note of appreciation is due those who made it possible for me to write *Words, Sounds, and Thoughts.* The help of Karen Leder, librarian at Woodland and Washington Valley schools, Warren, New Jersey, is sincerely appreciated. It was Ms. Leder who first used the book *Mushroom in the Rain* with Bach's "Air on the G String" and the film loop *Mushroom Growth and Reaction*, as described in chapter one. Special thanks go also to the students in my 1975 graduate seminar in language arts at Kean College of New Jersey; many of these students, who teach in elementary schools in New Jersey, served as sounding boards for embryonic ideas. Some, including Margery Frey, Nancy Pappas, Barbara Woods, and John Venezia, shared with me activities that had proved successful in their own classrooms. Similar thanks go to the teachers in Edison, New Jersey, with whom I share many ideas in workshop sessions and in whose classrooms the activities became more fully developed.

I thank also Vagn Söndeby of the Hotel Australia in Vejle,

Denmark, for supplying me with a copy of the helpful book *Language Service* (Copenhagen: International Language Service Ltd.), which gave me the idea of making language comparison charts. An appreciative thank you goes to Bente Bentsen for introducing me to the old tales of Mols found in the closing pages.

To my editor at Citation Press, Mary Allison, who supplied encouragement, ideas, and editorial assistance, I once again say a sincere thank you. And to my husband, George, who as always read, reread, proofread, contributed ideas too numerous to mention, and encouraged, I say thank you, thank you, thank you, repeating as the Ashanti do to emphasize the extent of my appreciation.

WORDS,
SOUNDS, &
THOUGHTS

Be patient, O be patient! Put your ear
  against the earth;
Listen there how noiselessly the germ o'
  the seed has birth;
How noiselessly and gently it upheaves its
  little way
Till it parts the scarcely broken ground, and
  the blade stands up in day.

"PATIENCE," WILLIAM JAMES LINTON

1. PUTTING YOUR EAR AGAINST THE EARTH: *Integrating Language Activities*

The window blinds in the story corner of Andrea Russell's classroom were drawn, hinting of interesting things soon to happen. Squatting on the carpet in various positions of repose were twenty-nine third graders; all were bright eyed with anticipation bred by previous sessions in the story corner. . . .

Traditionally the elementary language arts have been defined in terms of four basic skill and interest areas—reading and listening (often considered input or receptive skills) and speaking and writing (considered output or expressive skills). The advantage of this traditional conception of the language arts is that it clarifies the kinds of language learnings classroom teachers are responsible for helping youngsters acquire.

On the other hand, there is a serious disadvantage in conceiving of the language arts as composed of four major elements. Such a conception can lead to lessons that focus on just one of the language arts areas. The result is a program of unrelated reading sessions, composition times, oral reporting periods, and so forth. Clearly such fragmentation is not educationally desirable, nor is it necessary, as the following real-life examples indicate.

EXPERIENCES CAN MUSHROOM!

Ms. Russell, book in hand, placed herself on a low chair at the front of her eager third graders. "Are you ready for another excursion into story land?" she asked.

The children responded with an immediate "Yes!" And so she began. Holding the book with its cover facing the children, Ms. Russell read the title, *Mushroom in the Rain* by Mirra Ginsburg (Macmillan, 1974). Flipping to the first page and simultaneously lowering the needle onto a record lying in readiness on the player nearby, she started to read. The story was a simple one adapted from a Russian tale about an ant, a butterfly, a little mouse, a sparrow, and a rabbit who all take refuge under a mushroom cap during a rain shower. This is possible because mushrooms grow when it rains. The musical accompaniment provided by the recording, Bach's "Air on the G String," played with kotos, shakuhachi, guitar, bass, and drums to produce a "new sound from the Japanese Bach scene," harmonized perfectly with the rhythm and mood of the story.

When she finished the story, Andrea Russell snapped off the lights and switched on the Super-8 continuous film loop projector she had prefocused on a screen. To the continuing sound of kotos and shakuhachi, filmed mushroom spores sent out finger-like growths from which mushroom heads pushed their way upward, expanding in a dance-like rhythm that was almost hypnotic.

When the loop (*Mushroom Growth and Reaction,* Eyegate, Jamaica, NY 11435) came to the end and Ms. Russell stopped the Bach recording, the third graders clapped. Again without saying a word, she opened an ordinary brown paper bag that she had tucked under her chair. Out came a real mushroom and another and another. Eager hands reached out to grasp a mushroom until each held one.

Now came talk time. "What makes mushrooms grow in the rain? What do we mean when we say 'His problems mushroomed'? What do we mean when we say 'Money put in a bank will mushroom'? What words can we use to describe our mushrooms? What do mushrooms look like? What texture do we feel when we touch mushrooms? How are all our mushrooms similar? How do our mushrooms differ?" were just a few of the questions the teacher posed to trigger talk.

As the children brainstormed, their teacher wrote with a green flo-pen on a large piece of charting paper mounted on an easel, recording key words such as: *growing, soft, white, tossing, turning, brown-flecked, velvety, satiny, leaning, bending, dancing, protecting, tiny, gills, rain shower, dripping, dry, cap, stalk, moving, twisting, expanding.* Other words such as *orange, spotted, colorful, dangerous, hooded,* and *poisonous* were added as students began to talk about plastic models of several different poisonous varieties of mushrooms that Ms. Russell held up for all to see. A colorful mushroom poster mounted on a bulletin board ("A Guide to Edible and Poisonous Mushrooms," Garden Shop, Brooklyn Botanical Garden, 1000 Washington Avenue, Brooklyn, NY 11225) also stimulated discussion.

The chart was filled with words when Ms. Russell put down her pen. She lowered it to the floor, where it was still visible to the youngsters sitting there, and placed a fresh piece of charting paper on the easel. "Let's use some of these words to write a mushroom puff," she proposed. Writing the word *mushroom* across the top of the new sheet, she asked students to find words on the first chart that described the appearance of the mushrooms they still held in their hands. They picked *soft, white, brown-flecked, velvety, tiny* and then reordered them to read *tiny, velvety soft, white and flecked with brown,* which they said "sounded nice together and made sense." The teacher recorded these words as a second line.

Ms. Russell next asked students to give her *-ing* words that described what mushrooms do in the rain. They selected *growing, leaning, dancing,* and *dripping* in that order. Andrea Russell recorded these as a third line of the puff. She was about to go on when one boy suggested the need to add *in the rain* at the end of the line for "that is when mushrooms grow." Since these were his words, the youngster recorded them himself.

Moving to another idea, Ms. Russell asked her students to think of a real object that a mushroom looked like. The class answered almost in chorus, "An umbrella!" A girl noted that it was not a people umbrella but an animal umbrella. Another proposed that umbrellas could be called parasols, "Wouldn't it sound better to call a mushroom an animal parasol?" This could be the last line. A boy checked the spelling of parasol in the dictionary, and the last line was added to produce:

> Mushroom.
> Tiny, velvety soft, white and flecked with brown.
> Growing, leaning, dancing, dripping in the rain.
> An animal parasol.

When the students saw what they had produced together, they again clapped spontaneously. One youngster suggested they turn on the Bach record and read their piece in chorus to the Japanese sounds. This they did several times.

Then, because nonverbal expression was also a part of their classroom language activities, they became mushrooms to the musical accompaniment. Crouching low in huddled positions, they began to move slowly to simulate mushrooms growing, until all were fully upright with arms extended. They waved and bent to the music until they collapsed on the floor as they had seen real mushrooms do on the film loop. As a finale, one student read the poetic puff they had composed as a class, while others pantomimed mushroom growth to the now familiar sound of Bach's "Air on the G String."

After the third graders had repeated their brief pantomime for the sheer pleasure of it, their teacher described some related activities they might wish to try independently later on when time permitted. In a small box placed in a corner on the floor was a collection of other mushroom books. Some were imaginative tales such as Leo Lionni's *Theodore and the Talking Mushroom* (Pantheon, 1971) and Ruth Krauss's *Everything Under a Mushroom* (Four Winds, 1973). Others were more factual, such as Robert Froman's simple *Mushroom and Molds* (Crowell, 1972), Solveig Russell's more sophisticated *Toadstools and Such* (Steck-Vaughn, 1970), Dorothy Sterling's

The Story of Mosses, Ferns and Mushrooms (Doubleday, 1955) with its realistic photographs, and William C. Grimm and M. Jean Craig's *The Wondrous World of Seedless Plants* (Bobbs-Merrill, 1973) with its fine line drawings. Ms. Russell suggested that some children might enjoy going to the corner to read more about mushrooms and perhaps to draw diagrams of different kinds of seedless plants.

PURPOSE: To work with interesting words. To write sentences using these words.

DIRECTIONS:

1. Select a piece of colored construction paper.

2. Draw on it the outline of a large mushroom. Cut out the outline with your scissors.

3. On the perimeter, along the gills and under the cap, print words that have something to do with mushrooms. Use the dictionary to find and spell words correctly.

4. On an index card write a sentence describing your mushroom. Use words you have already recorded. Mount your card beneath your mushroom on the classroom bulletin board.

EXTRA ACTIVITY: If you finish your sentence writing and still have time, imagine what a growing mushroom would say if it could talk. Write a short story: "The Talking Mushroom."

She next described a word-art project they could pursue at the language and art station she had set up in another classroom area. This station presented an art-related activity with directions printed on a mushroom-shaped piece of orange construction paper tacked to a piece of scrap accoustical ceiling board placed on the floor. Students could work here individually or in pairs to produce their own mushroom shapes that they could mount on a nearby bulletin board.

Ms. Russell pointed to a corner station set up in what the third graders knew as their writing center. There on a large two-panel fold made from a cardboard box and covered with colorful contact paper was an activity titled Writing Nature Puffs. On the reverse side of the panels was a second writing option called Writing Nature Yarns. At least four third graders could undertake these two activities at one time.

WRITING STATION 1

WRITING NATURE PUFFS

A nature puff is four lines of writing.
Line 1 names an object found in nature.
Line 2 describes the appearance of the object.
Line 3 tells what the object does. It includes some -ing words.
Line 4 names something that the object is similar to or is like.

Here is an example of a puff.
Ferns.
Feathery, green, light.
Swaying, turning, twisting in the breeze.
Nature's fan.

PURPOSE: To learn to use words that describe.

DIRECTIONS: Select an object from nature such as an acorn, a snapdragon, an ant, a bee, a cactus, a fir tree, wheat, a jack-in-the pulpit, a palm tree, a coconut, a moth.

On one of the worksheets found below, write a puff about the object. Cross out and change words as much as you want. Then print your puff on a piece of colored construction paper. Put your finished work in the completed paper file.

WORKSHEET FOR PUFF WRITING

LINE I—Write the name of the nature thing.

_____

LINE II—Write some words that describe the nature thing.

_____

LINE III—Write some words that tell what the thing does. Use words that end in *-ing.*

_____

LINE IV—Write a creative comparison.

_____

WRITING STATION 2
(reverse of cardboard panels)

WRITING NATURE YARNS

In *Mushroom in the Rain* we read an imaginative story about a mushroom. We can write similar stories centered on some other objects in nature.

PURPOSE: To invent a story.

TASK: Decide upon a plant that can be the interest center of your story. If you need help, go through the slips of paper in the plastic bag at the right and select a plant from those suggested there.

Write a short story about something that could happen in, on, under, over, or by that plant. Use the paper found in the packet at the right. Put your finished paper in the pocket marked III. *Note:* You may draw some illustrations to help tell your story or write your story as a comic strip if you wish.

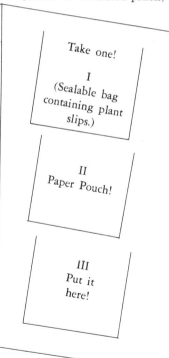

Take one!

I
(Sealable bag containing plant slips.)

II
Paper Pouch!

III
Put it here!

Some words to put on slips in the sealable plastic bag might be: dandelion, tree roots, moss, fern, blue spruce, walnut, decaying log, sunflower, lilac bush, cactus, lily pad, blade of grass, apple, tomato plant.

After explaining the reading, language and art, and writing stations so that youngsters who decided to work at these centers would know what they were expected to do in each case, Ms. Russell moved to a table in the classroom that had been pushed beneath a small bulletin board on which she had posted directions for this word-study station:

A WORD PUZZLE

PURPOSE: To identify relationships among words.

D
I
R
E
C
T
I
O
N
S

TASK A

INTRODUCTION: In English we sometimes call a mushroom a *toadstool.* In Dutch, the language spoken in Holland, the word for mushroom is *paddestoel. Pad* means "path" in Dutch; *stoel* means "chair" or "stool." In Danish the word for mushroom is *paddehatte.*

DIRECTIONS: Select any one of these words: *toadstool, mushroom, paddestoel,* or *paddehatte.* Write a story that tells how that word came to be used. Use your imagination to invent a way.

OR just write a sentence or two that explains why *paddestoel* or *paddehatte* is a good, sensible name for a mushroom.

Use the paper found on the table below. Put your finished papers in the basket on the table.

TASK B

DIRECTIONS: Look up the word *champignon* in the large dictionary on the table. On one of the index cards write down the meaning and the country of origin. Do the same for the word *fungus.* Put its meaning and the language from which we borrowed it on the other side of the card. Take the card to your desk and keep it safe until Friday. If you do this task, sign your name below:

> Sign here:

Andrea Russell reminded her third graders of the work the class had already done in finding out how certain words had come into the English language. She suggested that Kathie, Jeff, Pat, and Jake should try to come to this word station during independent study times, since these boys and girls were the class word detectives for the week—detectives responsible for tracking down word meanings, origins, and spellings. She assured the class that at this center they could either invent imaginative explanations of how mushrooms received one of their names or suggest entirely logical explanations.

Then Andrea Russell shifted gears and moved toward a science table. In individual sealable bags on the table were a pine cone, a pea pod, coffee beans, a sprouting onion, a piece of sassafras bark, a sprig of mint, a lime, a carrot, and a peach pit. On the table was a stack of mimeographed observation guides containing directions:

SCIENCE OBSERVATION CENTER

TASK: To learn to observe systematically.
To find words to describe firsthand observations.

DIRECTIONS:

1. Select one of the objects on the table. Take it from the bag. Examine its appearance, feel, smell, and heaviness carefully.

2. On the chart below, record words that describe these characteristics of the object.

3. When you have written down as many words as you can, combine the words into sentences. Write at least one sentence describing appearance, one describing feel or texture, one describing smell, and one describing heaviness.

4. Return the object to the bag and place your completed guide in the basket. You may repeat this activity several times, each time selecting a different object to observe.

Appearance Words   Texture Words   Smell Words   Heaviness Words

Sentences:

Ms. Russell briefly introduced this observational activity and named four students who definitely should add the science observational study to their independent study agenda. At this point she dismissed the youngsters to work at individual and group tasks. She herself moved with five children to the special instruction table to help them review how contractions are formed, a problem area she had noted in the written work of these girls and boys.

TAKING OFF FROM BASAL READERS

There are many different kinds of jumping-off points through which teachers can integrate language learnings. Ms. Russell jumped off with a story that had scientific overtones on which she could build both language skill and science understandings. She might just as well have chosen a story with social overtones such as portions of Richard Adams' *Watership Down* (Macmillan, 1972) or even a unit of work in the social studies. Working within a unit on Scandinavia, for example, children could have listened to fairy tales of Denmark and Norway, written their own, illustrated some, and gone on to make comparative studies of words in Scandinavian languages.

Another jumping-off point into integrated language arts experiences is the basal reader. Richard D'Angelo used this approach to integrate language learnings of fourth graders. The reader he used contained a brief introduction to Aesop's fables, followed by a selection of four fables. Rather than just having the children read, discuss the fables, and complete the related reading skill building activities in the accompanying workbook, he used the section as a springboard into listening, dramatization, oral interpretation of literature, writing, discussing, and thinking, as well as basic reading skills. Through this approach, he also helped students understand the fable as a form of literature possessing certain characteristics.

Mr. D'Angelo introduced the fable through a listening activity. The group listened to a taped rendition of "The Man, The Boy, and the Donkey," a fable not included in the basal, which the teacher had obtained from Educational Enrichment Materials (83 East Avenue, Norwalk, CT 06851). After the students had sat back and enjoyed the story, Mr. D'Angelo proposed, "We are going to listen again. This time after the story is finished, we are going to try to retell the story ourselves from memory. So let's listen to remember details." After re-listening, students tried to retell the story and did so rather successfully, even including the moral at the end.

Next the students turned to the first fable in their basal readers, "A Bundle of Sticks." Mr. D'Angelo suggested that they all read the story to see in what ways it was similar to the story they had just heard and retold. Students were quick to note that this story too had a moral lesson at the end. The words *moral, fable,* and *Aesop* were injected into the talk. The word detectives searched the large classroom dictionary for the meaning and origin of the words; they listed the words in a sentence on their New Words for the Week chart.

Instead of continuing the discussion to determine comprehension of the fable, the teacher moved the group into a spontaneous dramatization. Each student volunteered for a part, with one assuming the role of narrator. Because the fable as given in the reader was only a skeleton of the story with little dialogue and few details, the players had to extemporize and make up additional details and dialogue as they went along. In addition they had to invent their own non-verbal effects. The old man pretended to hold a cane and limped through his part; grunts, groans, and grimaces accompanied students' attempts to break the bundle of sticks.

When students had played and replayed "The Bundle of Sticks" for their own delight, Mr. D'Angelo showed them where they would find other fables in their books. He held up a box containing several books of fables. He suggested that each should independently read the three fables in the reader and at least one more fable from one of the books. Then individually or in small groups, they should select a fable to act out for the group. For instance, someone might select a single-character fable such as "The Crow and the Pitcher" to present as a monologue from the point of view of the crow. Two students might select a two-character fable such as "The Reed and the Oak" to present as a dialogue. Several students might pick a longer fable to dramatize as a group, or one student might simply prepare to read a short fable to a musical accompaniment selected from the record collection.

At the next formal lesson, Mr. D'Angelo helped with any logistical problems the fourth graders were encountering and then displayed the beginnings of a fable outline chart that looked like this:

FABLES WE HAVE WRITTEN			
Characters	Moral	Author	Title
1. Rooster, fox, dragon	A little knowledge is a dangerous thing		
2.			
3.			
4.			
5.			

"Today let's create our own fable as a group," he suggested. He gave a commercially produced hand puppet of a rooster to one child, a fox to a second, and a dragon to a third. (See Hammett's catalog, Vaux Hall Road, Union, New Jersey, for this type of puppet.) "Once upon a time and far away . . . ," he began, and then pointed to the boy holding the rooster to continue.

Tony added, "There was a rooster. . . ." After discussion, it was decided that to emphasize the moral with which this fable was to end—A little knowledge is a dangerous thing—the line should be revised to, "There was a silly rooster named Rick." Tony handed the puppet head to Stu.

Stu continued without prompting, "Rick lived in a barnyard and thought he knew everything there was to know about getting along." Passing the puppets from one to another, the students orally concocted a little story; they revised lines as they went along to add interesting details and to make the fable develop more logically. When they had put together a fable that led in a roundabout way to the moral, they talked as a group about a title for their fable. Following the pattern of other fables they had read, they decided that "The Silly Rooster" would serve quite well, and they recorded it on the Fables We Have Written chart. In the author column they recorded all their names. Two students who had taken a very active part in the oral story development volunteered to record their fable on tape. Incidentally, Mr. D'Angelo had selected this moral because *knowledge* was a word he wanted to stress with this group of students. By composing a story that led up to this word, students would deepen their understanding of it.

The teacher mounted the chart on the middle of three connected panels and told students that, as they could see, there was room for information about other fables that they could begin to write individually or in pairs. He indicated a listing of fable morals he had already prepared and mounted on the right-hand panel: "Don't put off until tomorrow what you can do today," "Live for today," "Look before you leap," "Where there is a will there is a way," and "In unity there is strength." Students could select one of these morals or invent one of their own.

Handing a stack of cards to two students, Mr. D'Angelo remarked that in order to write a fable, they would need to identify the characters involved. He suggested that the class brainstorm possible characters while the two scribes wrote the character names on cards, which would then be mounted on the left-hand panel. Students enjoyed calling out words such as moose, ass, mite, orangutan, and water buffalo, many of which had to be checked for spelling in the dictionary. Most were animal names. When asked why they tended to name animal characters, they replied that most of the fables they had read had dealt with animals.

Mr. D'Angelo asked, "What other kinds of characters have we encountered?" Students named characters such as reed, oak, old grandfather, mother, shepherd, and so forth. When a lengthy list of characters had been added to the left panel, Mr. D'Angelo reviewed the directions for this learning station. Students were to come to it individually or in pairs, select or invent a moral, decide on characters, and invent a fable. They could record their fable on paper or tape. When finished, they should think up a title and record it along with the moral, characters, and their names on the chart. A student quickly volunteered to write up a direction card and post it at the station.

Next the teacher held up several tapes of other fables. Two he had recorded himself; the others were from Educational Enrichment Materials. He announced he was putting them in the listening center so that students who needed some re- laxation could listen to an Aesop's fable once they had written fables of their own. Tapes the students made of their own fables would also be placed in the center.

Mr. D'Angelo also held up four filmstrips of fables he was putting in the viewing center. These strips had tape sound tracks; however, students could view them as "silents" and then try to devise their own sound tracks. Later they could share their sound tracks with other members of the group as they viewed a strip together.

The teacher reminded the students of one option that was always open to them—those who had completed the invention of a fable could go to the materials preparation center to prepare accompanying visuals. They could make transparencies to go with their fables, draw flat pictures, make puppet heads, or even produce a brief filmstrip by drawing with India ink or wax pencil on U-film (see Scholastic's catalog for information on filmstrip preparation materials).

Before dismissing the class, Mr. D'Angelo asked each student to announce where he or she would begin working. Two students who seemed a little unsure of what they were going to do during their independent study times stayed a moment longer with their teacher, who helped them write down an agenda to follow during work periods.

INTERACTIVE AND INDEPENDENT LEARNING ACTIVITIES

The wealth of commercially produced materials available is making an approach similar to Richard D'Angelo's and Andrea Russell's relatively simple today. The ease with which teachers can put together their own materials with the aid of technology simplifies the development of sequences integrating all the communication areas. Mr. D'Angelo used commercially prepared tapes and filmstrips to integrate listening and writing with basal reading activity and he used felt puppet heads to involve youngsters in oral story composing. In addition, he made some tapes of his own and urged students to make tapes and filmstrips as well as pictures and puppet heads.

The multitude of commercial learning materials and the comparative ease with which students and teachers can put materials together on their own also make possible the blend of guided interactive and independent activities so evident in Ms. Russell's and Mr. D'Angelo's classes. *Guided interactive* activities are those in which teachers lead students in conversing with one another. *Independent* activities are those in which students work on their own without direct verbal communication with the teacher.

Interactive sessions in which teacher and children talk and listen together as a class or in small groups are an essential aspect of language development programs. New words can be interjected into discussions by both teacher and children. Repeated in talk sessions, these words become an integral and meaningful part of children's speaking and listening vocabularies. Reinforcing words by writing them on class charts makes them useful additions to children's reading and writing vocabularies.

During talk sessions ideas can be brainstormed so that children feel the thrill of cooperative creation. Ideas formulated together can be ordered and recorded and used as a springboard for later individual creations. Thoughts can be shared so that children learn to respect and listen intently to the ideas of others. Spontaneous dramatizations can involve everyone, and composing together can make the process fun rather than tedious.

The benefits inherent in interactive teacher-led sessions have sometimes been underplayed when educators have stressed the value of independent learning activities. This may have come about because of the rigid manner in which interactive sessions have at times been structured. Too often they have been used for giving information to students sitting at desks in rows. In contrast the interactive sessions led by the two teachers in this chapter involved sharing, discussing, brainstorming, inventing together, spontaneous dramatization, choral speaking, direction giving, and so forth.

Interactive sessions are perhaps most successful when students gather together informally. Many teachers have found it convenient to have children sit on the floor for talk sessions or to arrange their chairs in a semi-circle around a central area of open classroom space.

Working with kindergarten groups of no more than fifteen, Ms. Lorraine Wilkening finds the latter conducive to maximum student participation. She also uses a rug at the center of her semi-circle as a composing stage on which to place word, sentence, and number cards as well as actual objects, all of which are clearly visible to each of the kindergarteners. Agile five- and six-year-olds can quickly leave their seats to move onto the rug to arrange cards and/or objects into related columns, rows, or whatever order is called for by the teacher's questions. Several students can work on the composing stage at one time. As they return to the perimeter, other students move forward to take their places so that there is the almost continuous action so necessary for young children.

Essentially the interactive sessions in this kindergarten, as in the third- and fourth-grade classes already described, involve talking and doing with the teacher guiding to develop specific language learnings. Often what young people talk about and do in the interactive sessions lays the foundation for related kinds of things they will be thinking about and doing independently. New skills, ideas, and materials are introduced; new processes are tried out.

Independent learning for which children have been sufficiently prepared is as important as interactive sessions. Independent reading in a wide range of materials builds vocabulary and comprehension skills as well as the reading habit. Individual and small group composing encourages the formulation of ideas and a logical organization that clearly communicates these ideas to others. Learning to research facts for writing and oral reporting can only occur through actual doing—by checking dictionaries, encyclopedias, and other references, by tracking down magazine articles for additional material, or by using card catalogs and bibliographical listings. These tasks are most successfully carried out by individuals or very small groups.

Activities carried on independently as part of a larger ongoing series of experiences make students assume some responsibility for their own learning. A young person must choose the activity or two on which to concentrate. He or she must decide the sequence in which to attack tasks to be done and the time to allocate to each aspect of a task. He or she must carefully listen and read to follow directions, since the teacher is not always available to give assistance or to repeat what has been previously stated.

To provide opportunities for in-depth investigations of ideas introduced in larger groups, many teachers such as Andrea Russell and Richard D'Angelo are setting up learning stations or centers in their classrooms. There tasks to be pursued independently are clearly described, and materials and equipment necessary for completing the tasks are available. These stations may present activities that are primarily for enriching ideas previously developed in larger groups. Children can choose from among several tasks those that appeal to them, or the teacher may indicate which students will find a particular task most rewarding. The teachers previously cited in this chapter used learning stations primarily for enrichment.

In addition, learning centers may present tasks that are basic components of a learning sequence and, therefore, are required for some students. This is especially true where tasks provide additional practice in a skill students are just acquiring.

Teacher Anna Dreschall set up such a station for a group of young students with whom she was working on the long and short *a*. Using a piece of red oak tag as the base for her floor-level station, she mounted directions, a sturdy sealable plastic bag containing slips bearing long *a* and short *a* words, two removable label slips, (one saying Short *a* Words; the other saying Long *a* Words), an answer pouch, and a sign-here paper. The directions stated:

1. Place the two labels on the floor.

2. Take the word slips from the plastic bag. Place each slip by the correct label depending on whether the word has a long or short *a*.

3. When you have placed each word slip by a label, take out the correction lists from the answer pouch. Check to see that you have placed each word under the correct label.

4. When you have corrected your words, place them back in the plastic bag. Return the answer lists to the answer pouch. Place the labels in the label pouch. Sign your name on the Sign Here sheet.

5. You can come back to this station to do the activity again. Sign your name each time you come.

All students in Ms. Dreschall's class who were being introduced to the long and short *a* were expected to include this station on their independent study agenda.

SETTING UP LEARNING STATIONS

In an average-size elementary school room, finding space to set up learning stations for independent study sometimes poses a problem. One solution to the space problem is to use bulletin boards to display the components of a learning activity. Pouches holding necessary materials and finished products, task cards outlining the purpose and directions for the activity, and related charts and explanatory materials can be mounted on the bulletin board surface. Sealable plastic bags, large manila envelopes, or file folders stapled along their sides serve adequately as pouches. The colorful file folders now appearing on the market are especially attractive for mounting and sealable bags are great for holding moist materials such as a clump of moss, a land snail, or even a goldfish swimming in its own miniature pond.

Callaway House (P.O. Box 1751-E, Lancaster, PA 17604) sells a sturdy pouch that can be attached to almost any upright surface. Made of heavy, simulated wood-grain cardboard, these pocket-like boxes can be used and reused.

To obtain additional upright surface space for mounting, a teacher can cut two or three connected panels from a heavy-duty cardboard carton. The unit will stand on the floor or a tabletop if the panels are spread out and angled. Tasks can be presented on both sides of the panels, which can serve also as room dividers to separate parts of a classroom into smaller, quiet, independent study areas.

Teachers who have used carton panels to provide additional mounting surface have found that covering the front and back surfaces with colorful, patterned contact paper makes them more serviceable. Smudges can be easily removed, and file folders and manila envelopes can be stapled or taped on, removed, and then restapled as the tasks are changed periodically.

Callaway House offers a sturdy simulated wood-grained room divider in two sizes, 48×54 inches and 30×108 inches. With a little ingenuity, however, one can make a permanent divider from three pieces of pegboard by attaching hinges between the panels so that they will stand free when spread at appropriate angles. With pegboard, of course, slip-on clips can attach materials.

Another way to use a smaller three-panel unit is to angle the component sides to form an individual study carrel or cubicle. Task-related materials can be mounted on the inside surfaces, while equipment such as filmstrip viewers and tape recorders is placed on the table on which the carrel-forming panels rest. A small rectangular white sheet can be mounted on an inside panel face, onto which film loops, 35mm slides, and filmstrips can be projected since the panels of the carrel will slightly darken the area within. Da-Lite Screen Co., Inc. (P.O. Box 629, Warsaw, IN 46580) supplies a 9 × 12 inch white, coated, fabric sheet with an adhesive backing that is especially designed for use in small viewing areas.

Again one can purchase sturdy cardboard, simulated-wood carrels from Callaway House. They come in two sizes and can be used over and over again, so the purchase of one or two is a worthwhile investment.

It is, of course, possible to eliminate carrels and room dividers and simply mount task materials on any flat surface or collect materials in an ordinary box. Flat work-display surfaces cut from oak tag, heavy-duty cardboard, wood, or even scraps of acoustical ceiling tile can be placed on the floor or a tabletop. Children particularly enjoy working at floor stations, for legs can stretch out and restless bodies can relax. Sometimes the materials of a floor station are placed under a table; a small piece of rug and a pillow make an under-table spot a particularly cozy nook for an informal reading center, especially for younger children.

Task-related materials can be laid on the surface of a tabletop learning station. Samples may be displayed for observation or paints and brushes, flo-pens, crayons, and paper made available. A wire basket serves as a repository for finished products. This setup is ideal if the task to be completed requires a flat, open work surface as is often true in art or science-related activities.

MAKING LEARNING STATIONS FUNCTIONAL

Teachers who have been successful in making independent learning station activities an integral part of their instructional program have generally found that the most functional learning center is one that projects a clear explanation of the task to be carried out. Therefore, include a task card to identify the purpose of the activity and outline step-by-step directions for what is to be done. In addition, try to make the station a self-contained unit. Make available all materials required including paper, crayon, flo-pens, and any necessary audio-visual hard and software. Indicate clearly what is to be done with a finished product—whether a student is to put it in a finished-product pouch or basket, mount it on a bulletin board, include it in a personal file, or retain it until a specific class talk time.

Try also to incorporate a self-correctional element. Having finished the activity as outlined, youngsters may reach into a correction pouch to check their answers against a master list or, in the case of a flat-surface oaktag station, they turn over the oak tag to find the answers on the reverse side. An easy way to keep a record of who has worked at a particular station is to include a Sign Here sheet. Upon completion of the exercise students write their names on the sheet mounted somewhere at the station; this is a particularly useful device when the task is one in which no permanent product results.

Provide variety in the tasks to be completed. With so many audio-visual materials on the market, it is relatively easy to find a tape, Super-8 film loop, or sound filmstrip that correlates with a particular subject and provides content for a station. Likewise, it is easy to gather together samples or models of real things or a collection of books that relates to a topic. Consider if a rock, twig, sprouting seed, or hardware items from kitchen or workbench drawer can be used; real objects provide the eyes with three-dimensional views, the fingers with tactile impressions of textures, and the nose with olfactory sensations. Working with a variety of materials like these, students listen, view, observe, handle, record, write, do, and make as well as read, in contrast to typical fill-in-the-blank seatwork that involves only limited writing experiences.

Try for variety in the format of the tasks. Mount some on bulletin boards and others on upright divider panels. Place some on carpeted areas of floor and others on tabletops. Just being able to leave one's desk and go to another area of classroom to sit in a different position offers a needed change to restless, growing students.

Perhaps most important, prepare students sufficiently so that they can work independently at stations. For very young children directions should be given orally to the total group so that everyone knows what is expected. Children can be taught how to operate the projectors and recorders they will be using at the stations; even first graders can learn to operate the newer kinds of self-threading models.

The work set out in learning stations should relate in some way to on-going topics, areas, and skills. Learning center activities should not be chosen because they happen to be accessible or are interesting or fun. Rather they should be an integral component of classwork; they build on and reinforce learnings being developed in large and small groups and in turn feed back into interactive sessions when students report on and discuss things they have done independently.

Timing is important in using learning stations. Students become bored with a station after it has been around much longer than three weeks. Frequent change is a must to maintain student interest.

When devising the activities at stations, remember that you need not prepare all the materials yourself. A number of companies supply kits, which provide a complete learning station activity that students can encounter independently. Some, such as those in the Instructo Learning Center series (Instructo Corp., 111 Cedar Hollow Road, Paoli, PA 19301) are colorfully presented and well packaged. Used as independent follow-ups to interactive sessions, pre-packaged stations are especially helpful to a teacher who is using independent learning activities for the first time. In selecting commercial materials, however, be wary of the kit that in essense presents a fill-in-the-blank activity sheet for student completion. Even though this type of kit comes with a tape, is packaged attractively in individual boxes, and includes a pre-test, post-test, and precisely stated behavioral objectives, it may actually be a workbook exercise in disguise and at higher cost. Instead of beginning with such routine materials, creatively adapt materials you may already have in your classroom. For example, many classrooms have boxes of synonym, antonym, and homonym cards similar to those produced by Milton Bradley and marketed by J. L. Hammett Co. (2393 Vaux Hall Rd., Union, NJ 07083). Teachers can devise tasks that upper-elementary students can complete independently with these cards. Picture series are generally available in schools, and these too can be a base for a station activity. Commercially sold charts and games can likewise supply content for a center as can the boxes of language arts curriculum materials such as *Aware,* a multi-sensory program about poetry, and *The Writing Bug,* "a swarm of writing experiences," both curriculum packages sold by Random House (201 East 50 Street, New York, NY 10022).

Students can help prepare learning station materials. Printing up sentence cards is a profitable activity for a child who needs additional penmanship practice. Printing directions given orally by a teacher is a worthwhile listening-writing activity. Locating related books to place in a reading center or a tape or record to place in the listening center is a purposeful context for developing library search skills. Actually designing a learning activity and devising a display for it can be adventures in creative thinking.

For the teacher who has had only limited experience in putting together independent learning activities, perhaps a final caution is advisable—in beginning, do not overextend. Introduce one or two center-type activities that really challenge students. Develop a schedule for student visits to the station by letting youngsters sign up for specific ten- to fifteen-minute visits. Supplement stations by setting off areas of the classroom for special purposes. One area can be set aside for independent reading, another as a place to play games, another for listening activities. Students who finish formal assignments can go to these spots to read, listen, and play instructional games. They may decide which area they wish to visit and when. Once one or two formal stations and several informal learning areas are functioning in your classroom, you can gradually introduce an additional station or two as you periodically change the on-going activities. You initially need to create only a few learning stations. Once you have introduced several activities, you will find that designing others is rather challenging. It becomes a process you will begin to enjoy and do quickly.

PUTTING IT TOGETHER

Blending independent activities with class interaction is the context in which to view the activities presented in the following chapters. Some are clearly intended for independent learning, others require more direct teacher guidance, and still others can be set up for independent or guided learning as the situation demands. In addition, readers should consider the activities in each chapter as sources of ideas from which to choose those that relate to on-going work of their classes, not as sequences to be followed. For example, building word ladders or theme charts as suggested in chapter 2 will be most meaningful if the substance of the ladders and charts is related to a theme or unit under investigation. Tracing word inter-relationships as suggested in chapter 7 will be most significant if placed within a unit in which word relationships are an integral part. By working with words in meaningful contexts, young people gradually acquire fundamental communication skills; they learn to use words to express their thoughts in written and spoken communication, to interpret meanings of words in communications directed toward them, and to enjoy word relationships.

The activities in *Words, Sounds, and Thoughts* focus on verbal communication—communication in which words play a major role. Activities for developing nonverbal communication skills have been described in a previous book, *Smiles, Nods, and Pauses* (Citation Press, 1974). Teachers interested in expanding their ability to involve children in creative dramatics and pantomime, oral reporting, and sharing are referred to that volume. Both volumes have been devised particularly for teachers who enjoy seeing how an idea planted in a classroom can mushroom as children toy with it through words and actions. They are for the teacher who wishes to put his or her "ear against the earth" and "listen there how noise-lessly the germ o' the seed has birth."

REFERENCES ABOUT USING
LEARNING STATIONS IN CLASSROOMS

Barth, Roland. *Open Education and the American School.* New York: Schocken, 1974. An introduction to open education with background theory.

Blitz, Barbara. *The Open Classroom: Making It Work.* Boston: Allyn and Bacon, 1973. A clear blend of theory and practice for the teacher who wants to integrate open classroom techniques in his/her classroom.

Bremer, Anne, and John Bremer. *Open Education: A Beginning.* New York: Holt, Rinehart, and Winston, 1974. Another introductory-type presentation on open classroom approaches.

Carswell, Evelyn, and Darrell Roubinek. *Open Sesame: A Primer in Open Education.* Pacific Palisades, Calif.: Goodyear Publishing, 1974. Specific ideas presented with a touch of humor that makes the teacher want to try them out in the classroom.

Fisk, Lori, and Henry Lindgren. *Learning Centers.* Glen Ridge, N.J.: Exceptional Press, 1974. Descriptions of specific ideas for learning centers that can be rather easily set up in elementary classrooms.

Forte, Imogene, and Joy Mackenzie. *Nooks, Crannies and Corners.* Nashville, Tenn.: Inventive Press, 1972. A popular book with teachers, chock-full of creative ideas for learning stations.

Kaplan, Sandra, with Jo Ann Kaplan, Sheila Madsen, and Bette Taylor. *Change for Children: Ideas and Activities for Individualizing Learning.* Pacific Palisades, Calif.: Goodyear Publishing, 1973. Lots of ideas for learning stations; try the one on tall tales!

Kaplan, Sandra, with Jo Ann Kaplan, Sheila Madsen, and Bette Taylor Gould. *A Young Child Experiences.* Pacific Palisades, Calif.: Goodyear Publishing, 1975. Descriptions of practical activities for individuals or groups, worksheets, learning centers, and task cards.

Stephens, Lillian. *The Teacher's Guide to Open Education.* New York: Holt, Rinehart and Winston, 1974. Provides practical suggestions on how-to-do-it.

Taylor, Joy. *Organizing the Open Classroom: A Teacher's Guide to the Integrated Day.* New York: Schocken Books, 1974. More suggestions on how-to-do-it.

Thomas, John I. *Learning Centers.* Boston: Holbrook Press, 1975. Ideas for learning centers in all areas of the curriculum.

IDEAS FOR ACTIVITIES
IN THE LANGUAGE ARTS

Allen, Roach Van. *Language Experiences in Communication.* Boston: Houghton Mifflin, 1976.

Coody, Betty. *Using Literature with Young Children.* Dubuque, Iowa: Wm. Brown, 1973. Puppetry, dramatics, storytelling, experience story charts, related art activities.

Greene, Harry and Walter Petty. *Developing Language Skills in the Elementary School.* 5th ed. Boston: Allyn and Bacon, 1975. A basic text in the language arts with chapters on dialects, planning, listening, speaking, creativity, and so forth.

Hennings, Dorothy Grant. *Smiles, Nods, and Pauses: Activities to Enrich Children's Communication Skills.* New York: Citation

Press, 1974. A source of activities that focus on nonverbal language development.

Hennings, Dorothy Grant, and Barbara Grant. *Content and Craft: Written Expression in the Elementary School.* Englewood Cliffs, N.J.: Prentice-Hall, 1973. Ideas for getting children to express themselves in written form.

Hopkins, Lee Bennett. *Let Them Be Themselves: Language Arts for Children in Elementary Schools.* 2nd ed. New York: Citation Press, 1974. Clear descriptions of ways to make language arts meaningful to children.

Petty, Walter, Dorothy Petty, and Marjorie Becking. *Experiences in Language.* 2nd ed. Boston: Allyn and Bacon, 1976.

Smith, James A. *Adventures in Communication.* Boston: Allyn and Bacon, 1972. An exceptionally practical language arts text that is filled with ideas that are easily implemented in the classroom.

Smith, James A. *Creative Teaching of the Language Arts in the Elementary School,* 2nd ed. Boston: Allyn and Bacon, 1973. A fine source of language arts activities that belongs on every teacher's bookshelf.

Tiedt, Iris, and Sidney Tiedt. *Contemporary English in the Elementary School.* 2nd ed. Englewood Cliffs, N.J.: Prentice-Hall, 1975. A basic language arts text that provides necessary theory and at the same time marvelous activities that are really great in elementary language arts classes.

"The time has come," the Walrus said,
"To talk of many things:
Of shoes—and ships—and sealing wax—
Of cabbages—and kings—"
    "THE WALRUS AND THE CARPENTER," LEWIS CARROLL

2. OF SHOES AND SHIPS AND SEALING WAX: *Activities for Word Building*

To talk and write about the world they live in, people must acquire a multitude of words—symbols through which they can express the real world "of shoes—and ships—and sealing wax—/Of cabbages—and kings." Word symbols make possible communication about objects, actions, feelings, events, and people. Word symbols allow the human mind to speculate about such complex ideas as "why the sea is boiling hot—/And whether pigs have wings."

How do teachers introduce young people to this ever-expanding world of words that mirrors to some extent the world of reality? How can we help students acquire their own repertoires of words?

In this chapter ideas for vocabulary building are presented. First are activities in which students search out related words and attach meanings to them; they compare and contrast meanings and categorize words according to these similarities and differences. Second are activities that aid students in finding more expressive words to substitute for overworked ones; the emphasis is on using words effectively to describe places and people. Third, students analyze words in meaningful contexts; they interpret context clues to figure out meanings to attach to words as they are being used.

SEARCHING FOR WORDS

MIXING COLORS AND SEASONS   Kindergarten teachers can cut out large colored shapes and suspend them as mobiles from the ceiling after labeling them—red, orange, yellow, black, brown, and so forth. By referring to the colors and the labels, children learn to attach verbal symbols to the colors with which they are familiar.

Each of the common colors, however, exists in a variety of shades, requiring more descriptive labels—chocolate brown, mauve, sea green, fuchsia, golden yellow, sand, apricot, robin's egg blue, and so on. Working in teams, older students can expand their color vocabularies to include these and other shades of color.

Each team concentrates on one major color group. For instance, the brown group searches for brown-related terms and may turn up such descriptors as beige, buff, tan, cocoa, toast, olive brown, golden brown, nutmeg, copper, chestnut, or cinnamon. The list is almost endless. With watercolors, they paint a brown wash onto a piece of large construction paper. The wash is shaded so that dark browns blend gradually into red browns, orange browns, and yellow browns. Brown words are lettered onto the shaded paper after the wash has dried to form a word poster.

Meanwhile the red group searches out red-related terms. They may identify such words as flame, maroon, cardinal, pink, ruby, claret, ruddy, lobster, vermillion, crimson, or cherry as well as other fiery words. They label their words on a large sheet they have washed down in various shades of red.

Display these color posters as a bulletin board at a writing center. Beneath the posters, mount a pouch of paper for students to use in their writing. On a table heap a stack of books that deal with color. The Peter Max books, *The Land of Yellow*, *The Land of Blue*, and *The Land of Red* (Watts, 1970), are particularly good for this purpose. So is Dr. Seuss's *Green Eggs and Ham* (Random House, 1960). Students working at the station read these books to find out what imaginative things can be done with colors. They then write their own color stories drawing on the posters for a wide range of color words to include. Titles that might be mounted along the perimeter of the board to trigger imaginative thinking are:

Adrift in a sea of _____	Flying in a sky of _____
Walking in a world of _____	Skating on _____ ice
Eating _____	Climbing a mountain of _____

Students can select one of these titles and fill in their own color words.

February words are groundhog, leap year, valentine, skating, freezing, Lincoln, or Washington, whereas April words are fools, umbrella, showers, spring, puddles, and crocuses. Because certain words are commonly associated with special times of the year, teachers can build an on-going calendar of words with primary school youngsters.

Keep a big piece of cardboard-weight experience paper on an easel. At the beginning of the month, you or a student prints the month's name at the top. Each day provide time for the class to add a word or phrase to the sheet, words students associate with that day or time of month. Encourage children to talk about each word so that they gain a concept of the variety of contexts in which it may be used.

Your class's on-going calendar of words can function as a simple writing station. Students working at a desk placed by the easel select chart words to write into calendar yarns. You may even tack to the base of the easel a pouch of cards listing possible topics. Students who have trouble getting started on their own can work from one of these suggested beginning points. Titles you might want to tuck into a February pouch are:

The Leap Year Valentine	Did the Groundhog See Its
The Day I Met Washington	Shadow?
February Thaw	Ice Storm
Storm Warnings	The Sign Said, "Thin Ice!"
	Groundhogs Are Woodchucks

Into an April pouch you could place:

Fools Under the Umbrella	Inside the Easter Egg
Puddle Hopping	Underneath the Yellow Crocus
Caught in the Rain	Bicycling in the Rain

BURROWING INTO ANIMAL AND THEME WORDS

Although not many people are familiar with puffins, many would recognize that a puffling is a little puffin, for very often in English the diminutive of an animal name is formed by attaching -*ling* to the word. The fact that in English there are words designating infant forms can be the base for an animal word search.

Students begin their search by brainstorming. They will probably think of such big/little animal names as:

pig/piglet	horse/colt	woman/girl
duck/duckling	lion/cub	man/boy
dog/puppy	frog/tadpole	sheep/lamb
deer/fawn	cow/calf	cat/kitten
chicken/chick	butterfly/larva	goose/gosling

Other words can be discovered by searching dictionaries and thesauruses and by keeping eyes and ears alert for several days.

When students have an extensive listing, they may compose a class animal booklet with each youngster contributing a page. Each student writes a simple statement; i.e., "A little frog is called a tadpole. Tadpoles _____." completes the statement with one idea about tadpoles, and draws a picture to illustrate that idea. The pages are compiled alphabetically according to adult animal names and fastened together as a booklet titled Little Animal Names.

Older students may enjoy the same type of activity carried out at a higher level of sophistication. Divide upper-elementary classes into animal word search teams with each working on one type of animal words such as:

Group and individual names (colony/ant, herd/cow, flock/sheep, covey/partridge)

Male and female names (gander/goose, bull/cow, rooster/hen)

Ordinary and scientific names (person/*Homo sapiens*, cat/*Felis*, horse/*Equus*)

Animal words applied to people (ratty, catty, bovine, bullish, clamish)

Animal appendage names (horns, talons, quills)

Animal home names (burrow, hill, lair)

Animal cover words (hide, scale, feather)

Animal locomotion words (slithering, hopping, flying)

A series of informative volumes called Animal Encyclopedia, with each volume bearing a series number and title, i.e., Volume I, Big/Little Animal Names or Volume II, Group and Individual Names, can be compiled.

Incidentally, if you are working with youngsters whose first language is not English, this activity is a good one for language comparisons. Spanish-speaking youngsters may be able to tell how diminutive forms are expressed in Spanish or French-speaking youngsters may be able to show how masculine and feminine are expressed in French.

There are countless other themes you can introduce to help children expand their repertoire of words to describe the world around them.

Some themes emerge from activities of high interest appeal to certain groups of children, such as sports. Each team of students concentrates on a specific sport; i.e., a football team identifies football words, a tennis team identifies tennis words, and a basketball team identifies basketball words. Using categories such as action words (tackle, pass), materials and equipment words (goalpost, racket), and rules terms (love, down, shortstop) may elicit more words, and searching books on the topic should produce even more.

Teams write their words on a large cutout that symbolizes the sport, i.e., a football, a tennis racket, or a swimsuit. When each symbol is chock-full of related words, teams present their cutouts to the class and talk about their word discoveries.

Playing with theme words may also be a productive way of investigating the sciences and social sciences. Students who are studying weather phenomena, for example, may culminate their investigation by making word charts on subtopics, i.e., cloud words, wind words, storm words, precipitation words, or temperature words. Such words can be lettered across a mural depicting clouds, storms, and precipitation. Or students who have studied community workers may put together a booklet in which each page names a worker, describes the things the worker does, and tells about the tools she or he uses.

Working systematically with theme words can be a helpful vocabulary building aid, especially with slower learners. A teacher of educable youngsters, who was helping students learn the names of common articles of clothing, cut from cardboard a large human figure and printed clothing names on slips of paper. As students talked about scarfs, boots, sneakers, sweaters, or gloves, they pinned each word card to the place on the figure where that piece of clothing is worn. After the class activity, the cutout and cards became a learning station in the corner of the room to which individual students could later go to reattach the cards to the cutout.

The theme word approach also has a place in bilingual classrooms. Words related to a central theme are lettered onto cutouts, murals, charts, and so forth in both the first language as well as the second or target language. Word stories can be written by students drawing upon words from both languages as in the type of story that goes: "Marie went to the supermarket. She bought grapes and pears and oranges and figs. She likes fruit." "Jose went to *el supermercado*. He bought *las uvas* and *las peras* and *las naranjas* and *los higos*. He likes *las frutas*, too." Students might play with words in this way after they have collected lots of supermarket or *supermercado* words—fruits/*frutas*, vegetables/*legumbres*, flowers/*flores*, and meat/*carne*. They can letter words from both the first and target languages on huge word charts and draw from these charts as they write their two-language stories.

Vary students' adventures with theme words by presenting a list of topically related words whose vowels have been deleted. Students must puzzle out what the missing letters are.

Write each word, minus vowels, on a card. Divide students into two teams. Hold up each card as it is pulled from a grab bag by a team member who must fill in the empty letters to earn a point for his or her team. If the player is unsuccessful, a student on the opposing team takes a turn at replacing the vowels. The team completing the word keeps the card, and the team holding the largest number of completed cards at the end is the winner.

Here is a brief listing of "kingdom" words to begin with. Students can produce their own lists of vowel-depleted words related to topics they are studying.

r _ y _ l	kn _ ghts
r _ g _ l	k _ ngsh _ p
m _ n _ rch	c _ stl _
c _ _ rtly	_ bs _ l _ t _
s _ v _ r _ _ gn	r _ l _ r
m _ j _ st _ c	cr _ wn
g _ v _ rn	h _ _ r
q _ _ _ n	pr _ nc _ ss
p _ l _ c _	l _ rds
pr _ nc _ ly	p _ rl _ _ m _ nt
l _ d _ _ s	c _ nst _ t _ t _ _ n

MOSAICS AND POSTERS   Tack a large piece of oak tag to a bulletin or chalkboard and print a title at the top identifying a category of words, i.e., holiday, geology, monster, apartment house, school, make-believe, happy, or miserable words. As an option during independent work time, students go to the word center and write related words into the developing chart. Keep a variety of colored flo-pens available to create a striking mosaic. An even more fascinating display can be produced by writing words so that they share a common letter in crossword-puzzle style.

Later hang the chart as the backdrop of a writing center. Students working at the center can draw upon words from the mosaic as they write on topics of their choosing but related to that category of words.

Or use the word mosaic as the backdrop for a thinking center. Youngsters at this station study the words printed on the oak tag and organize them into subcategories by writing related words in a series of columns, and devising labels that describe the quality shared by all the words in each list.

Such learning stations as these are easy to construct. Tape the word mosaic next to a clean sheet of oak tag, and on it print directions and affix a pouch for writing paper and another pouch for completed papers. Stretch both sheets out and tack to a bulletin board or stand the taped sheets on a table surface by folding the pieces inward.

WRITING STATION

AN EXCURSION INTO THE WORLD OF MAKE-BELIEVE

DIRECTIONS: Write a story using words from the mosaic. You may add more words to the mosaic if you wish.

Here Is Paper for You!

Put Your Finished Papers Here!

OUR MAGIC MOSAIC

Insight Associates (Essentia, The Evergreen State College, Olympia, Wash., 1974) has produced a poster captioned Ways of the Mind. In the center is the imprint of a girl's head, and surrounding it are words that have to do with the two functions of the mind. Words on the left include dream, sing, fantasy, invent, draw, space; words on the right include plan, reason, order, verify, read, write. At the bottom are the words "Together they create true art, true science, true being."

Students can design similar posters to depict word relationships. For example, students can select an easy theme such as cats and search for words that describe kinds of cats, cat actions, or cat appearance. They then arrange these words into a poster with the outline of a cat as the central object and with an interest-attracting caption at the top. To pull the chart together, they compose a short sentence summing up the theme and place it at the bottom.

Other words that could serve as the theme for a poster are dogs, trucks, horses, buildings, plants, or sea life.

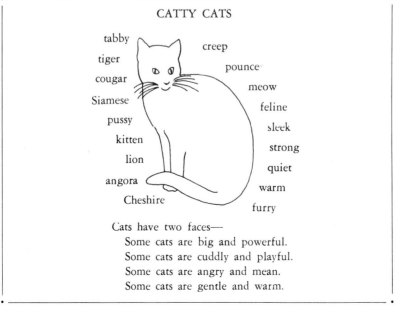

CATTY CATS

tabby
tiger
cougar
Siamese
pussy
kitten
lion
angora
Cheshire

creep
pounce
meow
feline
sleek
strong
quiet
warm
furry

Cats have two faces—
   Some cats are big and powerful.
   Some cats are cuddly and playful.
   Some cats are angry and mean.
   Some cats are gentle and warm.

A cover of a Sunday *New York Times Magazine* was a poster-like chart that depicted a pyramid of blocks of words related to success. Words such as fight, team spirit, and competitiveness related directly to the purpose of the chart, which was to show components of success in football.

Upper-elementary students can design similar theme pyramid posters that contain both words and definitions, based on the example adapted from the magazine cover. Students who have interpreted and discussed the success pyramid can go on to build their own love, peace, happiness, or humility pyramids. Conversely they can invert their pyramids and construct failure, hate, war, vanity, or sadness pyramids that point downward.

Once young people have designed their pyramids, two or three can be mounted on oak tag to form the sides of a learning station. Students can select an assortment of words from the pyramids to build into a paragraph on the meaning of hate, the meaning of war, and so on.

A SUCCESS PYRAMID

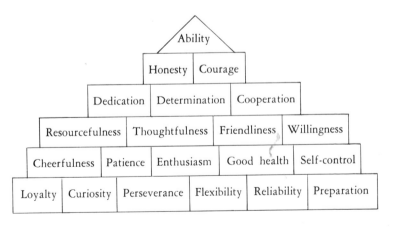

WORD WHIRLIGIGS   The dictionary defines *whirligig* as "something that whirls, revolves, or goes around" and as "a continuous round or succession." One kind of beetle has been named whirligig because it and its relatives circle rapidly about on the surface of a pool of water, rippling the water as they go.

A word whirligig is a whirl that begins with one word and keeps going round and round; words that relate to the initial word are added to the whirligig at each round. New whirls spin off as different types of related words are considered. The example shows a whirligig of ships and boats that began as youngsters searched for words related to the starter word *ferry* and then spun off new whirls as they added words that identified workers and actions.

Divide your class into three- or four-person teams to produce whirligigs. Give each team a large piece of brown paper, a dictionary, colored flo-pens, and a starter word such as: grasshopper, salmon, truck, hemlock, musk melon, sparrow, or wheat. For more sophisticated youngsters, skin, linen, buffet, cube, or chrysoberyl may be more challenging and mind expanding.

Allow students to spread their brown paper on the floor and have several thesauruses available. Suggest that they begin their first whirl in the center of the paper so that they can shoot off additional whirls of related words in all directions. You may want to help them identify the kinds of whirls they can build into their whirligig, i.e., whirls of object words, action words, people-related words, color words, feeling words, texture words, and so forth. Building whirligigs is an excellent review activity for students who have already had considerable experience searching out and categorizing words, for to put together a whirligig they must note similarities and also recognize differences among related words.

Whirligigs can form the content for at least two other dif-

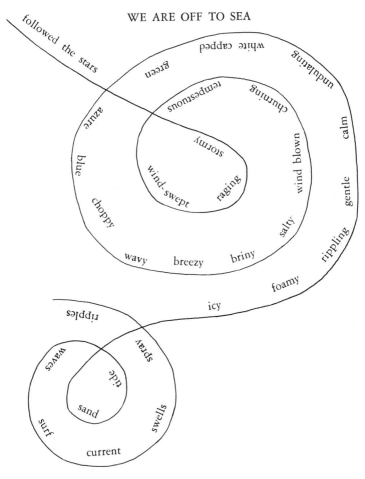

WE ARE OFF TO SEA

followed the stars

white capped
green
undulating
tempestuous
churning
azure
stormy
calm
blue
wind-swept
raging
wind blown
choppy
salty
gentle
wavy   breezy   briny
rippling
foamy
icy
ripples
waves
spray
tide
sand
surf
swells
current

ferent kinds of activities. Students can play Challenger using their whirligigs. Each team challenges other teams about the way words have been categorized or the meaning assigned to a word on a whirl. "What is a galleon?" a challenging team may query, or, "Why did you put *gondola* on that whirl?" a challenger who has confused *gondola* with *gondolier* may ask. To stand up to such challenges, teams must be certain of meanings before adding words to their whirligigs.

Completed whirligigs can form the substance of a writing station. A caption such as Set Yourself a Whirl, or Climb Aboard a Whirligig, or Whirlabout a Whirligig, will do nicely, or better still, ask students for a catchy caption. Stack first-draft paper on a writing table beneath the display, place a finished-paper pouch or basket nearby, provide an assortment of flo-pens for writing or a typewriter if you can manage to obtain one, and pin directions to the board:

WHAT
TO
DO

Jump aboard one whirl at any location on a whirligig. That word plus the two words before or behind it on the whirl is to appear in a story or a description that you will write.

If you want, you may jump aboard more than one whirl of a whirligig and select several strings of words to build into a story or description.

Now compose a story or description using the words you have selected. Help yourself to paper. Try writing your first draft with a flo-pen or on the typewriter.

When you have finished writing, go back and underline in your story or description all the words you have used that appeared on the whirligig. Check spelling of these words against the spelling of the words as they appear on the whirligigs.

Finished stories and paragraphs can gradually be added above or beneath the whirligig that triggered the writing. Compile the finished products book style so that a small volume of related stories begins to take form, which students at the learning station can read.

By the way, whirligigs containing just two whirls are a fun way to develop students' ability to work with words that are opposite in meaning. For example, there are loud words and quiet words. Loud words include racket, din, clatter, blast, hubbub, tumult, honk, and so forth, while quiet words are stillness, whisper, peep, quiet, hush, lull, and so forth. One group of words revolves on a whirl that connects to a second whirl containing the opposite group. Students may discover that there are many more words for one side of the whirligig; i.e., students doing the loud/quiet dichotomy will find it easy to think of noisy words but much more difficult to locate quiet words. Older students may find it interesting to hypothesize why this is so.

Other dichotomies upon which students can construct double-whirls are rough/smooth, fragrant/malodorous, bright/dull, pleasant/unpleasant, hot/cold, or old/young. Once again students' whirligigs can become the basis for writing stations at which other students extract a string of words to include in story or report.

Double-whirl whirligigs have a valuable place in bilingual classrooms. Students spin a whirl of words in their first language that is associated with a topic and connect this whirl to another containing the same words in the second or target language. When they write about the topic in the second language, they have a pool of words from which to draw.

FUN WITH ANTONYMS   Farfetched bragging about oneself is a fun form of word play that, according to Kenneth Koch, author of *Wishes, Lies and Dreams* (New York: Chelsea House–Random House, 1970), produces poetry-like pieces. It is also a different way through which students can encounter antonyms, words with almost opposite meanings.

Students writing brag poems operate within the confines of two sentences—I am not _____. I am _____. Repeating these two sentences over and over again, braggarts fill in the blanks, each time adding a different antonym pair. The results may resemble the following:

> I am not ugly. I am beautiful.
> I am not stupid. I am brilliant.
> I am not lazy. I am energetic.
> I am not hated. I am loved.
> I am not poor. I am wealthy.

After playing with bragging, they may enjoy further experimenting with antonyms with different base phrases such as, The storm was not _____. It was _____ _____. The ghost was not _____. It was _____. The sweater was not _____. It was _____. Inventive students can concoct their own base phrases.

A similar format for balancing opposites is the phrase _____ not _____. A sought-for quality is placed in the first blank, its opposite in the second. The frame is repeated, each time beginning with a different quality. With an original ending line affixed, the result can be quite poetic.

> Peace-making not warring
> Caring not hating
> Feasting not hungering
> Conserving not wasting—
>   We will live together.

Beginning lines to start students writing in this vein are: genuine not synthetic, friends not enemies, up not down, for not against, forever not just for a moment, or humility not pride.

Primary-grade children generally know the rules for playing Go Fish, a card game that can be adapted to learn about antonyms. Fish cards come in matching pairs, and six cards are dealt to each of four players. Upon receiving their cards, players check their hands to see if they can match any pairs. Then they replenish their hands from the remainder of the deck so that they each hold an unmatched hand of six cards. The first player asks any other player of his or her choosing a question such as, "Do you have a word meaning wide-awake?" The questioner holds a card meaning tired and must locate a wide-awake card to make an antonym pair. If the questioner is told, "No. Go fish." he or she draws a card from the remainer of the deck. If the questioner is told, "Yes," the questioner takes the card to make a matched pair. Then the next player takes a turn. The winner is the one who first matches all the cards in his or her hand or who has the largest number of matched pairs.

To prepare for antonym fish, print antonyms on small cards. At least twenty pairs of words are necessary to make the game fun. For your convenience in making antonym cards here is a list. In the left-hand column are words you might use with primary-level children; on the right are words to use with middle- and upper-grade youngsters.

Primary List	Middle- and Upper-Elementary List
sleepy/wide awake	tiny/enormous
quiet/noisy	troubled/peaceful
cold/hot	just/unjust
deep/shallow	bald/hirsute (hairy)
rough/smooth	clever/dense
tall/short	windy/calm
curved/flat	ferocious/tame
fat/lean	aggressive/timid
slow/fast	active/passive
big/little	frequent/seldom
good/bad	proud/humble
sweet/sour	good/evil
wet/dry	prompt/tardy
straight/curly	steep/gradual
healthy/sick	expensive/cheap
happy/sad	turgid/flaccid
rich/poor	liberal/conservative
early/late	ancient/modern
freezing/melting	shiny/dull
odd/even	fruitful/barren
many/few	positive/negative
full/empty	attractive/repulsive
easy/difficult	frugal/wasteful
heavy/light	cheerful/heavy-hearted

Variations of antonym fish are easy to prepare with different kinds of matching cards, i.e., synonym fish with pairs of synonyms, definition fish with one card containing a word and its mate containing its definition, or sentence fish in which one card contains a word and its mate contains a sentence with a blank into which the word fits.

Go Fish is effective too in bilingual classrooms. A pair of cards contains a word in English and in the first language.

SEARCHING FOR EXPRESSIVE WORDS

EXCHANGING SYNONYMS FOR THE BLAH   In the Churchill Film *The Story of a Book,* Holling C. Holling shows how he substitutes exciting words for less expressive words when he writes. He rewords the sentence "The fish *swam* through the water" to "The fish *streaked* through the water." He changes "*bit* the tentacles" to "clipped the tentacles." Holling does this because exciting words make exciting stories.

The notion of blah words can motivate children to search for exciting words. Blah words arouse little interest, for they communicate the mundane as in the following examples:

> An old man *walked* down the street.
> A girl *entered* the room.
> A boy *made* a box.
> The gong *made a noise.*
> Jack's car *went* through the intersection.
> The tree *fell over.*
> The horse *ran* across the field.
> The boat *moved* through the water.
> The football player *went* through the opposing line.

Write these blah sentences on strips of paper or on colored, lightweight cardboard. Beneath each strip attach an index card, which students can fill with interesting words to substitute for the blah word. Affix strips and cards to a bulletin-board learning station.

The car _went_ through the intersection.

crashed	ripped	sped
zigzagged	careened	charged
cut	mowed	jackknifed
	scissored	forged
	crawled	crept
jerked	navigated its way	
maneuvered	plodded	

Students who have searched for their own synonyms will enjoy Eve Merriam's "Be My Non-Valentine":

> I have searched my Thesaurus through
> to find a synonym for you;
> here are some choice words that may do:
>
> you're a hoddy-doddy, a dizzard, a ninny, a dolt,
> a booby, a looby, a fribble, a gowk,
> a nonny, a nizy, a nincompoop,
> a churl, a scrimp, a knag, a trapes,
> a lubber, a marplot, an oaf, a droil,
> a mopus, a flat, a muff, a doit,
> a mugwump, a dimwit, a flunkey, a swab,
> a bane, a murrain, a malking, a pox,
> a sloven, a slammerkin, a draffel tail,
> frumpery, scrannel, and kickshaw, too!

After listening to Ms. Merriam's poem, upper graders can try their hand at writing similar poems in which synonyms are used back-to-back to describe something particularly pleasant or repulsive. Subjects students can explore in this way might be food, weather, automobiles, school, teachers, friends, homework, or vacation.

Another approach to learning forceful synonyms is to build word cones. Sketch a large cone shape onto a sheet of paper and at the top print a common word such as *say*. Students search for more expressive synonyms and write the substitutes on lines inside the cone.

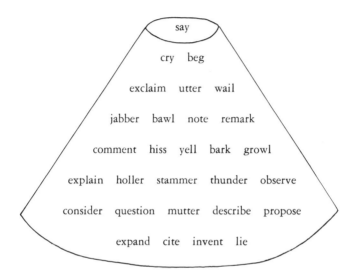

Other overused words to place at the pinnacle of a synonym cone are *go, do, nice, pretty, bad, good, make, put* or *got*.

By the way, encourage students who have devised word cones to write short pieces in which they use at least a half-dozen of its words. *Say* substitutes are fun to convert into short written pieces such as the following:

"You are a mean one," he *growled* at me.
I *thundered* back, "You're the mean one!"
"You are!" he *yelled*.
So I *barked*, "Stop *holler*ing at me. You sound like a *wail*ing wolf."
Then he *hissed*, "You are a snake in the grass."
Guess what happened next? We both turned into hissing snakes.

To extend students' understanding of synonyms, try pantomime play. Write a blah word at the top of a card and beneath it write a more expressive substitute. For example, to a number of cards with the word *walk,* add a more expressive verb such as tiptoe, skip, march, hurry, trudge, saunter, sneak, limp, strut, stalk, or stride. A student player draws from an envelope of prepared cards. Without allowing others to see the *walk* substitute noted on the card, he or she acts out the meaning. Watchers guess the word being pantomimed. The student to guess the actual word becomes the next performer and selects a card to pantomime.

You will find that as students play this game, they will suggest synonyms or close-synonyms for the word being pantomimed. For *hurry,* students may suggest *rush, run,* or even *scurry.* For *saunter,* older students may guess *stroll, amble* or even *loiter* or *wander.* This is good. When such alternates are suggested, students can consider differences in the ways such related words are generally used. You may wish to have students check a dictionary or perhaps a dictionary of synonyms to determine the fine distinctions among such synonyms or near-synonyms.

HANGING AND LISTENING TO SYNONYMS Students can arrange synonyms in the form of word mobiles. For a smart mobile, the word *smart* is lettered onto a strip of paper and affixed to the bottom of a clothes hanger. Students write sentences containing smart synonyms onto smaller strips and suspend them by threads from the hanger. In this case, synonyms could include keen, sharp, intellectual, brilliant, shrewd, clever, bright, or quick. Hang the mobile from a cord or wire strung across a corner of the room. As students unearth additional synonyms, they can write and add sentence strips to the mobile. Other overworked words to convert into mobiles are dumb, boring, silly, scared, ugly, or funny.

This activity functions well in an independent learning

center. Letter overworked words on strips of paper and attach each to a hanger. Start the activity by temporarily tacking the hangers to the backdrop of the station. Provide a stack of large index cards, mount a pouch beneath each hanger, and attach the following directions:

You may do either of two things at this station:

1. Select from a pouch a synonym card already started by another student. Add a sentence with the synonym and return the card to the pouch.

OR

2. Take a card from the stack of cards below. Write on the top a synonym for one of the hanger words. Then write a sentence using that synonym in a way that shows its meaning. Put the card into the pouch beneath the appropriate word. (*Reminder:* Before starting a new card, check the cards already in the pouch to make certain that there is no card for your word.)

When there are many cards in each of the pouches, the class is ready for mobile making. Assign a group of students to each pouch. The group selects sentences that best reveal the distinctive meaning of that synonym, prints them on strips of colored paper, and adds them to the hanger. Suspend the finished mobiles in some area of the classroom.

Students who have done some preliminary work with synonyms will enjoy visiting a word listening station in which the distinctions between synonyms are clarified. Troll Associates (320 Rt. 17, Mahwah, NJ 07430) sells a vocabulary development package called *Words, Words, Words* that introduces young people in grades three through six to the shades of differences in meaning among related synonyms. It consists of six sound filmstrips and a brief teacher's guide. The strength of this particular series is that words are presented in meaningful contexts in an interesting fashion. Students working independently can listen to the sound filmstrip and then write the related words into their own paragraphs.

FINDING DESCRIPTIVE WORDS   Looking at something from different perspectives is another way to trigger expressive words. Encourage students to do this by having them consider the smell, taste, sound, feeling, sight, and even happening words associated with a particular object.

For instance, let students listen to a suggestive recording such as *Chilling, Thrilling Sounds of a Haunted House* (Disney Land Records, #DQ1257). Open a brainstorming session with, "What are the sounds of a haunted house?" Participants will fire off squeal, groan, grate, creak, squeal, eeks, yikes, and a host of others. A scribe fills the chalkboard with brainstormed suggestions.

Continue with, "What are the smells of a haunted house?" Responses that may pop forth are musty, dusty, dirty, cob-webby, stale, damp, and dank.

"What are the feelings you would have in a haunted house?" This time words given may be heart beating, curious, numb with fear, quaking, shaking, trembling, curious, or adventuresome.

When ideas dry up, a student can search a thesaurus to un-earth additional words. Unknown words found this way are checked in a dictionary to determine their meanings before they are added to the burgeoning classroom listing. Finally, students talk about things that could happen in a haunted house and add key action words.

When you and your students have thought of a whole boardful of haunted-house descriptors, student volunteers copy the words onto sheets in their best handwriting. Sound words go on one sheet, smell words on another, and so forth. You could refer to these as class thesaurus sheets.

Next students write haunted-house yarns, using words from the class thesaurus sheets. Afterward, they check the words against the sheets to insure accurate spelling.

This activity, of course, is most appropriate as an October, pre-Halloween happening. However, similar materials are available to use at other times of the year. The recording *Sounds of Our City* (Scholastic Book Services, Englewood Cliffs, NJ 07632) can trigger sound, sight, smell, feeling, and happening words, and another Scholastic recording, *Insect Sounds,* can spark summer-related words.

You may, however, wish to start with sights rather than with sounds. To do this, use pictures or concrete objects as word stimulators. Students first give words that describe the appearance of objects, then move on to suggest sound, smell, and feeling words.

An individual vocabulary-building activity to try as follow-up to the preceding activity is I Can't Resist Chocolate Ice Cream. Students identify their favorite foods such as strawberry ice cream, chocolate pudding, fresh corn on the cob, spaghetti, pizza, peanut butter, watermelon, hamburger, angel food cake, or devil's food cake. They list the foods down the left side of a page. Across the top they label columns, How It Tastes, How It Smells, and How It Looks, and they write a descriptive word in each block about their favorite foods.

Foods	How It Tastes	How It Smells	How It Looks
Chocolate ice cream			
Spaghetti			
Peanut butter			
Hamburger			

Once students have selected taste, smell, and sight descriptors, they select a favorite food from the chart and write a paragraph describing the food they cannot resist. As a follow-up, students can list foods they dislike, find descriptors for how these foods taste, smell, and look, and write paragraphs of description.

DESCRIBING PICTURES   Magazines and newspapers can supply pictures of people. If a pile is available in a corner of the classroom, students can clip out pictures of unique people and tack them collage-style to a bulletin board. A people-crowded board converts easily to an independent learning station for upper-elementary students. Attach a shoe box full of index cards to the left base of the board and an empty box to the right base. Place a number next to each picture and staple to the board the following directions:

WHAT
TO
DO

1. On this board are many people. Select one picture-person as your own.

2. Take a blank card from the left-hand box. Write on it the number given next to the person-picture you have chosen. Fill your card with words that describe your person. Include words that describe his/her clothing, facial expression, body build, and stance. Then include a name that you think fits that person.

3. When you have completed your card, place it in the right-hand box in numerical order.

When most of the picture people have been chosen and described, change the board so that the box of completed cards is on the left, a pouch of paper is in the middle, and a pouch for completed papers is at the right. The directions now read:

WHAT
TO
DO

1. On this board are many people pictures. Select one person as your own and in the card file locate by number the card or cards containing descriptive words about that person.

2. Think about the words and names found on the cards. Then using those words and/or others you prefer, write a paragraph or two describing your picture person.

3. Place your paper in the finished paper pouch.

If you teach lower primary, you may wish to try a less

sophisticated version of this activity. Have students bring to school any large stuffed animals they may have. Each day select a stuffed animal and encourage children as a class to brainstorm words that describe it. Record the words on a paper or card that you then place near the animal. When you have brainstormed words about several animals, students can go individually to sit near the animal they like best and write about it, selecting words from the card as a writing aid. This becomes an independent writing activity.

Scenes of fields and farms, city streets, classrooms, mountains, seashores, suburbs, bridges, forests, or volcanoes can be found in magazines or on calendars, and the pictures can be tacked up on a classroom bulletin board as a collage of places. Use this collage the same way the collage of people pictures was used. Students select place pictures, write word descriptors, and finally write paragraphs that describe the places shown in their pictures.

You may prefer to offer this activity as an individual adventure. A student finds a picture he or she wants to describe, mounts the picture on construction paper, and labels related words around it. These words become the stimuli that lead to a short descriptive paragraph.

Or you may want to start the ball rolling by organizing the total class. Mount a calendar picture on oak tag. As youngsters call out words, print them around the edge of the picture, and then ask groups to write paragraphs of description.

A sound filmstrip series from Troll Associates (320 Rt. 17, Mahwah, NJ 07430) called *Getting Ready to Write Creatively* is a particularly useful box of materials to involve young people in description. The series consists of three cassette tapes and six color filmstrips that focus on describing objects, people, and actions as well as putting together stories from real experiences and imagination. An accompanying teacher's guide provides additional activities to supplement the film and tape experience. Use this type material either as the content of an independent learning station or as a springboard for group session.

Ms. Deborah Smith, working with three fifth- and sixth-grade girls in Elizabeth, New Jersey, invented the idea of a poem-allage to trigger a flow of words. She started with a collage of happy faces that she had put together from pictures cut from magazines. She explained that they were "loving faces," and the girls studied them and talked about what loving means. Then individually they printed on separate pieces of paper as many phrases starting with *Love can* or *Love is* as they could think of.

When each girl had written several slips, they worked as a group to organize their sentences into a sequence of ideas that they liked. When they had agreed on an order, they pasted the slips to a cardboard to accompany the collage of faces and called it their Love Poem-allage:

Love is accepting what you are.
Love is knowing why you're here.
Love is understanding other people.
Love is wanting to be loved.
   Love is accepting what you are.
   Love is the one you're with.
   Love is a good feeling inside.
   Love can mean almost anything.
Love is what I'm in.
Love is a creation of feelings.
Love is seeing and believing. Love is happiness.
Love is caring for others.
   Love is being together.
   Love is the color of my brothers' and sisters' skin.
   Love is a beautiful song.
   Love is a phantasil.

ADVENTURING WITH MULTIMEDIA   Andrea Russell, the teacher introduced in chapter 1, is a master of multimedia language adventure. Remember how she integrated a story, a Super-8 film loop, a musical recording, and concrete materials into a word adventure about mushrooms. You can borrow from her lesson-plan book by making use of the wide range of high-quality commercial materials available today—posters, films, filmstrips, records, and tapes.

Argus Communications (7440 Natchez Avenue, Niles, IL 60648) markets especially beautiful word-picture posters. Each expresses a thought through a full-colored, large picture and a short quotation of poetry or prose. Langston Hughes's "Hold fast to dreams for if dreams die,/life is a broken-winged bird that cannot fly" is lettered across a sky filled with hovering gulls, while a monarch butterfly perched amid a delight of blossoms is the background for L. Richard Lessor's

> Happiness is like a butterfly.
> The more you chase it, the more it will elude you.
> But if you turn your attention to other things.
> It comes and softly sits on your shoulder.

If you mount these posters on an easel chart in a learning station, students will have no trouble filling the surrounding space with their own words and lines.

Argus also sells a series called Posters Without Words. Black-and-white as well as some full-color posters depict men and women and boys and girls at play and at work. Ask students to supply the words that tell what the picture is about. Or mount a picture on a bulletin board, stack a pile of poetry books beneath, and let students search the anthologies for lines that best express the picture on display. They letter their discoveries on the surrounding bulletin board space. When the space is full, students can discuss the suggested lines and decide which one is *the one.* Place this line directly onto the poster.

You can use the pictures in the Weston Woods (Weston,

CT 06880) film *A Day Is Two Feet Long* in much the same way. The film juxtaposes one nature scene against another to create a mood about the peacefulness and magnificence of nature. Focus on just one scene—perhaps that of mallards paddling serenely across a pond—to induce words that describe both physical setting and mood. Or allow students to produce a potpourri of descriptive lines in reaction to the entire film. Meld the lines together as a class poem.

Use scenes in *Naturally Speaking* (Prima Education Products, Division of Hudson Photographic Industries, Inc., Irvington-on-Hudson, NY 10533) in a similar way to spark descriptive words and sentences. After viewing one of the strips titled "Sounds of Silence at a Pond," students will fill a board with phrases evoking the muted sounds and sights of a pond. For advanced students you may extend the experience by reading a few paragraphs of Henry Thoreau's *Walden* before they enjoy the audio-visual adventure. Other titles in this exceptionally expressive series are "Feelings in a Forest," "Water Brook Songs," and "The Working Sea, Wind and Sand." A bilingual narration in Spanish and English is available.

Two other sound filmstrip series distributed by Prima also are splendid for triggering talk about the world encountered by city students in early elementary grades. Real life pictures portray the beauty of each season in *The Four Seasons in the City*. In "Fall Comes to the City" young viewers see the change from summer to winter as the days shorten, the trees drop their leaves, and even the games of children change. In "The Sights and Sounds of Winter" viewers experience the cool cleanness of a newly fallen snow and the lights and decorations that transform city streets into a holiday wonderland. "Spring Comes to the City" is a profusion of flowers bursting into color, shown with time-lapse photography, and a downpouring of spring showers. "The Sights and Sounds of Summer" is filled with the joys of summertime play.

The second series is actually two, *Let's Talk About* and *More to Talk About*. Titles include "Let's Talk About Bridges and Boats," "Let's Talk About Signs We See," "Shapes We See in the City," and "Buildings We See in the City." If you are teaching in an urban area and are working with bilingual students, you will find this series particularly helpful. Some of the signs are in both English and Spanish in "Let's Talk About the Signs We See," and commonly encountered objects are shown to which English and Spanish names can be attached.

You may wish to experiment with a do-it-yourself approach. Scholastic (Englewood Cliffs, NJ 07632) markets a kit called Quick Slide. With it, students can convert small, colored pictures from clay-coated or slick magazines such as *National Geographic, Newsweek,* and *Time* into homemade slides that project with an ordinary slide projector. The kit consists of "film," plastic slide covers, a stick for rubbing, a sponge, and easy-to-follow directions. To determine if paper is clay coated, rub a wet finger in a small circle to see if a whitish film comes off on your fingertip.

Less expensive slides can be made with clear contact paper. Just cut a 35mm slide-sized picture from a slick magazine, and cut a similar-sized piece of clear contact paper. Carefully remove the protective cover, and stick the contact to the face of the chosen picture. Rub the slick outer surface of the contact paper with the edge of your fingernail or a discarded ice-cream stick to remove all the air from between the contact and the picture. Soak the slide in water until the clay coating of the picture dissolves. You may have to rub your fingers along the back of the slide to remove the clay backing. Adding a few drops of liquid detergent may help the backing to slip off more easily. Allow the slide to dry, spray the sticky side with hair spray to preserve it, and mount in a discarded slide frame.

Ms. Myra Weiger uses this type of homemade slide to trigger ideas for poetry writing. Students in her class make a series of related slides. As they project them, they read poetry-like lines they have written, which have been stimulated by the visual images they have chosen.

One can make full-sized transparencies in much the same way. One creative fifth-grade teacher, Ms. Patricia Baxter, cut from a newspaper an advertisement for carpet named after Jonathan Livingston Seagull. The ad was a profusion of golds, blues, and whites and depicted a bird in graceful flight. Removing the backing from a piece of contact paper she had cut to the picture's size, she placed it sticky side down on the face of the advertisement. After thoroughly rubbing the glossy surface to remove air bubbles, she soaked off the backing. Voilà—a transparent picture in color ready for projection. Ms. Baxter projected her version as she read soaring, diving gull sentences from *Jonathan Livingston Seagull* by Richard Bach (Macmillan, 1970). Her students quickly supplied other gull words to write into poems.

Kodak (Consumer Markets Division, Rochester, NY 14650) will send directions for making a simple, inexpensive camera from an ordinary film cartridge. Just write and ask for customer service pamphlet AA-5, *How to Make and Use a Pinhole Camera*. Students in upper-elementary grades will have no difficulty reading the brochure and following the directions. With their homemade cameras, they can snap photos, which must then be sent out for developing. Mount the pictures to a surface; as students talk about their snapshots, they record descriptive sentences. Of course, if you have access to an old Polaroid camera, you may prefer that students take pictures with it. In this case there is no waiting for developing and one gets on-the-spot pictures about which students can immediately project words and sentences. Encourage young-sters to take a series of pictures on the same theme, about which they then can write a number of descriptive sentences.

Suggest that they search for a musical selection on tape or disk to play as they display their pictures with an opaque projector while reading their words and sentences.

ATTACHING MEANING TO WORDS

CRUISING FOR WORDS   Some cruise ships offer trips to nowhere; they are just short excursions with no ports of call and with pleasure and relaxation as prime objectives. Teachers can take their students on cruises to nowhere with short walks along a path covered with fallen leaves, around the block, near a neighborhood construction site, through newly fallen snow, through a pocket park, across an empty field or vacant, littered lot, or just by a row of shops. If you combine talking with walking, you will offer pleasure and relaxation and at the same time help students identify words to use in verbalizing about things in their daily environment.

A cruise through fallen leaves can trigger such words as crunchy, crackling, crisp, decaying, and even pungent. A city cruise can produce littered, refuse, congestion, siren, or ear-shattering. These words surface naturally as youngsters talk about what they are seeing. You may aid the process by asking, "What is that pungent odor?" as you raise your head in a sniff, or you may ask students to look for pieces of refuse discarded by inconsiderate people. Use of *pungent* and *refuse* in meaningful contexts such as these can add these words to children's functional vocabularies. For reinforcement, try using the new words more than once and upon returning to the classroom, encourage children to record words talked about on the cruise. The resulting word chart can serve as an aid for later written expression.

"Cruises" to such places as airports, farms, zoos, nature reserves, train stations, shops, industrial plants, colleges, museums, aquariums, botanical gardens, public buildings and monuments, and historical points of interest allow young people to learn many new words. With little effort and generally with high interest, they attach meaningful verbal labels to things seen.

To prepare for such an excursion, sketch a map of the area to be visited. Young observers carry map sketches with them, and as they make stops to look, listen, and analyze, they add labels to their maps. A map of an airport will begin to bear labels such as observation deck, passenger lounge, check-in counter, lockers, boarding lounge, boarding gate, customs area, security check, shuttle bus, people mover, conveyor belt, runway, control tower, and hanger. A map of a nature reserve will begin to bear labels such as the blind, fern area, hemlock stand, marsh, beaver dam, and the names of specific kinds of fauna and flora.

For visits to industrial sites, you may find a flow chart a more useful device for student recording. Labels will clarify steps in the process being observed, and labeling done on site makes it more likely that students will attach meaning to a process.

And, of course, talking about visits after returning to the classroom will produce additional words. Compiling a glossary of terms after an excursion is a worthwhile summarizing activity. Each contributor must compose a brief explanation of a term, including pertinent facts and perhaps indicate pronunciation. The glossary becomes a ready reference for students participating in writing activities that stem from the excursion.

DETERMINING MEANING FROM CONTEXT*   A fun way to relate meaning to context is to play with nonsense words. Students study the way a nonsense word is used in an

*This activity is based on an idea described by Hayakawa in *Language in Thought and Action,* 2nd ed. (Harcourt Brace, 1963).

otherwise normal sentence and construct definitions for it. For example, print the following sentences on a large piece of charting paper:

He *grimpled* to his friend across the room, and his friend *grimpled* back.

Grimpling can give you a sore throat.

When he *grimpled* next to my ear, I thought I would be deaf for life.

It is not polite to *grimple* at the dinner table.

His constant *grimpling* got on my nerves.

What is a meaning for the nonsense word *grimple* as used in these sentences? Students in small groups can attempt definitions, i.e., to call out loudly, to shout, or, sometimes, to burp, and construct a proper dictionary entry. Suggest that each group check what goes into a typical dictionary entry and the order in which each item is given. Suggest also that the pronunciation can be found by checking the pronunciation of a rhyming word (in this case, *pimple*) and that the definition is written by checking the dictionary for the meaning of a word that appears to be used in the same way. Students write their dictionary entries on index cards similar to the following:

grim ple   (grim′ pəl), v.   grimpled, grimpling.
 1: to call out loudly.   2: to speak noisily.   3: to shout.
 4: sometimes, to burp.

On the reverse of the card, students compose additional sentences to indicate ways the word is used.

Other nonsense words are given below in sentence contexts that students can analyze. Type these sentences onto cards and place them in a learning station alongside a stack of blank index cards. Include this direction sheet:

WHAT   1. Read the sentences on card A. Figure out the meaning or meanings of the underlined nonsense word.

TO   2. On an empty index card write a dictionary entry for the word. You may check rhyming and related words in a regular dictionary.

DO   3. Turn over the index card and write other sentences that show how the nonsense word is used.

HERE   4. When you have free time, return to this station, and do the same for cards B, C, D, and E.

A

The car *trused* on the icy pavement.
He *trused* and fell, breaking his arm in the process.
Trusing on the freshly waxed floor, he grabbed for the table and knocked all the glasses onto the floor.
Sally hung on the rail for fear of *trusing*.

B

Bob was a particularly *juppy* boy.
The loss of his money made him *juppy*.
The girl who felt *juppy* walked slowly and wore a frown on her face.
Bill tried to laugh, even though he felt more *juppy* than happy.
Juppiness is contagious. Once one person in a crowd begins to feel *juppy*, others feel *juppy* too.

C

The long, sharp blade of the *krandy* can cut through the toughest material.
The handle of Joe's *krandy* broke off.
Don't swing the *krandy* so high when you use it.
He *krandied* his way through the pile of material.
I wouldn't use a *krandy*. It is too dangerous.

D

He always acted rather *fleapily.*
Morris crept *fleapily* into the room.
The thief looked *fleapily* down the hall before making a move.
Fran did not want anyone to see her, so she walked *fleapily.*
He made not a sound as he neared the open door. Each step was *fleapily*
taken.

E

Judy felt *gacky* that day. She had won the prize.
When I feel *gacky,* I can overcome everything and anything!
The *gacky* woman had the biggest smile on her face.
It is great to feel *gacky* once in a while, but it sure tires you out to feel
gacky all of the time.

FIGURING OUT REAL WORDS   Upper-grade elementary
students who have devised dictionary entries for nonsense
words can use the word analysis skills they have acquired to
figure out the meanings of real words encountered in reading
or listening.

Keep a supply of index cards available. Young people can
take a card when they come across an unknown word in their
reading, and from context clues, try to figure out its meaning
and write a dictionary entry. They check their entry against
an actual entry in a classroom dictionary and revise their own
accordingly. They write on the back of the card sentences
similar to the one encountered originally.

Because this is a thinking-discovery activity, students may
find it easier to work as word-detective partners. When either
partner finds an unfamiliar word, the detectives work together
to figure out a definition from context clues.

Detective partners who have analyzed word clues, developed definitions, and written sentences for previously unfamiliar words can become leaders of a classroom guessing
game. Partners write their new word on the board and read
their model sentences. Classmates try to guess the definition.

The student who first figures out the definition becomes the next leader.

Detective-prepared cards go into the classroom dictionary and can be the source of materials for a teacher-led guessing game when there are a few minutes to be filled between activities. The teacher draws a card from the file and throws out word clues, "I'm thinking of a word that is used for a badge. . . . It is sometimes a mark of honor. . . . It is used often to refer to military badges. . . . It has four syllables. . . . It starts with *i*."

After giving each clue, the teacher pauses to see if anyone knows the word by saying it and using it in an appropriate sentence; i.e., "Insignia. He wore a gold insignia on his jacket."

Students who have played this guessing game on several occasions may enjoy leading it themselves. Teacher takes a back seat as a student calls out clues, much in the fashion of some popular TV game programs.

Clues to help others guess words can be acted out as well as given orally. A student pantomimist might pretend he or she holds a badge in hand, pretend to pin it to a classmate, or make marching motions with the body to help guessers think of *insignia.*

Pantomiming is particularly effective when students are working with action, feeling, or object words. Action words such as collapse, clutch, snooze, ransack, shove, dawdle, investigate, or bustle are fun to pantomime. This activity will call forth synonyms of the word being enacted and will unearth related words.

Feeling words that are easily explored through pantomime include exhilarated, spiritless, quivering, flustered, jittery, tranquil, overjoyed, annoyed, downhearted, mirthful, nonchalant, and depressed. Equivalents for use with younger students are tired, sad, pleased, nervous, afraid, excited, and thankful.

Object words that lend themselves to pantomiming are

those having action associated with them, i.e., mural, propeller, whirligig beetle, and mound.

Vary the way clues are given. Some days ask for verbal clues, other days rely on nonverbal clues. Actually it is most fun to let the person directing the guessing game decide which kinds of clues he or she wants to give. The nature of the word itself may be the determining factor.

TALKING OF AND WRITING OF

In "The Walrus and the Carpenter" the walrus suggests, "The time has come . . . to talk of many things." Perhaps the time has come in classrooms to talk of many things as well, for it is through "talking of" that young people hear new words and gradually attach meaning to them. They gradually try out these words in their own conversations and make them part of their own vocabularies. Making word whirligigs, charts, mobiles, and so forth is really a means to an end—skill in handling the words listed.

Skill in handling these words is further developed by "writing of." The whirligigs, charts, and mobiles serve as jumping off places as young people attempt to consign their thoughts to paper. The charts spark composing; seeing a word and thinking about it trigger ideas that snowball into stories, descriptions, and reports. Word charts also serve as spelling guides for children writing on a particular topic. If a new word related to the topic is within easy view, children are more likely to use that word when "writing of" and to spell it correctly. This is a definite asset for young people who are becoming bilingual or bidialectal. It is an asset too for a youngster who has a mind full of exciting ideas but is unable to spell very accurately.

So fill your room with words. Fill it by "talking of" and "writing of" and splashing words—words—words onto bulletin boards and charts.

The muttering crow
Asked the stuttering crow,
"Why does the bee have a sword to his fiddle?
Why does a bee have a sword to his fiddle?"
"Bee-cause," said the other crow,
"Bee-cause,
B B B B B B B B B B B B B B B-cause."
Just then a bee flew close to their rail:—
"Buzzzzzzzzzzz zzzzzzzzz zz zzzzzzz zzzzzzzzzzzzzzz
    ZZZZZZZZ.
And those two black crows
Turned pale,
And away those crows did sail.
Why?
B B B B B B B B B B B B B B B-cause.
B B B B B B B B B B B B B B B-cause.
"Buzzzzzzzzzzz zzzzzzzzz zz zzzzzzz zzzzzzzzzzzzzzz
    ZZZZZZZZ."

"TWO OLD CROWS," VACHEL LINDSAY

3. B B B B B B B B B-CAUSE: *Activities with Word Sounds and Shapes*

Appearance and sound play an important part in a reader's enjoyment of a poem. Much of the effectiveness of Vachel Lindsay's piece, "Two Old Crows," is derived from the Bs and buzzes that resound throughout the lines. Much of the effectiveness comes too from the appearance of the string of zs spread across the page. "The Old Crows" is a harmonious blend of sight, sound, and meaning, a blend that tickles a reader's funny bone.

Although visual and sound qualities may not appear so strikingly in prose selections, such elements are important there also. Prose writers may use a series of harsh consonant sounds to build up tension or employ softer sounds to create a mellow mood; to produce a particular effect, they may turn to alliteration, assonance, and consonance, or they may create sentences that deliberately have flowing or jerky movements.

Read the following passage aloud to yourself to hear how essential sound is in conveying one writer's impression of October:

Now come the quiet days of Indian Summer and the quiet nights of starlight and leaf scuffle. October's magnificence comes without a whisper. Listen as you may, you never hear a maple leaf turning to translucent gold or an oak leaf turning from green to tan to purplish bronze. An October wind can bring them sailing from the trees and down the road, across the meadow, with a swishing crispness and a rustle. But no frog croaks, no green cricket drones, no harvest fly shrills. The quiet deepens toward the winter silence when snowflakes will whisper as they fall in the long night.*

The sounds of the season echo in a reader's ear—*w* in *without a whisper* (alliteration), the *ight* sound in *nights of starlight*

---

*From the editorial "The Quiet Comes," *The New York Times,* October 6, 1974.

(rhyming), the *f* in *leaf scuffle* (consonance), the short *i* in *with a swishing crispness* (assonance).

Teachers can introduce young people in elementary schools to an appreciation of sound and visual effects in oral and written communication by involving them in building sound meanings and visual meaning relationships. The result may not be many editorialists for *The New York Times* or many Vachel Lindsays, who can manipulate sight-sound/meaning relationships so effectively, but the result may be youngsters who find language intriguing.

PLAYING WITH SHAPES OF WORDS

FINDING PICTURES IN WORDS   A recent "Henry" comic strip shows young Henry in a classroom where one of his friends is writing the word *lion* on the board. Another follows with *elephant*. When Henry's turn arrives, his word is *camel*, and in typical humorous-Henry fashion, he writes a response that delights his teacher, who is pictured with a broad grin across her face.

Students can play with words Henry-style. Many words can be written to express their meaning visually. Try just a few. Ask, "Can you write *round* to show roundness? *tall* to show tallness? *fat* to show fatness? *rain* to show raining? *shaking* to show shakiness? *broken* to show brokenness? *climb* to show climbing? *crooked* to show crookedness? *slide* to show sliding? *tiny* to show tininess?" Ask students to reveal pictures in these words and others such as drop, leap, trip, smile, frown, corner, crowded, invisible, waver, tilt, snake, bend, branch, reversed, upside-down, flat, down, icicle, skyscraper, hole, bowl, or jump.

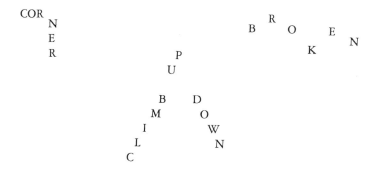

EXAMPLES OF WORDS EXPRESSED VISUALLY

Add a bit of color. Students with a variety of colored flo-pens can write colorful, rainbow, spectrum, dawn, sunset, autumn, kaleidoscope, or night, as well as the myriad of English color words, i.e., golden, rust, and sky-blue pink.

Try something slightly more complicated and even more fun—visualizing phrases. Students can write *column of smoke* so that the words communicate the meaning of the phrase. From there, go on to other phrases such as happy face, cup and saucer, a hole in the ground, sliding down the slide, on thin ice, ant hill, scrambled eggs, taking off into the sky, coming in for a landing, or falling down a flight of stairs. Encourage students to search out other phrases to present in concrete form. Ask those developing bilingual skills to express words and phrases visually in their first and target languages.

Once students have discovered the knack of creating pictures in words, a next step is to write short poems that communicate their meanings through words or phrases in picture forms. For instance, after playing with *a happy face,* they may write a concrete poem that actually smiles for Halloween:

JACK-O'-LANTERN

Let's carve
two eyes, a nose,
a crooked, crazy chin
and put a shining candle in
to give
our
Jack
a

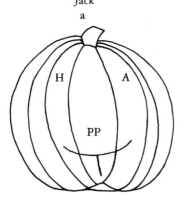

glowing grin*

Or if they have played with action words, they might devise a little piece such as:

---

*Dorothy Hennings, *Educational Projections,* volume 1, number 1, reprinted by permission of the editor.

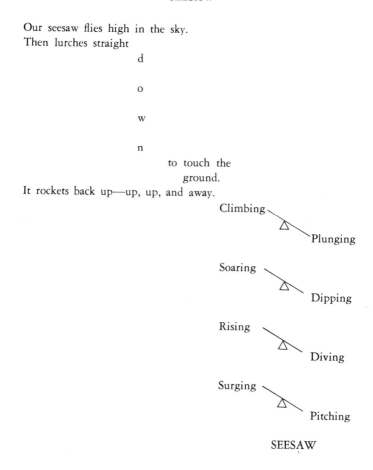

SEESAW

Our seesaw flies high in the sky.
Then lurches straight

d

o

w

n

to touch the
ground.
It rockets back up—up, up, and away.

Climbing
Plunging

Soaring
Dipping

Rising
Diving

Surging
Pitching

SEESAW

You can stimulate this kind of poetry writing by encouraging students to read concrete poems. An excellent source for youngsters in primary grades is Ruth Belov Gross's *The Laugh Book* (New York: Scholastic Book Services, 1971). In it is a delightful little poem about a roller-coaster ride that has always tickled the funny bones of students to whom I have read it. Another is an umbrella song filled with falling drops of wet rain in the shape of an umbrella. This book is a must for teachers in lower-elementary grades.

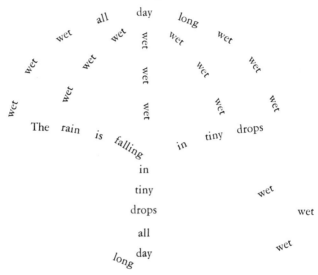

   To students in upper-elementary grades you will want to read and show poems from Robert Froman's *Street Poems* (McCall, 1971). According to the cover blurb, "*Street Poems* is what happens when you cross a picture with a poem." One of my favorites from this book is called "Blow Up":

                    B L O W   U P

                                                    higher

Wind

                                              and

      around

                                        higher

      the

                              and

corner,   higher

                  and

Blow

            high

the

      up

dust

In a similar vein but with a slightly different twist is Dexter Pease's unique combination of meaning and picture:

a
ap
app
appe
appea
appear
appeara
appearan
appearanc
appearance
        disappearance
        disappearanc
        disappearan
        disappeara
        disappear
        disappea
        disappe
        disapp
        disap
        disa
        dis
        di
        d

        r
        re
        rea
        reap
        reapp
        reappe
        reappea
        reappear
        reappeara
        reappearan
        reappearanc
        reappearance

Share this with students to see if they can devise similar word picture relationships by repeating a word or words. Lois Stevens's third-grade class did this and came up with these:

```
flag flag flag flag
l      f flag flag fl
a       lag flag flag
g flag flag flag flag        B
fflag flag flag flag         BU
l                            BUI
a                            BUIL
g                            BUILD
f                            BUILDI
l                            BUILDIN
a                            BUILDING
g                                          HAT HAT
                                           HAT HAT
                                           HAT HAT
                                     HAT HAT HAT HAT
```

SQUIGGLING   Hand out copies of this squiggles diagram. What do the squiggles represent—Plumes of smoke carried upward on a breeze? Fireworks spraying into the air? Kites dancing cloudward? Rockets heading toward the moon?

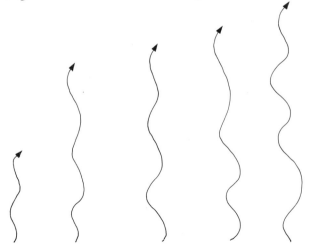

Streamers hurled skyward? Mice jumping on pogo sticks? Ants pouncing on a trampoline? Salmon jumping upstream?

Rotate the page clockwise ninety degrees. Now what do the squiggles represent—Worms burrowing through soil? Breezes moving over a landscape? Fish swimming through water? Cars spurting off at the Indianapolis Speedway? Waves racing toward shore? Sun rays dancing through a window?

Again rotate the page clockwise another ninety degrees. What do the squiggles represent now—Raindrops cascading down a windowpane? Icicles hanging from a roof? Anchors dropping from boats? Fish lines dangling in search of fish? Leaves falling to the ground?

Rotate the page once more and what do we see—Jet trails cutting the sky? Snakes slithering on the ground? Lines moving across an unsynchronized TV?

Brainstorm images like these with students who have copies of the diagram. One child serves as scribe, writing each image idea on a strip of paper. Then ask students to decide which image they think is the best and use it, with the squiggle held at the appropriate angle, to build a class image picture. The initial words are supplemented with other words written onto the lines of the squiggle.

Perhaps students decide they want to devise an image picture with the squiggles pointing upward with a fireworks theme. On the first squiggle they print upward the word fireworks; on the second they print the remainder of the phrase originally brainstormed, "spraying into the air." Then ask what fireworks do. Students may reply, "coloring the sky," or "lighting the sky" or "filling the sky with color." Write these onto the third line. Then ask what the sky is filled with or what colors fill the sky. Youngsters will probably supply lots of color words to write upward onto the fourth line. Then ask students to express how they feel when they see the sky filled up with colors for a feeling thought to write on the last line. The result may be something like

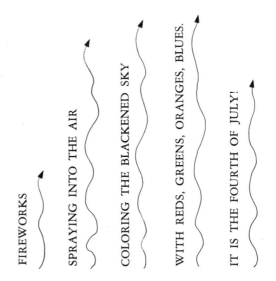

Another way to handle the session is to have students think of many words that describe the initial word. For example, *waves* may call forth dancing, playing, white-capped, powerful, rolls, rushes, jumps, pushes, foamy, misty, fast-moving, washing shoreward, striking the shore, eroding, watery train, and so forth. In groups students select from the brainstormed words and build them into a squiggle picture:

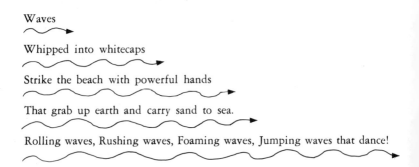

Create several of these picture images as a class or in groups. At a learning station stack extra squiggle diagrams and strips onto which all the brainstormed images were originally written, so that students can compose additional squiggle thoughts.

If you strike gold with line squiggles and your students produce some really creative images, try more complex squiggles. Lois Stevens invented a combination of lines and curves to which her mid-elementary students added words. They decided to add a start arrow to indicate where to begin reading:

THE OCTOPUS

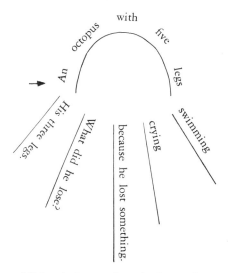

Make up additional sheets of squiggles and slip them into pouches in a learning center. Add a task card that states:

Choose a ditto from this pouch or create your own funny-shaped squiggle. Then study the squiggle from all different directions. First hold it with one side up. Then turn it upside-down. When inspiration strikes, add words to the squiggle.

Here are some ideas for squiggles:

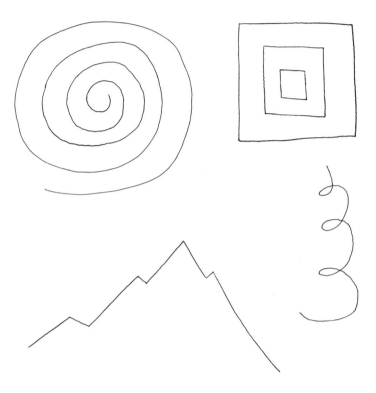

Incidentally, playing with squiggles is a good activity for youngsters developing bilingual skills. When brainstorming words and phrases as potential thoughts for a squiggle, they can give the words in both the first and target languages. Similar expressions from both languages are written next to each other on the board. Students then fill in the squiggle twice, choosing from words in both languages. When sharing their squiggles orally, they read both their first-language version and their English version.

SHAPING   The outline of a shape may spark word patterns as creative as those stimulated by imaginative squiggles. Students compose thoughts to write along the major lines of the shape or to fill in the open space within it. Here are just a few examples of shape thoughts to share with students. These shape thoughts were created by students in Ms. Lois Stevens's third grade:

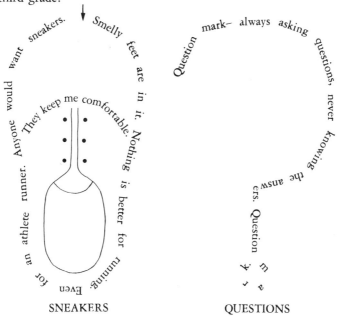

SNEAKERS   QUESTIONS

Other outline shapes for elementary students to fill with words are:

A hand, foot, or profile sketch: a student draws on paper an outline of his or her own hand or foot or stands before the projecting light of a filmstrip projector while another student draws an outline of his or her profile by tracing the shadow cast on a paper. The student then writes words "About Me" following the lines of the profile or hand or foot outline.

A pair of spectacles: a student who wears glasses outlines the rims on paper and then writes words about "What I See" into or onto the shape.

A light bulb, an automobile, a motorcycle, or any energy user: a student fills the outlined bulb or motorcycle with words "About Energy."

The dial of a clock: a student outlines or fills the shape with a thought "About Time."

Any animal: a student outlines or fills the shape of the animal with descriptive words, placing the words at the location on the animal being described; i.e., words about the long neck would be written along the extended neck of a giraffe.

Any symbol: a student outlines or fills the shape with words "About the Symbol." Good symbols are the peace symbol and holiday symbols such as a Christmas tree, Valentine heart, Chanukah candles, Washington's hatchet, Halloween witches and goblins, or winter snowmen.

Geographical areas as shown on a map: students fill or outline the mapped area with descriptive words, i.e., "About the Mississippi" or "About Australia."

SUBSTITUTING PICTURES FOR WORDS The eye-catcher for an advertisement in a Sunday edition of *The New York Times* was a cartoon-like sketch that depicted a dollar sign with human characteristics; the sign had legs that were propelling it along:

The attention-getters on a Citation Press book cover are drawings of letters of the alphabet in the shape of human figures with arms, legs, and head:

Both designs are examples of what might well be called "visual personification" or assigning human characteristics to inanimate objects in a visual image. Designing such visual images is a natural next step for upper-grade students who have worked with shapes and squiggles.

Start simply by asking young people to draw a human pencil. Encourage them to show their drawings to others to compare techniques employed. Continue by asking students to draw a human TV set, a human hand calculator, a human milk carton, a human Coke bottle, a human penny, a human tea kettle, or a human automobile. Once they have produced a visual representation, they can add a caption to extend the personification, or they can use their visuals as a jumping-off idea for storywriting.

A more difficult task is designing visual hyperboles or exaggerations. An advertisement for cruises aboard an ocean liner is one of the best examples of visual hyperbole I have seen. The huge liner is pictured standing on a New York City street amid skyscrapers and cars. It depicts the impossible, something that could never happen—an ocean liner parked on a city street.

To start young people creating visual exaggerations, help them to "dream the impossible dream." An opener might be, "Let's imagine impossible happenings. Close your eyes and picture an ocean liner parked on a big city street. . . . Close your eyes and picture a man carrying an elephant upon his back. . . ." After you have asked students to picture some impossible things, encourage them to suggest other impossibilities to visualize.

Once they have begun to imagine impossible happenings, they may be ready to convert their mental pictures into actual pictures on paper. As they sketch suggest that they think of a catchy phrase to add at the bottom; for example, the cruise advertisement commands, "Just add water."

COMPOSING ALPHABET POEMS

> Rain drops fall from darkened sky
> And paint the land in green of spring.
> I look up to see the sun
> Now smiling out between the clouds.

This little piece is a play with both visual and verbal images. The words themselves communicate, but so does the form of the poem with its key word spelled out in the first letter of each line.

Introduce this type of word experience by brainstorming with children words that begin with each of the letters in the chosen key word. For example, brainstorming *rain*, children might suggest the words river, rushing, raindrops, road, rope, running, riverlets, raining, resoaking, requiring, receive, raw, ravaging, rapture; alter, act, ask, apples, at, after, a, an, and, advent, advance, adapt, add; idle, I, if, it, in, into, involve, injure, inject, ice, immediate; and night, never, now, nine, no, nightingale, not, news, noon, or net. List identified words on the chalkboard or on a chart, and add more words by searching through the appropriate parts of a dictionary. Everyone will be amazed by the number of words that a dictionary check will bring to light.

List the letters of the chosen word vertically on a sheet. In groups of three, students can compose lines starting with the letters of the key word, choosing brainstormed words or others that surface as students begin to work the words into a meaningful context. The product is an ABC or alphabet poem, a form of poetry that even first-grade students can devise. First graders need only select one word per line as in:

> Icicles
> Cling
> Everywhere.

Third graders can work with more expanded thoughts in the form of phrases such as did the youngsters in Lois Stevens's class:

> Magnificent me
> Everyday person.

> Teaches very good
> Excellent speller
> Acts very good
> Comes when you need her
> Happy all the time
> Expert reader
> Runs very fast.

Older students may produce lines with more involved syntax as in:

> Bouncing
> Around—
> Light and
> Lively in
> Summer.

> Sleighing on
> Newly fallen snow—
> Oceans of fun in
> Winter.

They may enjoy using letters of their first and/or last names as line beginners, of a month, of a day of the week, of a holiday or of a season.

PLAYING WITH SOUNDS OF WORDS

CHANTING   Do you remember the nursery rhyme favorite:

> How much wood would a woodchuck chuck
> If a woodchuck would chuck wood?

This jingle and other equally well-known ones are especially appropriate introductions to the rhythmic patterns that are an important part of verbal communication.

Working from a wall chart on which a student has printed the jingle, have your class chant the lines together, choral-speaking style as you lead with your hands to maintain the beat. Repeat the lines several times until youngsters can chant them securely with real gusto.

Then distribute percussion rhythm band instruments such as drums, sticks, tambourines, and cymbals so that each class member holds something to bang as the class chants. The percussion instruments now are the rhythm keepers, with the largest drum starting and establishing the rhythm for the group.

To add interest, you may wish to divide the class into three groups and try the chant round-style. The first group establishes the basic rhythm by beating its instruments and chanting "woodchuck, woodchuck" over and over again, keeping a steady beat, not too slow nor too fast. Once the first group has established the beat, the second group joins the chant instrumentally and verbally by calling "chucky-chuck, chucky-chuck." This group is basically using a quick-quick-slow beat whereas the first group is doing a simple slow-slow beat. The third group joins by speaking the complete lines to the beat set by the first two groups.

As students acquire the feel for synchronized chanting, try subdividing into more chant groups. A fourth group can chant the quick-quick, quick-quick of woody-woody, woody-woody. A fifth group can chant the three-to-one beat of chuckety-chuck, chuckety-chuck. The following diagram shows how all the groups fit together:

How / much / wood / would a / wood / chuck / chuck /
Wood / chuck / wood / chuck / wood / chuck / wood /
Chucky / chuck / chucky / chuck / chucky / chuck / chucky /
Woody / woody / woody / woody / woody / woody / woody /
Chuckety / chuck / chuckety / chuck / chuckety / chuck / chuckety /

If a / wood / chuck / would / chuck / wood?
chuck / wood / chuck / wood / chuck / wood
chuck / chucky / chuck / chucky / chuck / chucky
woody / woody / woody / woody / woody / woody
chuck / chuckety / chuck / chuckety / chuck / chuckety

When all the groups are in action both vocally and instrumentally, participants will literally feel the rhythm flowing through their bodies. The sound is much like the monkey dance performed by Balinese men in Indonesia in which the men chant a rapid, staccato "Cha cha cha, cha cha cha" repeatedly, varying the loudness, tempo, and pattern, moving their bodies to the musical rhythm they are establishing with the repeated sounds and producing such a powerful performance that members of the audience feel the beat in their own bodies.

You can experiment with other nursery rhymes to achieve similar effects. Nursery rhymes work particularly well in this context, because they have such a clear, steady beat. "Hey Diddle Diddle" can simulate a barnyard. As one group of students chants:

Hey diddle diddle
The cat and the fiddle,
The cow jumped over the moon;
The little dog laughed
To see such sport,
And the dish ran away with the spoon.

a second group beats the rhythm out on percussion instruments. When groups know the words and the rhythm, introduce other parts. A small group makes cow sounds, another cat sounds, another fiddle sounds, and another laughter sounds. Add more animals and their sounds to the chant. Build toward five or six groups chanting different parts. The result is a barnyard ruckus.

Once youngsters have caught on to this technique, apply it to similar rhymes. For example, small groups can chant flower names to the basic beat while a group chants:

> Mary, Mary, quite contrary,
> How does your garden grow?
> With silver bells and cockle-shells,
> And pretty maids all in a row.

The effect is a garden bursting into flower.

Young children can play with "Jack, Be Nimble." As one group chants the lines, a second group beats the rhythm on percussion instruments while saying "Jump, Jack! Jump, Jack!" again and again. Or as one group chants the lines of "Little Miss Muffet," the rhythm keepers strike the beat with instruments and intone, "Tuffet, Muffet, Tuffet, Muffet." Once you have tried several of these with your class, place a copy of *Selections from Brian Wildsmith's Mother Goose* (Scholastic Book Services, 1964) on a table. Students can select rhymes and figure out a plan for converting them into rhythmic chants. Later they can lead classmates in chants that they have put together.

Print directions for the center on a half sheet of colored oak tag. Print with India ink and laminate the direction sheet if you have access to a laminating machine. This will make the station usable year after year without expending additional effort and materials.

TO DISCOVER THE RHYTHMIC PATTERN IN SOME POEMS
◄————— YOUR PURPOSE —————►

WHAT YOU WILL DO ————→ 1. Thumb through the book of rhymes on the table. Read some rhymes to yourself until you find one that has a clear, steady beat.

2. Repeat the poem you have selected as you tap out the beat with your hand on the table. Do this as silently as you can so you will not disturb others.

3. Next think of a snappy phrase that fits the beat and that a group might chant as the rest of the class chants the rhyme. Write it on an index card so you will not forget it. Write the poem on the index card too.

4. Think of at least one more snappy phrase that also fits the beat. Record the phrase or phrases on the card as well as your name. Drop the card in the little box.

WHAT WE WILL DO ————→ At the end of the week, you may be the one chosen to lead the class in your chant with the phrases you have designed. We will be doing lots of chants on Friday, so read your rhyme several times. You will want to be able to repeat it without looking at the card too often.

A second-grade teacher, Margaret McGuigans, encouraged youngsters to write variations on nursery rhymes that they had previously chanted as a class. The variations—actually parodies of the rhymes—maintained the same beat as the original, and the children created snappy phrases that a group could chorus as the rest of the class chanted the lines of their rhyme. One child paraphrased "Hickory Dickory Dock":

> Hickory dickory tease
> I heard my brother sneeze.
> "Ka choo ka choo and God bless you."
> Hickory dickory tease.
> (Chanting phrase: ac-choo! ac-choo!)

Another child, who was almost a nonreader, produced:

> Moodily moodily moo
> The cow went into the shoe.
> The shoe turned blue. The cow said "moo."
> How moodily, moodily moo!
> (Chanting phrase: moo-oo! moo-oo!)

Still another created:

> Hickory stickory stew
> A monster once turned blue.
> He ate some goo, got stuck with glue.
> Hickory stickory stew.
> (Chanting phrase: yum-yum; yum-yum)

Ms. McGuigans, the teacher, reports that her students were ecstatic when their written words became a total class oral production. The writing station at which the children produced their parodies was one of the most popular work areas in the room.

TRANSLATING SOUNDS INTO WORDS   Have you ever run a stick along an iron fence to produce ear-tingling zings and clacks? In the little poem that follows, the sounds are translated into "words" that can be uttered aloud to recreate the actual experience:

ZING

> Clang a stick on an iron gate.
> Clickety Clackety
> Zing-Zippity Zing-Zappity
> Now run that stick fast along an iron fence.
> Clickety Clackety
> Zing-Zippity Zing-Zappity
> ZZZZZZZZZZZZZZZZZZzzzzzzzzzzzzzzzzzzzing

Young people enjoy word play that involves *onomatopoeia.* As an opener have students recreate common sounds on paper and then read them. Start simply with bumblebee songs, which are easily translated as bbbbuuuuuzzzzzzzzzzzzzz. Shift to similar mosquito hums, which may be closer to zzzzzzzuuuuuuuuzzzzzz. Listening to portions of the recording *Sounds of Insects* (Scholastic Records, SX 6178, Englewood Cliffs, NJ 07632) will encourage students to listen closely to differentiate among insect calls. This recording is a collection of insect voices including the familiar cricket, hornet, mosquito, and the less familiar longhorn beetle, click beetle, and dragonfly in flight.

Refer back to some of the phonics generalizations students have been learning to apply. What graphemes represent the first part of the hornet's voice? The middle part? The ending part of the cry?

Once students have translated insect voices into graphemes and have a collection of sounds written down, suggest they write one extended sentence describing the activity of one insect. They then split the sentence into segments, each of which becomes a line in a poem that is followed by a line of the insect's sounds, as in the following:

> The bumblebee searching for nectar
> BBBBBBUUUUZZZZZZZZZZZZZZZZZZZZZZZZ.
> Lands upon a bursting rose,
> BBBBBBUUUUZZZZZZZZZZZZZZZZZZZZZZZZ.
> Drinks its fill of nature's sweet,
> BBBBBBUUUUZZZZZZZZZZZZZZZZZZZZZZZZ.
> And buzzing bumbles off.

Or students can combine different insect voices into one piece. Each line describes a different insect and is followed by a line of its song sound.

Shift next to other organisms, i.e., frogs croaking, birds singing, or farm animals vocalizing. These are just as easy to translate into graphemes as are insect voices. Move on to sounds produced by inanimate objects, i.e., an ear-shattering jackhammer in operation, waves striking a shore, paper being wrinkled, rain striking earth, a motor running, a car starting up on a cold morning, a man clearing his throat, a jet taking off, or drums beating. You may wish to develop one of these into a group sound-piece. Write down the sound as an extended first line and follow with a line or two of descriptive words:

hhhhhhhhhhhmmmmmmmmmmmmmmmmmmmmmmmmmmm
My Mazda hums along the road
Smooth and quiet like a cat.
hhhhhhhhhhhhhhhmmmmmmmmmmmmmmmmmm

Design follow-up task cards for students who have already worked with onomatopoeia.

TASK: To write down common animal sounds and use the written sounds in composing beginning poems.

STEPS TO FOLLOW: 1. Here is a list of animals you may have heard calling out:

bluejay	gull	rooster	donkey
frog	horse	chicken	monkey
owl	crow	dog	canary
cat	duck	lion	pig

Select one of these animals or another one you know. Think about the sound it makes. Write the sound on the scrap paper on the table. Try writing the sound in several different ways. Vary the letters you pick to express the sound.

2. Write a long descriptive sentence about the activity or appearance of the animal you have selected. Now combine your sound words with the long sentence. Break up the long sentence into segments as we did in class. Write each segment as a line of poetry, followed by a line of the animal voice sound.

3. Copy your final piece on a card. Post your completed card (with your name on it) on the bulletin board with our class publications.

TASK: To think of sounds heard at different places and events; to write down these sounds using letters; to use these sound words in a beginning poem.

STEPS TO FOLLOW: 1. Here is a list of places or events where you hear numbers of sounds:

city street	4th of July celebration
seashore	airport
farm	expressway
pond	thunderstorm
forest	fire
harbor	railroad or subway station

Select a place or event from the list or make up a place of your own. Then think of all the sounds you would hear there. As you think of a sound, write it down with letters that make the same sound. Record your sounds on scrap paper.

2. When you have recorded at least three or four different sounds, think of a line describing each sound. On your scrap paper write each line down, following it with a line of the related sound words just as we have done in class.

3. Give your piece a title.

4. Copy your six- to eight-line poem onto an index card. Attach your card to the publications bulletin board, with your name at the bottom.

Students who have completed these tasks will be able to undertake a search for words that imitate the sounds of things they designate. For example, some birds have been named with words that imitate their calls, i.e., whippoorwill, cuckoo, bobwhite. The pronunciation of some verbs imitates the associated sound, i.e., pop, splash, trip-trap, whistle, click, clatter, drone, and buzz. The game Ping-Pong has a name that expresses the sound associated with it. A thesaurus is a helpful reference for locating other noisy words.

REPEATING SOUNDS

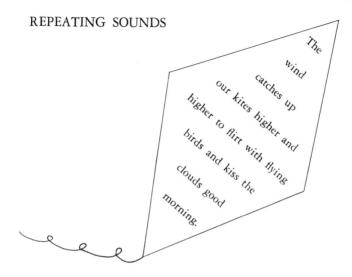

The wind catches up our kites higher and higher to flirt with flying birds and kiss the clouds good morning.

In this piece the shape into which the words have been placed projects part of the image; sound plays an equally important role. The hard *c* sound echoes throughout in catches, kites, kiss, and clouds. The *f* repeats too in flirt and flying. The result is a sound picture, a kind of poem students can play with while simultaneously learning about alliteration.

Alliteration, of course, is two or more words that begin with the same sound or contain the sound on an accented syllable. It is a device employed for effect both in poetry and prose writing.

Motivating students to design alliterative phrases is easy. Begin with writing sound pictures. Ask students to focus on an object that you hold in your hand, a large feather, for example. Ask them to think of other words that start with the same sound. In the case of feather, brainstormers will suggest and record falling, floats, free, forever, fast, friendly, flies, flits, flick, flexible, fancy, fine, fresh, flash, fleck, flight, and flirt. A dictionary check will provide others.

Now sketch a feather shape on a chart. Students in groups build some of the brainstormed words into a feather sentence and fill the feather shape as in:

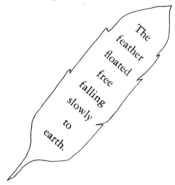

The
feather
floated
free
falling
slowly
to
earth.

Class brainstorming of words and group writing of lines can be a springboard for individual composing. Scatter on a bulletin board colored cutouts of shapes such as balls, gulls, clouds, bees, bubbles, chickens, keys, rabbits, trees, cars, witches, ghosts, circles, doves, robins, balloons, suns, moons, stars, and leaves. As a model, add a kite shape filled with the words above and add a task card with brief directions:

WHAT TO DO: 1. Select a shape. On a piece of scrap paper list words that start with the same sound as the name of the shape.

2. On your scrap paper write a thought about the shape. In composing your thought, include a few of the words that start with the same sound. Edit your piece so that all words are spelled according to the dictionary found on the table.

3. In your best handwriting copy your edited piece onto the shape. Sign your name. Pin the filled-in shape back on the board.

Incidentally, suggest to sophisticated students that they include on their lists words in which the repeated sound is within a word starting an accented syllable. For example, a good *b* word when working with buzzing bees or bouncing balls is *about*.

The book *Noisy Nancy Norris* by Lou Ann Gaeddert (Hale, 1965) can stimulate a different form of alliterative play: humorous naming. Read the story to second, third, or fourth graders. Then suggest that they invent a similar sound play upon their own first name. As an example start with your own name. My name is Dorothy so I usually begin with the name Dottie. Youngsters help me invent a new last name for myself, a name that also begins with *D*. Names commonly suggested are Doodle, Doolittle, Droodle, Dumbwit. Then youngsters help me locate an adjective to go before my new name; the adjective must also begin with *d*. The result is an alliterative name such as Daring Dottie Doodle. Students next consider all the things that Daring Dottie might try to do, especially looking for actions that begin with *d,* i.e., drop, dive, drive, decree, and so forth. Orally as a group the youngsters build a story about Dottie, using some of these words.

Students will be eager to play with their own names in the same way. Just push a table into a corner area, stack up paper and flo-pens, and explain to youngsters that they can go to the corner to write their own humorous name stories. Set aside time for students to read their stories to others. Since most stories will be slightly silly, story sharing is a fun activity, so you might wish to reserve it for Friday afternoons when students are more restless than usual.

To primary-grade youngsters read storybooks that begin with "A is for _____" and continue with "B is for _____." Children can write their own lines following this pattern through all the letters of the alphabet. Encourage them to find several words that go with each letter, as "A is for ants, alligators, and apples," and "B is for buckets, boxes, and bottles." Intermediate-grade youngsters can add an A adjective before each A word, a B adjective before each B word, and so forth; i.e., A is for active ants, ancient alligators, and acid apples; B is for bulky buckets, bottomless boxes, and broken bottles. Students will quickly discover that the dictionary is a handy aid in finding suitable words. By the way, the results will probably be humorous, which upper-elementary-grade students will appreciate.

Numbers in sequence can produce similarly amusing results. Two or more words in each line must contain the same sound as the number that starts the line as in:

> One wonderfully wicked witch with work to do.
> Two twisting twirling trees that tilt.
> Three thirsty trembling thieves out on the town.
> Four fretful foolish folks frozen stiff....

Again the dictionary is a handy tool for finding words that begin with the desired sound, and upper-grade students will enjoy the humorous elements of this writing activity.

Use a participation sound story to extend youngsters' appreciation of how repetition of sounds and words can build up an effect in a story. The old tale of Henny Penny is good for this purpose, because it is filled with rhyming name pairs and repeated phrases.

In preparation, make a copy of these five participation cards:

HENNY PENNY

1. Good morning.
2. Good morning.
3. Good morning.
4. Oh dear! I do believe I have been hit on the head by a piece of sky. This is a disaster! I must go and tell the king that the sky is falling.
5. Ducky Lucky, you will not believe it. I have been hit on my head by a piece of sky. This is a disaster! Will you come with me to tell the king that the sky is falling?
6. Yes, but if there is a disaster, we will need food.

DUCKY LUCKY

1. Hello.
2. Yes, if you have been hit on the head by a piece of sky, it must be a disaster. I will go with you to tell the king that the sky is falling.
3. Goosey Lucy, you will not believe it. Henny Penny has been hit on the head by a piece of sky. This is a disaster! Will you come with Henny Penny and me to tell the king that the sky is falling?
4. Yes, but if there is a disaster, we will need food.

GOOSEY LUCY

1. Hello.
2. Yes, if Henny Penny has been hit on the head by a piece of sky, it must be a disaster. I will go with you and Henny Penny to tell the king that the sky is falling.
3. Turkey Lurkey, you will not believe it. Henny Penny has been hit on the head by a piece of sky. This is a disaster! Will you come with Henny Penny, Ducky Lucky, and me to tell the king that the sky is falling?
4. Yes, but if there is a disaster, we will need food.

TURKEY LURKEY

1. Hello.
2. Yes, if Henny Penny has been hit on the head by a piece of sky, it must be a disaster. I will go with you and Henny Penny and Ducky Lucky to tell the king that the sky is falling.
3. Foxy Loxy, you will not believe it. Henny Penny has been hit on the head by a piece of sky. This is a disaster! Will you come with Henny Penny, Ducky Lucky, Goosey Lucy, and me to tell the king that the sky is falling.
4. Yes, but if there is a disaster, we will need food.

FOXY LOXY

1. Yes, if Henny Penny has been hit on the head by a piece of sky, it must be a disaster. I will take all of you—Henny Penny, Ducky Lucky, Goosey Lucy, and Turkey Lurkey— to tell the king that the sky is falling.

2. It is a long walk to see the king. Henny Penny, Ducky Lucky, Goosey Lucy, and Turkey Lurkey, will you be my guests for lunch this noon? My den is just down this lane. Come with me. If there is a disaster, we will need food.

Also prepare five signs: Foxy Loxy, Turkey Lurkey, Goosey Lucy, Henny Penny, Ducky Lucky. Give a story participation card to each of five children, but keep the name signs in reserve until later.

Now tell the story of Henny Penny to the class. When you get to the lines said by a character, gesture toward the student who holds that character participation card. The youngster speaks the lines with as much expression as he or she can muster.

If you are working with bilingual students, prepare two sets of cards, one in the native language, one in the target language. Tell the tale in the native language first with student participants interjecting dialogue in their own language; then switch to the target language with youngsters interjecting the dialogue in that language. Repeat several times. Someone once called this kind of practice "creative repetition."

The simplified version of the tale I have used goes like this:

Once upon a time in the barnyard lived a foolish hen. Her name was Henny Penny.

One day Henny Penny was making the rounds of the barnyard. She walked by the duck yard and said ... (gesture to Henny)

to her friend Ducky Lucky, who was just waking up and stretching.

Ducky Lucky quacked, ... (gesture to Ducky)

to Henny Penny.

Then Henny Penny strolled over to the pond where the geese liked to swim. She said ... (gesture to Henny)

to another friend, Goosey Lucy, who was already swimming around the edge of the pond.

Goosey Lucy clucked ... (gesture to Goosey)

to Henny Penny.

Finally Henny Penny hopped over to the turkey pen where the turkeys lived. She clucked ... (gesture to Henny)

to her dear friend Turkey Lurkey.

Turkey Lurkey called back ... (gesture to Turkey)

Then Henny Penny strolled back across the yard. As she was walking along, Penny chanced to pass under a large oak tree that spread its branches in all directions. She was just passing under the tree when she felt a large piece of something hit her on the head. Henny Penny exclaimed ... (gesture to Henny)

Henny Penny scurried off. The first one she happened to meet was her friend Ducky Lucky. To Ducky Lucky she cried out . . . (gesture to Henny)

Ducky Lucky was as excited as Henny Penny. He quacked . . . (gesture to Ducky)

So Henny Penny and Ducky Lucky scurried off. They had only gone a short distance when whom should they meet but Goosey Lucy. Ducky Lucky called out to Goosey Lucy . . . (gesture to Ducky)

Goosey Lucy was as excited as Henny Penny and Ducky Lucky and immediately agreed . . . (gesture to Goosey)

So Henny Penny, Ducky Lucky, and Goosey Lucy scurried off. They had only gone a short distance across the yard when whom should they meet but Turkey Lurkey. Goosey Lucy called to Turkey Lurkey . . . (gesture to Goosey)

Turkey Lurkey was just as excited as Henny Penny and Ducky Lucky and Goosey Lucy, and he exclaimed . . . (gesture to Turkey)

So Henny Penny, Ducky Lucky, Goosey Lucy, and Turkey Lurkey scurried off. They walked and they walked and they walked and they were a long distance from the barnyard when they met Foxy Loxy. Turkey Lurkey called to Foxy Loxy . . . (gesture to Turkey)

Foxy Loxy was just as excited as Henny Penny and Ducky Lucky and Goosey Lucy, and Turkey Lurkey. He cried out . . . (gesture to Foxy)

So they scurried off together. They had only gone a short distance along the road when Foxy Loxy stopped short and said . . . (gesture to Foxy)

Now Henny Penny, Ducky Lucky, Goosey Lucy, and Turkey Lurkey were feeling like lunch. They had been traveling for a rather long time. They replied together . . . (gesture to Henny, Ducky, Goosey, and Turkey)

Henny Penny, Ducky Lucky, Goosey Lucy, and Turkey Lurkey trotted with Foxy Loxy to his den just down the lane. First, Henny Penny went into the den. Then Ducky Lucky went into the den. Next Goosey Lucy went into the den. And then Turkey Lurkey went into the den. Finally, Foxy Loxy went into the den.

And do you know, no one ever heard from Henny Penny, Ducky Lucky, Goosey Lucy, and Turkey Lurkey again. No one ever warned the king that the sky was falling. But someone did spy Foxy Loxy, who had a very satisfied grin on his face.

When you and your five storytellers have shared the story of the foolish fowl with the class, ask the other students to name all the characters in the story. List the names on the board and ask, "How are these names similar?" When students have identified the fact that each animal's first name rhymes with its last name, ask, "What sound do we think of when we think of each of these animal characters?" List the sounds on the board next to the names:

> HENNY PENNY: Cheep, cheep, cheep
> DUCKY LUCKY: Quack, quack, quack
> GOOSEY LUCY: Cackle, cackle, cackle
> TURKEY LURKEY: Gobble, gobble, gobble
> FOXY LOXY: Woof, woof, woof

Divide the remainder of the class, excluding the five storytellers, into five groups. Give to the leader of each a sign bearing a character name. Everyone in that group makes the designated sound whenever that name is mentioned by the storytellers, who pause after saying a character name to allow the sound-effects teams to interject the appropriate sounds. This is essentially a listening activity for the sound-effects children, for they must attend carefully in order to come in at the right spots.

When students have enjoyed this participation sound story several times, encourage them to brainstorm character names that rhyme like those in Henny Penny, i.e., Andy Dandy, Murtle Whurtle, Nellie Kellie, Dickie Lickie, Jackie Lackie, Barbie Karbie, Tillie Nillie, Billy Silly, Dottie Lottie.

Write the rhyming pairs suggested on cards. Put them into a sealable plastic bag and attach it to a learning station board. Add another plastic bag of cards with characters, such as wolf, crow, cat, duck, hippopotamus, elephant, horse, giraffe, boy, girl, bear, and so forth. Affix a task card:

TASK: To write a story with characters who have rhyming names and to use a storyline that repeats.

STEPS:

1. Draw several cards from each pouch. Match rhyming names to characters you have chosen.

2. Compose a story about these characters. Write your story on scrap paper.

3. If you want to share your story with the class as a sound participation activity, write the words spoken by each character on separate cards. The cards will serve as the script for the activity, so write neatly.

4. List the characters on a separate card. Next to each character name write the sound you associate with the character. Groups will speak this sound when you share the story with the class.

Another different kind of follow-up asks students to build meaningful word pairs that rhyme. Introduce pairs such as willy nilly, pell mell, fat cat, pot shot, June moon, helter skelter, which are in actual use. Then suggest that students invent their own rhyming pairs such as fast blast, devout scout, coy boy, tight knight, gal pal, and so forth. Students print their pairs on slips of paper, which they pin up around the classroom.

RHYMING Dr. Seuss makes writing rhyming lines seem easy. His pieces flow along so naturally that rhyming words just tumble out line after line, making the reader feel that those words have always belonged together. For those without Seuss's talent, however, building pairs of rhyming lines is difficult, and the search for line-end rhymes can actually interfere with the expression of a thought.

On the other hand, writing short humorous rhyming pieces is an activity that delights youngsters in upper-elementary grades. Several forms of humorous verse are particularly manipulatable by students with a developing sense of humor: the limerick, the punctured poem, and the clerihew.

The *limerick* consists of five rhythmic lines with a rhyming pattern of aabba as in:

> There once were two lazy old cats,
> Who no longer chased after rats.
> They just slept and they ate
> And got so overweight
> That their heads grew too big for their hats.

A technique for encouraging this type of poetry play is described in *Content and Craft: Written Expression in the Elementary School* (Hennings and Grant, Prentice-Hall, 1973, page 184). Give youngsters short phrases with a list of accompanying rhyming words to motivate limerick writing. Base phrases and rhyming words suggested include:

Base Phrase	Rhyming Words
Plain Jane from Maine	rain, attain, champagne, complain, Spain, train, drain, cocaine, domain, abstain, hurricane, vain
Some merry mice	slice, dice, twice, ice, rice, precise, spice, sacrifice, suffice, nice, advice, lice
Mixed-up chick	brick, sick, lick, trick, hick, quick, kick, slick, stick, thick
Lady of Kent	bent, gent, scent, circumvent, vent, cement, descent, invent, lent, rent, spent, went
Man called Jake	bake, ache, shake, mistake, sweepstake, awake, brake, cake, lake, flake, make
Musketeer	fear, insincere, volunteer, severe, steer, beer, cheer, clear, dear, queer, spear
Bashful bride	side, chide, pride, broadside, ride, decide, stride, slide, confide, tide

Students who have trouble getting started can work within the framework of the sentence pattern, "There once was _____." They complete the first line by selecting a base phrase from the list supplied and go on to write a second line, choosing an end-rhyming word from the list. Lines three and four are short ones that limerick writers must supply on their own. For the final line, the writer looks for a rhyming last word from the list. By the way, students may enjoy adding their original phrases and words to this list of base phrases and rhyming words.

Punctured poems are an invention of Richard Armour. They consist simply of two lines of rhyming verse: a line from a well-known verse followed by a new line that twists the original meaning as in:

> Flow gently, sweet Afton! among thy green braes,
> Just loaded with litter and pollutants these days.

> Mary, Mary, quite contrary, how does your garden grow?
> No silver bells, no cockleshells, just lots of weeds to mow.

To encourage this type of sound play, provide collections of poetry books to scan and search for lines to twist. Lines from Robert Louis Stevenson, Mother Goose, and Dr. Seuss are easy to convert.

The *clerihew* consists of four lines that rhyme in an aabb pattern and contain a real or imaginary name as a first line. Each line is relatively short, and at least a little humor is attempted as in:

> Archie Bunker   Richard Nixon
> What a clunker!   Tried some fixin'
> TV bigot,   Now embarrassed
> Does not dig it.   Will be harassed.

To prepare for clerihew writing, students brainstorm names of political figures, sports personalities, and TV and movie performers. Students should search for names that have an interesting sound such as Englebert Humperdink, Freddie Prinz, Mohammed Ali, Big Bird (from Sesame Street), Henry Kissinger, Spiro Agnew, Evel Knievel, Joe Namath, and

Hubert Humphrey. A dictionary of rhyming words is a useful tool for locating words that rhyme. Remember that in this context writers can take liberties with the English language as in using *fixin'*, instead of *fixing* and can throw in a slang expression or two.

Here is a sampling of clerihews written by students in Barbara Block's class at James Monroe School, Edison, New Jersey.

Cher
wears clothes that flair.
Day and night
they are bright.

Jerry Lewis
is the newest.
In town
he's a clown.

Winnie the Pooh
    likes you!
If he had money,
he would buy honey.

Charlie Brown
What a clown!
He's a cupid.
Too bad he's stupid.

FINDING "POEMS"

LEFT OVER

In the hard-packed dirt of the midway,
After the glaring lights are out and
The people have gone home to bed,
You will find a veritable treasure of
    Popcorn fragments,
    Frozen custard dribblings,
    Candied apples abandoned by tired children,
    Sugar fluff crystals,
    Salted almonds,
    Popsicles,
    Partially gnawed ice cream cones, and
    The wooden sticks of
    Lollipops.

FROM *Charlotte's Web* BY E. B. WHITE
(HARPER & ROW, 1952)

Is "Left Over" poetry? Certainly the piece is written in the form people have come to expect in poetry. Its image-packed words paint a picture so vivid that the reader has a sense of being the only person left on a midway after the glaring lights have gone out. The description is filled with the hard sounds associated with a midway.

Is "Left Over" prose? Actually the piece was written as prose by E. B. White; it is part of a larger paragraph of description found in *Charlotte's Web* that was "edited" into poetry form by breaking lines into segments. The fact that some prose can so easily be transformed into poetry suggests that the distinctions between the two forms are not as clear cut as is sometimes thought. Transforming prose to poetry is an activity that forces a writer to search out visual and sound patterns hidden in some prose selections. The resulting piece is generally called a *found poem.*

Myra Weiger has described the way she introduced found poems to her upper-grade class in "Found Poetry" (*Elementary English,* December 1971, pp. 1002–4). She took her students to the library, asked them to "find" poetry in prose they had read, and to rearrange the prose lines to "bring out their poetic quality." Students quickly located books by authors who handle language in a particularly creative way, i.e., E. B. White, Kenneth Grahame, A. A. Milne, Beatrix Potter, and B. F. Beebe. Other youngsters "found" their poems in magazine stories or works of nonfiction.

Once students have had an opportunity to search out prose selections to transform into poetry, you may wish to set up a Found Poetry Center. Fill a large box with books and magazines that contain prose written in poetic styles. Include books by White and Grahame as well as some best sellers such as Richard Bach's *Jonathan Livingston Seagull* (Macmillan, 1970) and Richard Adams's *Watership Down* (Macmillan, 1972). Include also some picture books such as Pat Hutchins's *Rosie's Walk* (Macmillan, 1968). Throw in some *National Geographic* magazines and some newspapers, especially Sunday editions. Students can go to the center to thumb through the materials to locate lines to convert into poetry. Keep plenty of large paper and flo-pens available so that they can print their found poems as charts. Results may resemble some of the following:

> Winter
> still seems the most vibrant season
> to me,
> for it holds the sleeping breath
> of new life.
> The earth
> drinks in moisture, and
> buds form unnoticed
> under their blankets
> of snow.
> —"WHERE SOLITUDE IS IN SEASON" BY HUTSON,
> *National Geographic,* APRIL 1974, P. 572.

> WARNING:
> The Surgeon General
> Has
> Determined
> That
> Cigarette Smoking
> Is Dangerous
> To Your Health.
> —REQUIRED STATEMENT ON CIGARETTE ADS

For students whose first language is not English, include in the box books and magazines in the students' first language as well as books and magazines in English, the target language. They can "find" poems in the prose of either language, print their pieces on large paper, and share them during a talk time. You may find it helpful to talk first about pieces written in the first language in that language and follow with talk in English about the same ideas.

STARTING FROM EXPERIENCES

When we manipulate the sounds and shapes of words, we

are actually working with what Lord Chesterfield has called the "dress of thoughts." How we dress our thoughts is an important consideration in writing and speaking; aspects of sound and shape may determine how others receive our words and phrases and whether they accept the messages we are trying to communicate.

In working with youngsters in elementary schools, however, teachers must remember that thoughts and feelings are the core of any communication. Unless a person has interest-attracting ideas to express, all the "dressing" he or she employs may be for naught.

Thoughts and feelings, of course, spring from experiences, actual or simulated; they come from firsthand involvement in events or activities or from watching, listening, reading, or discussing. Such experiences need be an integral part of language programs if young people are to have thoughts and feelings to "dress" appropriately in a covering of words.

SELECTED REFERENCES

Four books of verse are "musts" on a classroom library shelf as children play with the sights, sounds, and meanings of words:

Merriam, Eve. *It Doesn't Always Have to Rhyme.* New York: Atheneum, 1964.
Merriam, Eve. *There Is No Rhyme for Silver.* New York: Atheneum, 1962.
O'Neill, Mary. *What Is That Sound?* New York: Atheneum, 1966.
O'Neill, Mary. *Words Words Words.* New York: Doubleday, 1966.

In addition, the following short books will delight ears and eyes:

Ciardi, John. *An Alphabestiary.* Philadelphia: Lippincott, 1965–66.
Ferguson, Charles W. *The Abecedarian Book.* New York: Little, Brown, 1964.

Do not overlook "The Poetry Place," a full page of well-selected poems appearing monthly in *Instructor.* Almost every month there is a poem or two that plays with word meaning-sound-space relationships.

. . . we say

WARM AS TOAST,
QUIET AS A MOUSE,
SLOW AS MOLASSES,
QUICK AS A WINK. . . .

Is a mouse the quietest thing you know?
Think again, it might not be so.
Think again: it might be a shadow.
Quiet as a shadow,
quiet as growing grass,
quiet as a pillow,
or a looking glass.

SLOW AS MOLASSES,
QUICK AS A WINK.
Before you say so,
take time to think.

"A CLICHE," EVE MERRIAM
It Doesn't Always Have to Rhyme, ATHENEUM, 1964

4. IS A MOUSE THE QUIETEST THING YOU KNOW?
Activities in Creative Use of Language

Words are great fun to play with. Words can be used creatively to "hear a tree bark" or "watch a cookie box." Words can describe people in animal terms— "He badgered me," or "She weaseled out of it"—and, conversely, words can describe inanimate objects in human terms —"The moon danced across the sky." One may remark that a man enjoyed a square meal, when obviously the meal did not have four corners, and a boy may be told to hold his tongue without meaning that he should grab hold of it.

When we speak or write such figurative language, we are departing rather radically from fact. We do much the same thing when we use words that cast what we do or feel in a favorable light or express our feelings about people and things. Adults admit to "touching up" or "rinsing" their hair rather than "dying" it. They snarl, "You are a crackpot," or purr, "You are delightful," which are both expressions of opinion, not fact.

There are many exciting ways to use language and avoid ordinary expression such as slow as molasses or quick as a wink. Some activities for getting children to "think again" about language are described in this chapter.

CREATING WITH WORDS

IMAGINING   "Let's imagine what it could be" can be a productive opener to start students building imaginative comparisons that are the essence of good metaphors and similes. One could begin by holding up a puffy piece of cotton wool and asking, "What is it?"

"Yes, it is a ball of cotton. But let's imagine what it could be. Let's list all the things you think it could be." Students may respond with a cloud in the sky, powder puff, sea foam, sponge, candy cotton, bunny's tail, heavenly chariot, ghost's face, shaving cream, smoke, or whipped cream.

Try the same thing with objects such as a pencil, red-and-white striped candy canes, a wastebasket, or a light bulb, and encourage students to imagine what these things could be. Candy canes become letter Js, barber poles, reindeer horns, or skiis, while a pencil becomes a rocket ship, lighthouse, magic wand, baton, or an arrow.

Pantomime has a place here. Give a student an old aluminum pie plate and tell her or him to imagine that it is something else and use it in a pantomime while other class members guess what is being imagined. The discarded pie plate can become a cap, an umbrella, or a throwing disc. The student who guesses what the pantomimist is imagining takes the plate and becomes the next performer. Now the plate becomes a mirror, an immense diamond, or even a shield from medieval days.

Many objects can serve as the stuff of imaginative pantomime. Try an ordinary household broom, which can become a dancing partner, a shovel, a rifle, a lance, a witch's chariot, even the pendulum of a clock. Try a book, which can be a hat, a block of gold, a step, or Atlas's world. Or try an umbrella, which can become almost anything the imagination wants it to be.

Students who have stretched their imaginations to convert an ordinary object into something else can do the same with words. "Let's imagine feet. They are the biggest feet in the whole world. What do they look like?"

Sketch a scale balance on the board. On one balance pan write the words *big feet*. As students supply "look-like" words, write them on the opposite balance pan, i.e., giant canoes, *Queen Elizabeth I* and *II* tied up at a wharf, two pink pigs in need of a bath, two immense dump trucks loaded with dirt, or a pair of rockets taking off. To help students to think beyond the ordinary, ask them to amplify their words. You might ask a girl who says simply, "two dump trucks," "What would the trucks be fillled with?" Or you might ask the youngster who suggests "two pigs," "What color were the pigs? What kind of pigs?"

Looked Like

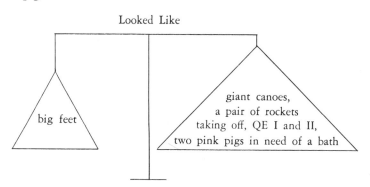

You might prepare a series of Balance Sheets for students to play with.* Prepare a ditto of a pan balance and print a word or phrase on the left pan; students write creative comparisons on the right balance pan. Good starters include her teeth, his nose, a river, the moon, a mountain, her eyes, falling snow, a broken umbrella, straight-back chair, a rocket ship standing on the launch pad, and an airplane sitting on the runway.

Introduce the sheets first as a group activity in which three or four young people work together to complete a sheet. The groups then pool their efforts to produce a master sheet containing all their creative comparisons. It is probably wise to start with an easy opening phrase such as falling snow or her teeth, which are conducive to many kinds of creative phrases.

Sheets with different starting words can be placed in a learning station. Include one pouch of sheets with no starting word for students who want to go it alone. Directions for this

---

*Idea contributed by John Ramos, Associate Professor, Kean College.

station read simply: "Select a balance sheet and complete it by dreaming up as many creative comparisons as you can. Put your name on your finished paper and place it in the finished pouch." In playing with words in this way students are becoming involved with similes. As youngsters devise their creative comparisons, it is not necessary to explain the term or differentiate between a simile and a metaphor. Knowing the terms will not help boys and girls think creatively as they use original figures of speech, and thinking creatively with words is, after all, the desired goal.

GOING BEYOND "LOOKS LIKE"   The question, "What does it look like?" can easily turn into "What does it smell like? What does it taste like? What does it sound like?" or even, "What does it feel like?"

I have found that upper-elementary-grade youngsters particularly enjoy creative comparisons involving smells. A fun one is the sentence, "There is a bad odor in the room," which can be converted into, "This room smells like a glue factory" or "This room smells like a garbage dump." Ask students to brainstorm other comparisons for a chart such as the following one:

A SMELL-LIKE CHART

Ordinary sentence: There is a bad odor in the room.
Converted sentence:

This room

smells like

a glue factory.
an onion inferno.
a pickle jar.
an outhouse.
a garbage dump.
a decaying swamp.

Other ordinary sentences that students can convert into powerful images are:

Ordinary Sentence	Beginning of Converted Sentence
My typewriter is noisy.	My typewriter sounds like ____
This bread tastes stale.	Eating this bread is like _____
I have a headache.	My head feels like _____
Our car consumes a lot of gas.	Our car acts like _____

Write the opening phrase of a simile on a large index card and fasten it down on a tabletop in a learning station where individual students can print creative endings. When a number of endings have been added by different children, one student shares the card with the class. You will probably need a minimum of five cards, each with a different opening phrase to make this activity effective. Suggested opening phrases are:

The wind was blowing. It sounded like _____

He was proud. He strutted about looking very much like _____

She was angry. The expression on her face made her look like

_____

The sea was wild. The ship rolled back and forth very much like a/an _____

The air was foul. It smelled like _____

My sandwich was bad. It tasted like _____

Mike's bike is noisy. It sounds like _____

Her voice was harsh. It sounded like _____

The dragon's breath was foul. It smelled like _____

The way he gulped his food down looked like _____

The soup had a strong taste. It tasted like _____

Claire's face was pale. It looked like _____

After I got my paper back and saw I had failed, I felt like _____

If you are working with bilingual students, prepare two cards for each opening phrase, one in the first language, the other in the target language. A youngster may add a phrase ending to either or both cards.

How is a song like a spinning top? Let's see. . . . A song
has rhythm; so does a top. We can write, "The rhythm of the
spinning top was like a song, repeated over and over." A
song may go in circles; so does a top. We can say, "The song
seemed to go in circles just like a top spinning." How else is
a song like a spinning top? Can your students dream up an
unusual relationship?

Upper-grade students can make a game of finding unusual
relationships between objects not generally associated together.
To get them started, give them the song–spinning top comparison, and ask them to think of relationships as a class
talking-together endeavor.

Prepare for the next session by writing the following questions on individual slips of paper:

> How is a flag like a fan?
> How is a toaster like a pistol?
> How is an automobile like a magnet?
> How is an orange like a department store?
> How is a mirror like a piece of blank paper?
> How is a TV set like a calendar?
> How is a basket like a kangaroo?
> How is a giant like a computer?
> How is toothpaste like a snake?
> How is a typewriter like a magnifying glass?
> How is a dishwashing machine in action like a battle?
> How is a brain like a calculator?
> How is a lighted lamp like a companion?
> How is a plow like a dog?
> How is a camera like a psychologist?
> How is a banana like a deathtrap?

Divide the class into three- or four-person teams and deal
a slip of paper to each. Students identify different relationships
for the two parts of their comparison, and after a short period of
time, pass their slip to a team nearby and receive in turn a slip
with a different question. When each team has worked on several comparisons, schedule a class talking-together time in

which each comparison is discussed. You may wish to appoint a discussion scribe to list all the suggested relationships on the board. You will find that as the board begins to fill up, students will suddenly spot relationships they had not perceived before.

As a follow-up, encourage students to invent their own questions, i.e., "How is a dog like a kite?" and to decide on a desired response such as, "They both wag their tails." Use these question-answer sequences developed by individuals as time fillers when you have two or three minutes available between activities. A student who has invented two halves of a question-answer sequence asks his or her question, which has really become a low-key joke. Other students throw out answers. If nobody guesses the intended answer, the inventor must give his or her own response.

TURNING ROADS INTO RIBBONS   "The road was a ribbon of moonlight." When Alfred Noyes wrote that well-known line in the poem "The Highwayman," he was essentially writing a word equation: road = ribbon (of moonlight). Upper-elementary-grade students may enjoy writing similar creative equations.

Start with half the equation: This car = _____. Suggest that students think of words conveying the idea of speed to fit in the blank, i.e., This car = a bullet streaking through the air; This car = a rocket taking off; or This car = a deer in flight. Each of these comparisons conveys a message of speed.

Now convert the equation to convey different ideas:

This car = _____ (for important people)
This car = _____ (rugged)
This car = _____ (beautiful)
This car = _____ (uses lots of gas)

Let the class brainstorm possibilities for each equation.

When students understand word equations and know that

they can convey different messages, divide the class into writing groups and give each a card:

Our razor blades = _____ (sharpness)
Our razor blades = _____ (last a long time)
Our razor blades = _____ (for important people)

Each group devises two or three creative comparisons to complete each equation and shares their products by reading them to the class.

Here are some additional equations for continuing the activity either as a group or learning station adventure:

This room = _____ (beautiful)
This room = _____ (messy)
This room = _____ (crowded)

My bicycle = _____ (fast)
My bicycle = _____ (sleek)
My bicycle = _____ (beautiful)
My bicycle = _____ (beat up)

Our town or city = _____ (dirty)
Our town or city = _____ (crowded)
Our town or city = _____ (lighted at night)
Our town or city = _____ (noisy)

For older students
Life = _____ (sad)
Life = _____ (happy)

More sophisticated phrases to use in building metaphors are:

Papers blowing in the wind = _____
Mosquitoes buzzing in the night = _____
A river rushing to the sea = _____
A saw grinding through the wood = _____
A woodpecker pecking at the tree = _____
Cats meowing in the night = _____
Fireflies glowing in the dark grass = _____
Oatmeal bubbling in a pot = _____
Fire burning in the hearth = _____

MAKING FILMSTRIPS OF CREATIVE COMPARISONS

Order a roll of frosted U-film from Prima Education Products (Irvington-on-Hudson, NY 10533). U-film is available in 25-, 100-, or 1000-foot rolls. One can type or print with a ball-point or Leroy marking pen directly on the filmstrip. Color can be added to any frame with a wax pencil or crayon. Adding color makes the strip more interesting and also separates the frames if the colors are different. Incidentally, when making a filmstrip, you may find it helpful to divide it into sections to facilitate assigning work.

A suggested script to place on a filmstrip is:*

Frames	Content	Color
1. (title)	Creative Comparisons I	Orange
2. Frame 2	as fast as a fox as _____ as a	Green
3. Frame 3	as busy as a bee as _____ as a	Orange
4. Frame 4	as slippery as _____	Green
5. Frame 5	as warm as _____	Orange
6. Frame 6	as fleeting as _____	Green
7. Frame 7	as angry as _____	Orange

*A reliable student can prepare the strip for the class if you give her or him this book, a pen, and a filmstrip.

8. Frame   8   as sure as
                      _____   Green

                                Creative
                              Comparisons   Leave this frame
9. (title)   II   uncolored

10. Frame 10   An inchworm is
                      _____   Orange

11. Frame 11   An alligator is
                      _____   Green

12. Frame 12   Wind is
                      _____   Orange

13. Frame 13   A windmill is
                      _____   Green

14. Frame 14   A turtle is
                      _____   Orange

                                Creative
                              Comparisons   Leave this frame
15. (title)   III   uncolored

16. Frame 16   The tornado came
                           like a _____   Green
                      _____

17. Frame 17   The wind roared
                           like a _____   Orange
                      _____

18. Frame 18   The trees swayed like
                      _____   Green
                      _____

19. Frame 19   Cars were tossed
                           around like _____   Orange
                      _____

20. Frame 20   The earth looked as if
                      _____   Green

Set up a filmstrip viewer at a table learning center. Supply paper cut in strips for students to write down their creative comparisons as they view the strip. Later students talk together in groups, expanding their comparisons as they review the strip. Encourage student groups to select a number of their comparisons to incorporate into a creative composition.

EXPANDING METAPHORS   Students who have played with creative comparisons may enjoy writing stories and poems in which they convert one object into another so that throughout the story or poem the first object consistently performs like the second. For example, in the well-known Sandburg poem fog becomes a cat, a cat who creeps about, sits on its haunches, and is silent. In a story, a car might become a demon whose headlights are staring, glassy eyes, whose front bumper is a jutting lip, and whose tires are giant legs that mow down everything in sight. The car talks too, emitting monster-sounds that frighten everyone in sight. These two examples can introduce student writers to the expanded metaphor.

GIVING OBJECTS PERSONALITY

> The sun woke up,
> stretched,
> yawned,
> and called to all of us,
> "Wake up, you lazy world!
> It's time to go!"

When composing this little piece, the writer gave the sun human attributes and described it with people-action words.

Brainstorming is an amazingly easy way to involve students in the elements of personification. Ask them to produce as many words as possible to describe the sun. Words they may toss out are bright, shining, yellow, golden, and warm as well as many others. Student scribes can list the descriptors on the board.

Then ask students to think of words that tell what the sun does, i.e., rises, sets, shines, and burns. Suggest that they think of phrases or groups of words such as moves across the sky, sets in the west, warms the earth, or burns my skin. If a word such as creeps, rushes, hides, runs, or plays is suggested, record this word on a different section of the board. Ask if the sun actually performs this action. Ask students to suggest other words that usually describe human actions but could also tell what the sun does. If no one thinks of a word of this type, suggest one yourself and ask students to think of other people-related words. With luck and prodding, there will be a flood of words and phrases that describe in people-terms the sun's actions.

Returning to the list of descriptive words the class originally compiled, students can add words that are generally applied to people but could be used to describe the sun, i.e., friendly, joyous, rambunctious, playful, sweating, tired, and worn-out. If they run out of words, they can search a dictionary for synonyms of words already identified.

Next ask them to think what the sun might say if it could talk. "Sun talk" is added to the category listings on the board.

When you have a boardful of words, write an experience "thought" with the class. Begin by writing SUN at the top, and ask students to select human words from the lists to compile a sun-thought. You will be amazed at the result.

As a next step, ask students whether the sun they have described is happy or sad. Suggest that they individually write a similar sun-thought, drawing from the words brainstormed.

A writing station activity sheet can follow the format of the class brainstorming. Prepare a sheet with the word Wind at the top and divide it into six blocks: wind describing words, wind action words, human-wind describing words, human-wind action words, wind talk, and a wind thought. Students can go to the station, complete a Wind Sheet, and place it in a Finished Products pouch.

Other words to spark descriptions of inanimate objects in human terms are moon, river, snow, ant, or winter, which can be used for learning center sheets. Students may enjoy working out this activity in pairs so that they can brainstorm together.

MAKING IT HUMAN OR BEAST-LIKE A thoroughly dunked and dried-out teabag and a discarded tomato-soup can may at first glance appear improbable objects to inspire creative use of words, yet enthusiasts of the Andy Warhol-style of artistic expression know that objects such as these have been the stuff of innovative composition. Upper-grade students who are beginning to develop a sense of humor may be similarly inspired by mundane objects.

Imagining that a discarded teabag is a tired being who wants to tell its story can be a promising beginning. How would the bag describe its trip through scalding water and its drying-out experience? How does it view its inglorious end? What words can describe it? dejected? worn-out? exhausted? tea-less? drained? strained? Answering these questions is an adventure in extended personification.

Students who have been challenged by topics like this can write up their dejected-teabag thoughts, their squashed-squash thoughts, their drying-onion thoughts, their banana-peel thoughts, their junk-car thoughts, their Coke-bottle thoughts, and so forth as scripts for a monologue that can be delivered orally to the class. A scriptwriter may wish to wear an appropriate costume as he or she speaks the monologue sitting crosslegged on the floor or perched on a stool or desk top.

Students with an artistic bent can try to be Andy Warhols and design posters to accompany their pop thoughts. If they are composed in poetry-like lines, they can be lettered onto the posters to add a verbal dimension to the visual message.

If upper-elementary students find personification fun to work with, you may wish to construct a bulletin board to encourage them to think of additional, more complex relationships. Little is needed, since this is really a participation activity that requires a brief explanation, directions, and materials.

MAKING IT HUMAN

EXPLANATION:

People speak, laugh, shiver, get angry, weep, burp, cry, whisper. However, we can describe some objects with these action words, as in these sentences:

The trees spoke to us as we passed.
The car got angry and stubborn and would not start.
The laughing soda lost its spark and became sad.
The tired train slipped into the station with an exhausted gasp.

DIRECTIONS:

1. Try your hand at writing sentences in which objects act like people.
2. Objects you may wish to use are listed on slips of paper in the object pouch.
3. Write your sentences on paper in the paper pouch.
4. Write your name on your paper. Put your completed people-sentences in the finished-products pouch.

OBJECT
POUCH

PAPER
POUCH

FINISHED-PRODUCTS
POUCH

Words to list on slips and place in the object pouch include: mailbox, saxophone, drum, light on the street corner, speedometer, sink, clock, table, calendar, windmill, flag, airplane, engine, horn, pencil, chair, and ship.

In *Carolina Tips* (Burlington, NC 27215), a Carolina Biological leaflet, Kenneth W. Perkins comments that, "Man's lively interest in the beasts of the field is shown by his constant use of their names in everyday speech." He suggests that many action words used to describe human endeavors are "direct steals from the cages of the zoo." In a sense, when people employ such words they are doing the opposite of personification—something that could well be called "beastification."

Examples that Perkins cites include:

to ape	to badger	to buffalo
to bull	to clam up	to chicken out
to dog	to fox	to hog
to horse around	to hound	to louse up
to monkey around	to parrot	to pony up
to rat	to snake	to sponge
to squirrel away	to skunk	to weasel
to wildcat	to wolf	to worm

Perkins rules out verbs such as *to fish* meaning to catch fish, because it is a derivative verb that actually has something to do with fish. He also rules out *to bug,* which is of doubtful origin, and *to fly,* which is a verb in its own right and is not derived from the tiny insect that is bothersome in summer.

Give a few of the above examples of "beastification" and see how many others students can unearth.

EXAGGERATING A BIT

> I am so short that grass looks tall to me.
> I am so short that I look up to see a caterpillar.
> I am so short that no one sees me.

Students who wrote these lines were using exaggeration to create an image of shortness. Working in small groups, students invented new relationships and concocted hyperboles.

To involve your students in writing hyperboles, prepare 5 × 8 inch index cards containing a beginning phrase for an exaggeration such as: I am so cold that _____. On other cards write: I am so tall that _____. I am so brilliant that _____. I am so strong that _____. I am so ugly that _____. I am so rich that _____. I am so dirty that _____. I am so beautiful that _____. I am so tired that _____. or I am so frightened that _____.

Introduce the phrase, I am so short that _____, and suggest an ending such as, "I can walk under mushrooms or crawl under a closed door." Ask students to dream up equally outrageous endings to convey the impression of extreme shortness. You may want to record suggestions on the board; from these, students can select the four or five they think most effective and compose a poetry-style piece on a bulletin-board chart.

Now divide the class into four-person writing groups. Give each group a prepared card. After the group completes the hyperbole, it passes its card to a nearby group and receives a card from another group. Each group adds a second hyperbole to the card received. Circulate the cards in this manner so that at least four groups work on each card and on at least four base phrases. The chairpersons of the groups working on the last cards read the entire series to the class.

As follow-up, prepare additional cards with a base phrase for a hyperbole. The ones already used in the group activity may be repeated and/or other phrases added such as, I am so sick that _____. I am so hot that _____. I am so tiny that _____. I am so huge that _____. or I am so happy that _____. Make pouches labeled Happy Hyperboles, Huge Hyperboles, Tiny Hyperboles, and so forth to hold the cards. In addition, make a pouch labeled Original Hyperboles for blank cards. Mount the pouches on a learning center board captioned Exaggerating a Bit. Students can go to the station individually, select a card, write an original series of huge, tiny, sick, or happy hyperboles, and leave their cards in a pouch marked Our Exaggerations. Students selecting a blank card from the Original Hyperbole pouch invent their own base phrases and add on their own endings.

If you find that students enjoy this activity, you may wish to offer it a second time, employing base phrases that do not start with "I" but phrases such as, The mud was so gooey that _____. The water was so cold that _____. The wind was so strong that _____. The music was so loud that _____. The picture was so ugly that _____.

Remember you do not have to prepare the cards yourself. A student who needs penmanship practice can write the phrases on index cards, trying to use his or her best handwriting. Because the cards are to be a part of classroom activity, they may feel responsible for writing clearly and neatly.

Upper-grade students may enjoy writing exaggerated claims for commerically sold products. The claims may be so outrageous that they are actually humorous. An example to get them started is, "After only one week of taking our vitamin supplement, you will feel like Atlas and be able to lift the world on your shoulders."

Suggested products to play with include: cough medicine, fertilizer, tires, margarine, gasoline, light bulbs, batteries, floor wax, film, detergent.

PLAYING WITH FIRE *Amelia Bedelia* by Peggy Parish (Harper & Row, 1963, Scholastic, pap.) is the popular tale of a housemaid who interprets literally her list of chores. Told to dust the furniture, Amelia discovers a pleasant smelling powder, which she procceds to dust liberally on the furniture. Told to dress a chicken, she attires the bird in short pants. This all happens because Amelia Bedelia speaks English as a second language and is unfamiliar with English idioms.

Use *Amelia Bedelia* as a springboard to work with idiomatic expressions. Either share the story orally with youngsters in grades two through five or show the sound filmstrip distributed by Teaching Resources Films (Station Plaza, Bedford Hills, NY 10507). Older student viewers can identify the words in the story that the maid misunderstood to form the beginning of a list of idioms.

A fun activity that students in grades four through six particularly enjoy is drawing literal interpretations of commonly used idioms. Provide a chart of idioms, including their figurative meanings. Students select an idiom, draw with crayons its literal meaning, and add a caption that includes the idiom as it generally is used in a sentence. If each student works on a different idiom, the resulting drawings can be attached together as a class booklet.

One fifth-grade youngster captioned his drawing, "John had his heart set on a new bicycle." The drawing depicted a heart sitting on a bicycle seat. Another student wrote, "The man got tangled in red tape," and her drawing showed a man wrapped in a long strip of tape colored vivid red.

Give young people an opportunity to share their drawings with their classmates, which will lead to talking about language and laughing about some of the strange ways it is used.

Here is a list of common idioms to facilitate your planning:

Idiom	*Figurative Meaning*
Walk on air	Be overjoyed, extremely happy
Lower the boom	Put a stop to something
Bite the bullet	Do something that hurts
Run in circles	Do a lot and accomplish little
Tighten one's belt	Economize; do without
Sweep under the rug	Hide something
Steel oneself	Harden oneself against adversity
Eat a square meal	Eat a large, nutritious meal

Mend one's fences	Repair relationship with someone
Play with fire	Dabble in something that could go out of control
Spill the beans	Give out restricted information
Add fuel to the fire	Make worse
Be in the doghouse	Be in trouble
Be up a tree	Be without a solution
Hit the ceiling	Get angry
Drop a line to	Write a letter to
Cost a pretty penny	Be expensive
Gather wool	Daydream
Have a green thumb	Be able to make plants grow
Chickenhearted	Scared, afraid
In hot water	In a lot of trouble
All ears	Listen to everything said
Caught short	Unprepared, especially not to have enough money
Have butterfingers	Be clumsy
Jump from the frying pan into the fire	Make matters worse
Toe the line	Do what one is supposed to
Steer clear of	Avoid
Give someone a piece of one's mind	Bawl out
Bury the hatchet	Forget about old arguments and become friends again
Wash one's hands of	Give up responsibility for
Bark up the wrong tree	Be on the wrong track
Put one's foot in one's mouth	Say the wrong thing
A heavy heart	Be sad
On pins and needles	Be anxious
Turn over a new leaf	Make a new start
Have one's hair stand on end	Be scared
Paper over	Conceal

Incidentally, if you have joined the teachers who find learning stations a way to involve youngsters in independent activity, mount strips of paper bearing these expressions on the backdrop of a learning center. Students can help themselves to a strip and draw the literal meaning of its phrase.

HEARING A TREE BARK   The fact that one word may have several different meanings is the reason one can listen to a wedding ring, and see a stair stoop. It makes possible amusing plays on words such as, "Where does a weatherman put his money? Answer: In a cloud bank." It also makes possible puns such as Senator Birch Bayh's description of President Ford's 1975 economic program as "gerry-built."

The did-you-ever? format is an easy way to start composing plays on words. Students find *homophones,* words with double meanings, to fill the blanks in the following:

> Did you ever hear a tree bark
>   or watch a cookie box?
> Did you ever _____
>   or _____?
> Did you ever _____
>   or _____?
>   and so forth

Phrases that your word players may uncover include:

Did you ever—

watch a voice box?
see a house fly?
watch a sugar bowl?
hear an ear ring?
see an ocean wave?
watch a stocking run?
watch a finger tip?
see milk shake?
see a butter fly?
see a brick walk?

see a house dress?
watch a bed roll?
hear a house call?
watch a fish bowl?
listen to a waist band?
hear a bathtub ring?
see ice skate?
see a lemon twist?
watch a cigar box?
listen to a rubber band?

By the way, this is not a sit-down-and-get-the-job-done-fast activity. Rather it should be ongoing for at least a week with phrases coming to light as students listen and think. Keep paper available, and as students discover word pairs, they can sketch a picture showing the literal meaning of the phrase. For example, a house can be drawn with wings flapping frantically or a fish can be shown sending a bowling ball down an alley. Artists share their pictures with the class as fellow students try to guess what words are being depicted.

One clue may prove helpful in explaining the exercise. The last word of most pairs functions as a noun in the common expression; i.e., in *house dress*, *dress* is a noun, and to transform a word pair to a word play, convert the last word into a verb. The change is made orally by pausing briefly between the two words of the pair and raising the voice slightly upward on the second word. Read aloud several of the phrases given, first as the common expression and then as a noun-verb sequence that alters the meaning of the expression. Incidentally, this is an ideal time to help students discover the relationship between vocal intonation and meaning.

Playing with words is playing with sound and meaning. One form of word play is punning—using a word in two different senses. As Joseph Shipley has pointed out in his delightful book *Word Play* (Hawthorn Books, 1972), "Puns are double-tongued creatures; they seem to say one thing, then flash! we discover that they mean another." Shipley supplies two thought-tickling ones you may want to share with students as examples:

"I see the horse you've drawn, but where is the wagon?"
"The horse is supposed to draw that."

There are so many birds offshore that often buoy meets gull.

In a similar vein, Alice and Martin Provensen suggest in the introduction to their book *Play on Words* (Random House, 1972):

Watch out for words!
SOME WORDS make sense.
SOME WORDS make no cents.
This foreword has three more (not four) words:
LETTUCE GO FORWARD.

The Provensens have achieved a humorous effect by playing with words that are identical or nearly identical in pronunciation but different in spelling, words such as bored/board and so/sew/sow that are called homonyms.

Students can write riddles as well as silly conversations, stories, and poems using homonyms to add a pinch of humor. A splendid resource containing numerous examples of this type of word play is Harold Longman's *Would You Put Your Money in a Sand Bank?* (Rand McNally, 1968). Longman gives young readers such riddles as:

> Why was the mountain top flat when the mountain climber came back?
> Because he took a *peek* from the top.

nonsense conversations:

> *Phew!*
> You have only a *few?*
> No—I'm *through.*
> You *threw* something?
> No—I just set a *stake* near the *creek.*
> It must have been too tough to eat. I never heard a *steak creek* before.

and fun poems:

> A *bear* runs around in a *bear* skin
> To keep himself warm when it's freezing.
> If you run around in a *bare* skin
> You soon will be coughing and wheezing.

Share pieces like these and others from the volume with students and see if they can discover for themselves the source of the humor. When they perceive that humor is derived from the fact that some words spelled differently are pronounced similarly, encourage them to create their own riddles and silly conversations. Mount homonym word cards on a bulletin board or stack them on a table. Students select a homonym or two to manipulate and produce a humorous effect. A set of homonym cards sold under the Milton Bradley label is marketed by Hammett (Vaux Hall Road, Union, NJ 07083).

Incidentally, student products can serve as a springboard for talk sessions as well as motivation for clear handwriting. From Hammett can be purchased flip-chart tablets containing twenty-five 1-inch ruled 24×16 inch sheets of white paper, spirally bound (#9210). As students complete riddles based on either homonyms or homophones, they write the edited question portion on a page of the tablet. During a talk time a riddle-maker flips to his or her page, reads the riddle, and waits while classmates decipher the play on words.

You will find that some students take to riddle making and punning as naturally as ducks take to water. Generally these are students who are always tickled by knock-knock jokes and riddles. Encourage these punsters to listen for puns delivered by TV stand-up comedians and even by TV movie critics who often make puns around the name of the movie they are reviewing. Gene Shallit, the NBC critic, is a master punster.

Another intriguing activity is playing with number/letter sounds. Can students read "I C D 4 Cs"? Read it fast and they will hear the message, "I see the four seas." To introduce this kind of word play to upper-elementary-grade students, make available the little book *C D B* by William Steig (Windmill Books/Simon and Schuster, 1968). The total book is written in letters and numbers, and reading it is like figuring out a puzzle. Absolutely do not read the book to your students. Let them figure it out in small groups or individually.

Maxwell Nurnberg in *Fun with Words* (Prentice-Hall, 1970) dedicates an entire chapter called N E (1) 4 (10) S? (Anyone for Tennis?) to this type of word game. He gives lists of E′z words such as D K′ and R′ T, more E′z words such as T′ P and 4′ M, and lists of other examples to match with listed definitions. The latter are far from E'z. For example, there are O B' C T and X (10)' U 8. To help with these—two clues! In the Nurnberg system, 1 and 10 are placed within parentheses to prevent confusion and the accented syllable is indicated. Order the book for your school library. It is a gold mine of exercises youngsters can decipher.

ALLUDING TO THE FAMILIAR   A headline in *The New York Times* (January 19, 1975, section 4, page 2) announced, "Congress's Old Order Changeth Very Quickly"; another (page 1) proclaimed, "Ford's Fingers Are in the Dike." Both these headlines attempted to make a point by alluding to a literary piece. An alert *Times* reader recalled Alfred, Lord Tennyson's lines from *Morte d'Arthur:*

> The old order changeth, yielding place to new;
> And God fulfills himself in many ways.

Another pictured the storybook Dutch boy who plugged his fingers in the hole in the dike to prevent the sea from flooding his homeland. Such recollections help readers perceive current conditions in terms of other events with which they are familiar. In this case, the events were literary; such a reference is called a *literary allusion.*

Writers and speakers commonly allude to lines, characters, places, and titles from a variety of literary forms—myths, fables, songs, stories, poems, and even the comics. For example, *Newsweek* (January 20, 1975) described the wealthy Malcolm Forbes, "as a Walter Mitty dreamer with a solid Midas touch," alluding to the mythical king with the golden touch and to a James Thurber character. In the same issue a headline screamed "Henry the K: 'Don't Fence Me In,'" alluding to a popular song of the forties that asks for "room, lots of room" in which to maneuver, something that Dr. Kissinger was trying to manage for himself. The article itself referred to Kissinger as Super-K, a suggestion of the names sometimes attached to

Kissinger—Superman and Clark Kent, names from a comic strip.

Robert Lipsyte, writing on women in sports, concluded an article with, "More likely, however, the feminist revolution in sports will mean a fresh pool of cheap, eager labor for *Sports World*—Nimble Noras out of the dollhouse to join the Hammerin' Hanks in that Sweaty Oz of our dreams" (*The New York Times,* January 12, 1975, section 4, page 17). To make his point, Lipsyte drew on references from Ibsen's play *A Doll's House*, and a popular film and book *The Wizard of Oz*.

Encourage students to be on the lookout in their reading and listening for characters, places, words, and titles that pop up commonly in allusions. Studies of Greek mythology, fables, and even fairy tales are fine contexts in which to introduce literary allusion, for many names from these sources are alluded to in current books and papers, i.e., Pandora, Neptune, the boy who cried wolf, and Cinderella, to name just a few. Be ready to ask upper-grade students, "What is meant when one says that she is a modern-day Cinderella? that he opened a Pandora's box? that she cried wolf once too often? or that King Neptune swallowed him up?" Be prepared to help young people formulate creative comparisons that are the essence of good literary allusion. Ask, "Who could be called a contemporary Jack the Giant Killer? Who recently put on seven-league boots to go striding across the world? Is there anyone today who could be said to be balancing the world on his or her shoulders like Atlas?"

One kind of allusion that is easy to spot is the allusion to things popularized by the media—TV shows, advertisements, songs, or movies. Listening for such references is a productive activity for fifth and sixth graders. They may hear "We live in an Archie Bunker house" or "She is a Rhoda type," referring to two popular TV personalities. They may catch, "We're only number two; we try harder," an allusion to the Avis rent-a-car commercial, or "She spent all afternoon tying yellow ribbons

on the old oak tree," an allusion to a popular song title that
has become a welcoming thought.

Political and historical allusions abound and are even easier
for young people to spot. For example, when President Ford
announced his economic policy early in 1975, a political op-
ponent compared Ford to a man rearranging deck chairs on
the *Titanic.* Many speakers allude to Watergate in a variety of
different contexts. Some political analyists suggest that Americans need a Pearl Harbor to shock them into action against
economic problems.

Keep long strips of paper ready in the classroom. After
spotting an allusion, or better still concocting one, a student
records it on a strip and attaches it to an on-going bulletin
board. Allow them time to explain their findings to the class.

Reporting on political, sports, weather, and amusement
events is an ideal context in which to compose one's own
allusions, and a TV news program is an effective format for
presenting such reports. To prepare students listen to the
nightly news and identify members of the TV reporting team:
anchor person, weather analyst, news analyst, entertainment
critic, sports commentator, consumer critic, on-the-spot news
reporter, special features reporter, and so forth. In class they
divide into production teams, each of which focuses on one
subject area. Because there will be numbers of news stories,
several teams will probably work on current happenings, with
each specializing in local, national, or international news.
Teams identify stories to be written and prepare a script. At
this point remind scriptwriters that they may want to allude to
a literary or historical incident to make their newscasting more
clever and forceful. To help students work more effectively
with allusions, have available

Bartlett's Familiar Quotations
Books of popular songs from the twenties, thirties, forties, and fifties
Review books in history, literature, and political science
Television guides

If scriptwriters have difficulty seeing the relationships that are at the heart of creative allusion, brainstorm with small groups. Choose an event, such as the first visit of an American president to Japan, and discuss its purpose, significance, and outcomes. Ask, "Are there any other people who made first visits to Japan to whom the president can be compared? Are there any other openings to which this opening can be compared? Are there any references to peace-making that can be alluded to? Are there any lines of poetry or song that refer to taking a trip? making peace? being friends? Are there any elements in the background of the president—in this case, Ford—to which we can allude." Brainstorming may produce references to Admiral Perry, General MacArthur, I'll be seeing you in cherry blossom time, go the United way, tossing a football, opening up the doors and letting the sunshine in, there's a Ford in Japan's future, or making friends—but not haikus. Each student selects one of the references to write into a paragraph describing the event. Remember, just one, for excessive use of figures of speech can become deadly.

Once students have composed allusions and have written news scripts containing them, organize an evening news program. A set designer arranges desks to simulate a TV news studio. An associate producer plans the sequences of stories. Volunteers from the writing teams become the anchor person, weather analyst, and so on; they practice reading the scripts so they deliver them with appropriate phrasing and intonation.

When all is ready, the show goes on. Record or videotape the production so that students hear themselves in playback. Follow up with discussion on ways to write more interesting scripts and to speak so that the intended message comes across.

While younger students can draw literal interpretations of idioms or word plays as suggested in a preceding activity, more sophistication is required to handle allusions. Play with allusions is probably most effective with bright young people in grades five and above.

EXPESSING FEELINGS WITH WORDS

SEARCHING FOR GRANDEUR AND PROPRIETY   In *The American Language* (Alfred Knopf, 1963, p. 339), H. L. Mencken wrote:

The American seldom believes that the trade he follows is quite worthy of his virtues and talents; he thinks that he would have adorned something far gaudier. Since it is often impossible for him to escape or to dream plausibly of escaping, he soothes himself by pretending that he belongs to a superior section of his craft, and even invents a sonorous name to set himself off from the herd. Here we glimpse the origin of characteristic American euphemisms, *e.g., mortician* for *undertaker, realtor* for *real-estate agent, beautician* for *hairdresser, exterminating engineer* for *rat catcher* and so on.

Not only have we developed words to make people's work sound more impressive, but we have developed words to make ordinary or unpleasant things sound more pleasing. False teeth have become dentures; used or secondhand cars have become previously owned, late models; and buses have become deluxe motor coaches.

Students in upper grades can have fun searching for *euphemisms.* Start by suggesting a few examples on a classroom chart. A student who locates a euphemism writes the less impressive word on the chart while classmates guess the euphemism. As an alternative, you may want to set up a card game. Print an ordinary word on a card; on a second print the euphemism for it. Do this for at least fifteen sets of words so that there are thirty cards in the deck. The cards are dealt to four or five students, who match the pairs they hold in their hands. Then a player draws a card from a neighbor's hand and tries to match it with a card in his or her own hand. If this is impossible, the next player draws a card. When one player has paired all his or her cards, she or he is declared winner.

Here is a list of common euphemisms to print on game cards:

custodian/janitor

demolition engineer/wrecker

domestic engineer/housekeeper

podiatrist/foot doctor

section manager/floor walker

loan office/pawnshop

mobile home/trailer

industrial park/factory district

gown/dress

casket/coffin

memorial park or cemetery/ graveyard

pass away/die

chef/cook

hair stylist/barber

restroom/public toilet

unmentionables/underwear

touch up hair/dye hair

maitre d'/head waiter

Substituting words from another language for ordinary words in one's own language is another way to add glamour to what one does and says. When we order roast beef, we ask for it *au jus*. When we make a mistake, we call it a *faux pas*. One serves *hors d'oeuvres*, buys *haute couture*, and acquires an *objet d'art*. We categorize someone as being *nouveau riche* and announce that a friend has graduated *cum laude*, *summa cum laude*, or *magna cum laude*. We speak of *laissez-faire* economic policy.

Words such as these that have not been completely assimilated into the English language are printed in italics in books and magazines and underlined in handwritten or typed copy. Newspapers tend to omit italics.

The use of italics makes foreign words easy to spot in books and magazines. Searching fashion, travel, and cookery magazines will produce a good listing of foreign words and is an uncomplicated project for students in upper-elementary grades, who may want to hypothesize why most of the words found have either French or Latin origins.

Sometimes organizations to which people belong are named with letters and words from other languages. Sororities and fraternities as well as honor societies usually have names consisting of a series of Greek letters, i.e., Phi Beta Kappa, Sigma Chi, and Kappa Delta Epsilon. Other organizations give themselves impressive titles such as The Exalted Order of Royal Crowns. Again a search for examples of status-seeking names is an individual project for a budding linguistic investigator.

A few more word-conscious students may wish to investigate still another way in which people attempt to place what they are doing in a more favorable light—the development of a specialized vocabulary within a trade or profession. Often the first step in gaining access to a particular occupation is learning these specialized words or *jargon.* To borrow a word from publishing jargon, the "in-house" language distinguishes those within the profession from those on the outside.

Jargon changes periodically; words that are "in" one year may be "out" the next, and new "in" words take their place. For example, educators formerly talked of their goals, later goals became objectives, still later objectives became behavioral objectives, and more recently behavioral objectives have become competencies.

Through interviewing, upper-grade students can identify words that are part of the specialized vocabulary of some trades and professions. Students can interview construction people, demolition engineers, editors, accountants, computer programmers, veterinarians, principals, sales representatives, or any worker in a trade or profession requiring considerable training. Interviewers can ask, "Do you have any specialized words associated with your occupation? What are some of these words? What do these words mean in everyday language?" A simple interview guide will help them structure their interviews:

INTERVIEW GUIDE

Name of person interviewed _____

Occupation of person interviewed _____

Number of years person has been in the occupation _____

Name of person conducting the interview _____

Date of interview _____

Specialized Words Associated with Occupation	Meaning of Words in Everyday Terms

If a number of students are working on this project, it may be possible to pool their results. Several who have interviewed principals and teachers—who, of course, are easily available—may compare their lists to find words that more than one person identified and compile composite listings.

Interview results should be shared orally so that students who have not had an opportunity to interview anyone may pick up new words that have moved from jargon to general usage. Data processing words such as input, output, and programmed are examples of such words.

DISTINGUISHING BETWEEN FACT AND FEELINGS

Identifying euphemisms and jargon is an easy introduction to the idea that words do not communicate just factual information but often feelings as well. Studying the relationships between concrete and relative words will help upper-elementary students enlarge upon this concept.

Work out this activity as a total class experience. Pick up a book and ask, "What is this?" Repeat the question, and each time hold up another book. Each time, of course, students will respond, "book." Write book at the top of a piece of charting paper labeled Concrete Words.

Next work with a word with a less precise meaning such as *heavy, pretty,* or *rough,* a relative rather than a concrete word. A noun such as *book* refers to a definite object, but a word such as *heavy* has a relative meaning, i.e., to a weak person, one object may be heavy, and to a stronger and larger person, the same object may appear light. Applying an adjective such as light and heavy to an object is more a judgmental act than using a term such as book.

Hand a large dictionary to a student and ask, "Is the book heavy?" Hand the same dictionary to another student and repeat, "Is the book heavy?" Do this several times. Some students will respond, "Yes," whereas others will respond, "No."

Write the word heavy at the top of a second piece of charting paper labeled Relative Words.

Start again by pointing to a picture. Ask, "Is this pretty?" Encourage several students to express an opinion. Now ask, "Is the word *pretty* more like the word *book* or the word *heavy*?" and follow up with the how question, "How is *pretty* like *heavy*?" Record the word *pretty* beneath *heavy* on the Relative Words chart.

Repeat this sequence several times, starting with different concrete or relative words such as:

Concrete Words	*Relative Words*
book	pretty
hammer	heavy
clock	happy
rug	slow
dog	old
ear	pale
table	friendly
blanket	rickety
pen	cold

As students analyze these words, add them to the appropriate word charts, and help students understand the labels heading the two columns.

COMMUNICATING WITH FEELING   One's feelings toward someone or something influence the words chosen to describe that person, object, or event. A thin person can be described as lanky, lean, scrawny, skinny, slender, slim, or even svelte, depending on one's perception of the person and her or his attitude toward slimness. Conversely a fat person may be called big, plump, portly, stocky, stout, chubby, fleshy, corpulent, obese, or just plain fat. Within these descriptors are some words that carry a negative connotation and some that carry a more positive one. Chubby is a rather positive way of viewing fatness, while obese expresses more negativeness. Svelte is an extremely favorable way to view thinness; scrawny is extremely unfavorable.

In *Language in Thought and Action* (2nd ed., Harcourt Brace, 1963), S. I. Hayakawa suggests an activity that can help students comprehend the connotations that closely related terms communicate. He "conjugates" words starting with one that has a favorable connotation and ending with one that carries a more negative message, giving the following series as an example:

I am firm.   You are obstinate.   He is a pig-headed fool.

This series was originally given by Bertrand Russell on a British Broadcasting Company radio program called "Brains Trust." Hayakawa quotes a whole series of similar word conjugations originally published in *New Statesman* and *Nation:*

I am beautiful.   You have quite good features.   She isn't bad-looking if you like that type.

I am righteously indignant.   You are annoyed.   He is making a fuss about nothing.

I have about me something of the subtle, haunting, mysterious fragrance of the Orient.   You rather overdo it, dear.   She stinks.

Ask students to analyze first examples that are relatively simple:

I am determined.   You are stubborn.   He is an obstinate fool.

I always do the proper thing.   You are a prude.   She is a strait-laced goody-goody.

I am very careful before I make a move.   You are overly cautious. He is a pussyfoot.

I enjoy taking a chance.   You are reckless.   She is a foolhardy daredevil.

Toward whom are people generally most positive? Who is described in words that carry the most positive message? Toward whom is one most negative? Why are we inclined to pick more positive words to describe someone with whom we are speaking (you) than to describe someone who is not present?

When students have grasped the concept that the words a speaker selects not only supply information about a person or thing being described but also about the speaker's own point of view toward the person or thing, suggest they try conjugating words:

VERY FAVORABLE VIEW	LESS FAVORABLE VIEW	VERY UNFAVORABLE VIEW
I evaluated.	You gossiped.	She was catty.

Some starting phrases are listed below. You may want to type them on U-film, one to a frame, and place the homemade filmstrip in a learning station where students can view the strip and write the conjugations on strips of paper. Later they can compare their conjugations with those of others who have worked at the station.

> I always speak my mind.
> I am a practical person.
> I am a born leader.
> I am very friendly.
> I like to talk.
> I am very well organized.
> I run a tight ship.
> I enjoy a good fight.
> I always stand up for what is right.
> I generally know what I am talking about.
> I always do things in a wholehearted way.
> I rarely forget anything.
> I am a conscientious person.
> I am slightly plump.

Students who have played with these beginning sentences can then devise their own by writing original conjugations on squares of different colored construction paper and mounting their squares on an on-going bulletin board captioned Your Words Give Away Your Point of View.

In *Writer's Guide and Index to English* (4th ed. Scott, Foresman, 1965), Porter Perrin writes that words such as slender, scrawny, thin, and so forth not only suggest an attitude on the part of the person using them but usually arouse a similar feeling in most readers or listeners. In other words, the connotation attached to a word, either negative or positive, is generally shared by most speakers of the language.

Encourage students to examine their own perceptions of certain words and to test Perrin's generalization by playing a question game called Negative or Positive. Students given a particular word must categorize their reaction to it as positive, negative, or neutral. Words might include: vacation, detention, failure, french fries, recess, lunch, homework, assignment, chores, friend, McDonald's, report card, test, art, guilty, summertime, and cheat.

After every youngster has reacted on paper to each word, a group analyzes the unsigned sheets by tallying the number of times each word was given a positive, negative, or neutral rating. It then draws a conclusion about how widespread feelings associated with these words are.

Students who have analyzed their own feelings about certain words may wish to investigate further. They draw up a list of terms they think may elicit positive or negative reactions from adults such as: fat, scrawny, fussy, cheerful, dependable, wealthy, drunk, frivolous, demanding, elegant, young, vacation, holiday, inflation, pollution, marriage, home, recession, hospital, dentist, and taxes. Next they interview adults, asking whether these words have a positive, negative or neutral connotation. All data obtained by interviewers are combined and compiled in a composite table. Students study the table to determine whether there is any evidence that most adults react similarly to certain words.

Words often communicate explicit judgments about people and things. One may explode, "You low down double-crosser," or may compliment, "He is such a personable young man." These are not statements of fact but rather of opinion. S. I. Hayakawa, author of *Language in Thought and Action* (cited earlier) equates the first statement with animal growls and terms it a snarl. He equates the second statement with animal tail wagging and terms it a purr.

Hayakawa believes it important that people understand the difference between thoughts expressed in snarls and purrs and thoughts expressed more factually. Unless we understand the difference, we possibly may not "allocate the meaning correctly." One should be aware that such snarl words as hard-boiled landlord, greedy monopolists, underhanded communists, hippies, lady drivers, crackpots, suckers, or foreigners do not reveal facts but are judgments of a speaker. Likewise, we should understand that such terms as great statesman, lovable child, dedicated public servant, sweetest girl in the world, or great music indicate that the speaker is expressing approval, not relaying facts.

Use Hayakawa's terms—snarl words and purr words—to get the ball rolling with students. Young people keep their ears alert for words that express approval or disapproval. They will locate snarl words galore if they start with terms of derision people throw at one another: tyrant, tramp, Hitler, dictator, scum, scab, radical, pig, red, knucklehead, meathead, or wino. A TV program such as *All in the Family* is a gold mine of snarl words, for Archie Bunker, the lead character, is a conglomeration of prejudices that he expresses verbally. His counterpart, Mr. Jefferson on the program *The Jeffersons*, is a similar gold mine of snarls. Listening to people express themselves about the TV nightly news is another activity bound to produce a lengthy list of words expressing disapproval.

Sometimes an expression of opinion is not obvious. If one says, "She spends her time gallivanting around town" or "He is a scoundrel," it may appear at first that the speaker is stating facts. Actually through the choice of words, she or he tucked opinion in too. *Gallivant* implies that the lady in question gads about with little or no purpose. To suggest that she has no objective makes an inference and then judges her activity worthless. The word *scoundrel* implies that the gentleman in question deliberately misbehaved. Hayakawa cautions against using such words in factual reports. Essentially these are snarl words, though less obvious ones.

Sophisticated upper-grade students can search out hidden snarls words that at first glance appear to convey facts but actually convey opinion. Letters to the editors of magazines and newspapers are a storehouse of hidden snarls. So are some editorials and feature columns. Keep a stack of index cards available as well as recent issues of *Newsweek, Time,* and local newspapers. Students can go to a Hidden Snarl Center to dig out snarls and record them on cards for later sharing with classmates.

PROJECTING POINTS OF VIEW   Give upper-elementary students a list of characteristics possessed by a hypothetical person such as:

A man about twenty-five years of age: wears jeans and a plaid shirt with a rip in it; shoulder-length hair with an Indian-style headband; wears metal-framed glasses; enjoys reading; is unemployed; travels around by hitchhiking.

Divide the class into writing groups of three or four students. Half write a paragraph describing this person as an individual whom they dislike intensely and for whom they have no respect. Their descriptions must contain some snarls. The other groups write descriptions showing that they like and respect the individual. Their descriptions must contain some purrs. Groups may add details not contained in the original information, but they should try to avoid using the exact words contained in it.

After groups have written their descriptions, they read them to classmates who try to identify words that convey positive or negative messages.

If students enjoy writing "prejudiced" descriptions, set up a writing station where individuals go to write more of the same. Mount cards containing information about characters on the backdrop of the center. Students read the stereotyped information, select a character, toss a die to determine whether they will like or dislike the character (an odd-number toss requires a like point of view; an even toss requires a dislike point of view), and write a paragraph of prejudiced description. Here are some stereotypes to present:

A younger brother or sister: everyone is always remarking how "cute" he or she is; says things that make people laugh; has a little dog that always follows him or her around; knows how to get his or her own way.

An eight-year-old girl: is best baseball hitter in the class; always plays practical jokes; tells funny stories and has to stay after school a lot; is shorter than most of the others in the class; wears a shirt with UCLA across the front.

A ten-year-old boy: always turns homework in promptly; always pays attention in school; is good looking; has lots of pocket money; is liked by adults.

A twelve-year-old: trips over his or her feet; knocks things over; very tall and thin; involved in many activities; never gets his or her work done on time; always losing things.

An older brother or sister: tells you what to do; knows a lot of things; receives very good grades in school; gets to do what he or she wants; is always on the go; drives his or her own car; stays out late at night; goes to college.

A great-grandmother: about eighty-five years old; has white hair pulled back in a bun; holds a cane in her hand; sits in a rocking chair; talks slowly; smiles a lot at you.

A grandfather: about sixty years old; always wears a navy blue suit with a white shirt and tie; has gray hair and walks with a slight limp; points with his finger as he talks to you.

A workingman: about forty years old, very tall and very big; wears overalls and a hard hat; talks with a loud voice; has very rosy cheeks and a suntanned look.

Students who have written prejudiced descriptions may enjoy writing favorable descriptions as a culmination to their study of how feelings can be communicated with words. Print on a chart a series of words that are not especially complimentary when applied to a person. Words that work well in this context are: dumb, hot-tempered, stubborn, greedy, stingy, dictatorial, self-centered, and timid. Each student selects a word and writes a description of a person, making her or his unpleasant characteristic sound positive. Encourage students to share their descriptions orally. Hearing how easy it is to turn the bad into the beautiful makes listeners comprehend what can be achieved through masterful manipulation of words.

LINGUISTIC SEXISM   Growing concern has been expressed about sexism inherent in the English language. This sexism is evident in several ways. First, when describing activities performed by both males and females, in the past the masculine pronouns *he*, *him*, and *his* have been used exclusively, i.e., "Will everyone raise *his* hand," when addressing a group comprised of both men and women. In like manner, masculine pronouns have been used to refer to certain things or occupations and feminine pronouns to refer to others. Farmers, bankers, doctors, and lawyers have been treated as if they were all men; while feminine pronouns are used when talking of ships, hurricanes, librarians, nurses, and elementary school teachers.

Since such instances abound, students can collect samples of linguistic sexism with relative ease. Mount a piece of oak tag on a classroom wall on which linguistic researchers can print examples they find. Schedule a talk time when students can consider the implications of such usage.

In English people are just beginning to move from terms such as *chairman* to sexless terms like *chairperson*. This trend can be the basis of a memory game in which young people pair terms in the style of the TV game "Concentration." Word pairs to use for the game include:

police officer/policeman
letter carrier/postman
people/men
maintenance person/maintenance man
radio engineer/radio man
weather forecaster/weather man
hunter/huntsman
cowhand/cowboy
worker/workman
humankind/mankind
launderer/washwoman

the common people/the common man
fire fighter/fireman
garbage collector/garbage man
sound-effects technician/sound-effects man
newscaster/newsman
assembly person/assembly man
person-like/man-like
craftworker/craftsman
prehistoric person/prehistoric man

Select fifteen pairs of words from the above list or others you can think of. Print each member of a pair on separate index cards and shuffle them. On the reverse side stick masking tape on which is written a number from 1 to 30. Spread the cards on the floor, five across and six down, numbers up in the manner of the concentration board.

Divide the class into two teams. In turn a player from each team calls out numbers on two cards. The cards are turned up and then promptly turned down again unless they are a pair i.e., a sexist term and its nonsexist equivalent. If a player correctly calls a matching pair, it remains face up and the team to which the player belongs is awarded a point. Play continues until all cards are matched by the power of concentrated memory. The team with the largest number of points is winner.

A CONCENTRATION PLAYING BOARD
WITH CARDS FACE UP

To play, turn cards over so numbers on reverse side are visible.

To rearrange the cards for other rounds of concentration, peel off the masking tape numbers and renumber the cards. If you can laminate your cards, they will remain in good playing condition for many rounds, and peeling off the number tapes and renumbering will be easier.

You can make similar concentration games to teach a variety of word relationships:

> Matching synonyms, antonyms, or homonyms
> A word on one, its definition on another
> A euphemism on one, its less fancy equivalent on another

PLAYING WITH MEANING

Metaphor, simile, personification, hyperbole, idiom, jargon, euphemism, literal allusion, connotation, and denotation are words that identify some of the creative ways language is used.

Should teachers define these words explicitly for children in elementary school classrooms so that they can differentiate between a simile and a metaphor, between connotation and denotation? I think not! To stress distinctions among ways of using language in many instances kills the joy of playing with language. Students memorize definitions and that becomes the sought-after end. Rather, emphasize the ability to express meaning in a variety of patterns and the pleasure of working creatively with words.

So encourage young people to imagine what a broomstick could be, to see similarities between a flag and a fly, to describe people in animal terms and inanimate objects in people terms, to pun, to invent prestige-carrying phrases. In the process, if you wish, use terms such as hyperbole and allude, but keep terminology in the background so that it does not interfere with the sheer pleasure of word play.

'Twas brillig, and the slitby toves
Did gyre and gimble in the wabe:
All mimsy were the borogoves
And the mome raths outgrabe.
"JABBERWOCKY," LEWIS CARROLL

5. ALL MIMSY WERE THE BOROGOVES: *Activities in Sentence Building*

People put words together in a variety of patterns—in short sentences or lengthy ones, in simple patterns or complex ones, in repetitive patterns or varied ones, in typical noun-verb word order or flip-flopped reverses, or perhaps in groups of words that are not sentences at all. The manner in which words are arranged is part of one's speaking and writing style.

The previous two chapters have considered three aspects of verbal style: choice of words, sound-shape relationships, and figurative language. The present chapter treats a more basic element of style—the sentence patterns available in the English language. Attention will focus on parts of speech and kinds of sentences, since both areas tend to be included in elementary language programs today.

One caution before beginning! When involving students in English sentence patterns, teachers should not push them to produce prose ladened with unnecessary complexities, polysyllables, figures of speech, or words. Such "purple prose" is generally pompous and often unclear. Rather, teachers should provide young people with opportunities to handle a variety of patterns so that they can gain skill in putting words together and become sensitive to the use of diverse patterns in the written material they encounter. In the process they may gain an appreciation of the power inherent in their language and an increasing ability to tap that power for themselves.

MASTERING THE SENTENCE

DEVELOPING SENTENCE SENSE   Help youngsters begin to recognize sentence units by playing orally with the two major building blocks of the sentence—subjects (or noun phrases) and predicates (or verb phrases). Distribute at random word cards bearing simple noun phrases or simple verb phrases such as:

Noun Phrases (Subjects)	Verb Phrases (Predicates)
a dancing monkey	tilted downward
the wild horses	roared down the street
Mary and Bob	took off
the speeding cars	rushed along
Susan	came home
those excited girls	tore up the pavement
two diesel engines	crashed into the window
four buzzing bumblebees	threw up dirt
the seagulls	circled around
a swirling hurricane	spun up and around
a tiny hummingbird	shot into the sky
two hungry and tired boys	glided to a halt
a rocket ship	stood motionless
twenty airplanes	tumbled to the ground
the first helicopter	came into the room
spinning wheels	swished by

Keep one noun phrase in hand to start the sentence building. Perhaps begin with *the speeding cars.* Place that phrase card on the floor and ask if any student can build a sentence from it by placing his or her card on the floor next to it.

the speeding cars	roared down the street

You may wish to add appropriate punctuation and capitalization. Cuisenaire rods can be used as capitalization and punctuation markers. Just use the small beige cubes to represent periods and the light green pieces to represent commas. Set the long pieces across letters to indicate capitals.

Another student may suggest that his or her words also fit. If this happens, simply move the phrase *roared down the street* to a position below and substitute the new phrase, perhaps, *swished by.*

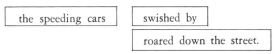

Now ask for words that could fit in the slot in front of *roared down the street*. Students may suggest *those excited girls* or *two diesel engines* or *the wild horses*. Keep building simple sentences in this way by juggling noun and verb phrases. Since most of the noun phrases are interchangeable, additional switches may be made as noun and verb phrases form columns on the floor.

Hold in readiness cards with these labels: Sentence, Noun Phrase, Verb Phrase, =, and +. As students build sentences from their cards, place the Noun Phrase label at the top of the first column and the Verb Phrase label at the top of the other. Labels can also produce an equation for sentences:

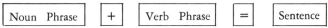

To reinforce understanding, give students basic kernel sentence cards such as:

The mountain appeared in the distance.
The wall clock chimed loudly.
The house burned to the ground.
Grapefruits are expensive.
The dictionary weighed a ton.
One hundred elephants walked by.
Jack threw the football over the goalpost.

Ask them to cut the cards into two parts, one to place under the Noun Phrase label and one to place under the Verb Phrase label. Supply many simple sentences for children to play with in this way.

Extend the activity by asking groups to write their own sentences comprised of noun and verb phrases. They can be written onto cards, cut into phrase parts, and placed on the floor under the appropriate labels. Once students have laid out many sentences in this manner, suggest that players interchange the noun phrases of their sentences to create additional sentences that could make sense.

In this activity an open area of classroom floor serves as a composing stage. Noun phrases can be set down and shifted around as verb phrases are added. Youngsters sitting around the composing area, either on the floor or on low chairs, can manipulate the cards with relative ease and interchange components to form a variety of fun sentences.

A floor area can also serve as a composing stage for an individual student who needs additional work putting noun and verb phrases together into sentences. Just gather all the phrase cards developed in previous activities into a box and put it on the floor in the corner. A student goes to this learning center to build phrase cards into sensible sentences. This type of follow-up is particularly valuable for students who are learning English as a second language.

BUILDING WORD LADDERS   Ms. Marjorie Frey encouraged fourth graders in Westfield, New Jersey, to build interesting sentences by helping them construct word ladders. Starting with a word such as *car*, which she had printed on a card, she asked her students to think of words that describe a car. They proposed big, new, comfortable, unusual, shiny, economical, compact, fancy, classy, expensive, and sports and wrote each word on a card of a different color, which were taped ladder-style above the word *car*.

Then Ms. Frey asked the children to think of words that tell what a car does. They suggested stalls, speeds, slides, skids, crashes, and so forth. Again each word was written on a card of a different color, and they were attached ladder-style beneath the word *car*. Ms. Frey attached a string to the top word card and hung the series so that one could read the words from top to bottom.

In groups students constructed more word ladders. Key words used as starters included cat, dog, girl, train, baby, and flower. Each group thought of words that described a starter word and taped them above the starter; they then thought of words that told what the starter word did and taped those beneath. The word ladders were suspended with strings from the lighting fixtures.

As follow-up, Ms. Frey gave her students strips of paper. Students selected words from any of the ladders to build into sentences, adding other words where necessary. They wrote

A WORD LADDER

lightfooted
alley
elegant
sly
stray
calico
Siamese
scrawny
finicky
c a t
meows
purrs
prowls
climbs
runs
scratches

sentences such as The elegant Siamese cat meows, Colorful wild flowers droop and die, and The naughty dog nips, growls, and barks.

Ms. Frey's activity can be extended with older students by adding words laterally to the ladders. For example, cards such as very, loudly, contentedly, at night, in the dark, or up trees can be added to the cat ladder by attaching the side of a card with string or tape to the side of an original card. Students attach as many cards as they can fit onto the orginal ladder and then create sensible sentences from their expanded strings of words.

MANIPULATING WORDS   Ms. Elizabeth Murray, a co-ordinator of language arts in Chelmsford, Massachusetts, explained in *Instructor* (March 1975) an activity that stimulates young people in grades three and four to write expanded sentences. To prepare for her activity, make cards labeled

Actor	Action	What Kind?	How?	Where?	When?

Ms. Murray suggests taping the Actor and Action cards to a large chalkboard surface and beginning by printing the word *snowflake* beneath the Actor card. Ask children to brainstorm words that tell what snowflakes do; list their responses in a column beneath the Action card.

Now mount the What Kind? card in front of the Actor card, ask for words that tell what kind of snowflakes, and list word responses.

What Kind?	Actor	Action
white	snowflakes	danced
cold		swirled
tiny		fell
lacy		melted
soft		whirled
huge		spun
		fluttered

Continue by mounting the How? card after the Action card. Again encourage students to think of words that tell how snowflakes act. Do the same with the Where? and When?

cards. Students supply words that answer these questions, suggesting both individual words and phrases. The final result in Ms. Murray's class was this extensive chart:

What Kind?	*Actor*	*Action*	*How?*	*Where?*	*When?*
Tiny	snowflakes	danced	merrily	by my window	as twilight approached.
white		swirled	quickly	in the yard	yesterday
cold		fell	slowly	on Santa's tiled	on Christmas
tiny		melted	quietly	roof	this morning
lacy		whirled	fast	on her freckled	when the sun set
soft		spun	softly	nose	in the afternoon
huge		fluttered		on the church	before the sun
				steeple	rose
				in the lamplight	
				over the town	

This board contained many of the ingredients of interesting sentences. Choosing words from each category, students created other sentences structurally similar to the one at the top of the chart. They built sentences through both oral and written activities.

Ms. Murray found that youngsters enjoy manipulating the labeling cards to investigate other word orders in sentences. They can try placing Where? and When? words at the beginning rather than at the ending of their sentences. They can try placing How? words before Action words. They can look for other locations where What Kind? words fit.

Through activities modeled after Ms. Murray's, students will gain an understanding of the basic ingredients of sentences. They write sentences and begin to experiment with words to produce interesting ideas—all without using the terminology of parts of speech. Such experiences are particularly valuable for the young person developing skill in English as a second language.

EXPANDING SENTENCES   A sentence such as *The police officer stopped the bandits* can be expanded by adding words at a number of locations, i.e., at the beginning, before and after *police officer*, before and after *bandits*, and after *stopped*. Working with a model sentence similar to this one and cards on which additional words are written, youngsters can expand the sentence to produce one that gives more information.

Teams start by writing the model sentence on a paper strip and then cutting the sentence into individual words, which they place on any flat surface. They prepare word and phrase cards to insert into the sentence. Remind them that an insertion can be a single word such as *fleeing* before *bandits* or a group of words such as *Pushing the police car to top speed* at the beginning of the sentence.

When team members complete an expanded sentence, they staple or paste it to a large piece of charting paper. Then they start again with the same base sentence and expand it with other words and phrases. All the completed sentences are stapled to the charting paper, which quickly fills up with many variations of the base sentence.

Mount the group charts across the front of the room. By analyzing them, students can identify the kinds of information they have interjected at each location in the sentence and can attempt to generalize about where certain kinds of ideas tend to be placed within sentences.

Once students have completed this activity as part of a group, they can go on to try their hand individually at writing variations, each time introducing different ideas and types of words. Sentences useful for such follow-up study of sentence expansion are:

> The horse wandered into the cornfield.
> The icicle dripped.
> The television set blared.
> Miriam won the award.
> The pitcher threw out the ball.

Just print one sentence on the top of a duplicating stencil, and run off multiple copies to stack in a learning station. Using a fine-line flo-pen, students fill the sheet with expanded versions of the sentence.

During a talk sesssion, youngsters can share and compare their sentences with what classmates have written to learn new ways of incorporating ideas into sentences.

WORKING WITH WORD ORDER   Part of the meaning of sentences in English is communicated through word order. To help young people comprehend this fact about their language, begin by cutting apart the words in sentences such as: The mighty elephants pulled a log across the clearing or The hungry dog munched a steak bone or Twenty monkeys devoured all the bananas on the banana tree. Give individual word cards from these sentences to students and ask them to arrange themselves so that the words they hold will make sense. The sentences in this group are all in a noun-verb-noun (or subject–verb–direct object) pattern. Ask youngsters to decide in each case who is the actor, what the action is, and who is receiving the action. You may wish to use the Actor labeling card from a preceding activity as well the Action label; an additional card labeled Receiver of Action can be made to identify the second noun.

Once children have played with putting words back together into sentences, they can go on to write or speak other sentences patterned after the model ones. Encourage them to write their sentences on strips, cut the strips into individual words, and see if other students can put them back together again.

A fun follow-up that Sandy Ozolins uses with her fifth graders is writing nonsense sentences by reversing actor and receiver nouns in a sentence. The result can be something as foolish as: All the bananas on the banana tree devoured twenty monkeys. Ms. Ozolins has her students draw pairs of pictures—

one showing the meaning communicated by words in normal English sentence order and one showing the meaning communicated when actor and receiver words are reversed. By doing this, children begin to understand the importance of word order in communication. This is especially important for a child whose first language is not English.

Much the same thing can be done by working with other English sentence patterns, i.e., noun-verb-noun-noun. Cut into individual words the sentence Mary gave John an apple. Students arrange the words properly and draw a picture depicting the action. They then switch and reswitch the words to form sense and nonsense: John gave Mary an apple. An apple gave John Mary. John gave an apple Mary. They draw pictures to depict the crazy action in some of these sentences.

A fun sentence to twist in this way is Martha gave Sally Jill. Assign a student to be Martha, a second to be Sally, and a third to be Jill. Each student wears a name sign, and they pantomime various versions of the sentence. Classmates must guess which sentence is being pantomimed.

Another approach to a study of English word order is using sentences from magazine and newspaper advertisements. Just cut up large print sentences from advertisements, shuffle the words to put them into random order, and toss them one at a time onto an open floor area around which young participants squat. As each word flutters to the floor, students try to order the words that have been dealt so far. Toward the end, they guess what the remaining words must be for the sentence to make sense. Good advertisement headlines to use are: "Our status symbol is under the hood, not on it," "Get a grip on yourself with Lifestride," or "You know us by our reputation."

"This year you should be wearing last year's sandal." works well with sophisticated students. Through manipulating rather creative sentence patterns, young people will begin to see original ways of working with words. They can go on to invent sentence patterns of their own similar to advertisement sentences.

IMBEDDING SENTENCES   Students can generate one sentence from two by imbedding the ideas of one inside the other. For example, the two sentences, The man dropped a bottle on the floor and The man was angry can be combined into The man who was angry dropped a bottle on the floor. Or The man who dropped a bottle on the floor was angry. Or even into the less wordy form The angry man dropped a bottle on the floor.

Give students working as "baseball" teams sentence pairs similar to the preceding one. Write both sentences on a pitcher's card. Place many pitcher's cards in a box. A "pitcher" pulls a card from the box and "pitches" it to the opposing team. The team sends its first batter to home plate, where a large piece of manila paper has been placed. The batter must write on the paper a sentence containing the ideas of both sentences pitched. A three-person group of umpires standing by home plate judges the validity of the combination. The next batter runs to first base; on a large piece of manila paper there, he or she must write a second variation of the two sentences. Again the umpires judge the validity of the "run." The team sends a third batter to second base to try to write still another variation, and the umpires check the sentence. Finally, a fourth team member attempts to write yet another combination of the sentences on manila paper located at third base.

The team chalks up one point for all runs judged acceptable by the umpires. Record points on a score board. Once a team has written four variations of the sentences pitched to it, it retires; and the opposing team comes up to bat, and the process is repeated. The same group of umpires judges the acceptability of the sentences and assigns the points for the second half of the inning.

Suggested sentence pairs for pitcher's cards are given below:

The dog barked at the moon all night.
The dog was a collie.

Tim hit the ball across the fence.
Tim wore a baseball uniform numbered 1.

The trees whistled and twisted in the wind.
The trees were in my back yard.

The garbage cans rolled down the street and struck a car.
The garbage cans were shiny and new.

The light bulb burned out.
The light bulb was at the top of the dangerous stairway.

The kangaroo has short forelegs.
The kangaroo hops high into the air on its rear legs.

The clock ticked off the minutes and chimed every hour.
The clock hung on the wall.

The bicycle race took place in Monaco.
The bicycle race was won by a French boy.

The battle was fought in Lexington.
The battle was the first one in the War for Independence.

The dinner was served at six o'clock.
We had spaghetti and meatballs for dinner.

Twenty horses escaped last night.
The horses were all white stallions.

The waves crashed toward the shore.
The waves were whipped by the powerful wind.

Just write each pair on an index card or give this page to a youngster so that he or she can practice handwriting skills by preparing the cards. Label the bases on manila sheets and sketch a scoreboard on a piece of oak tag. You may also want to ask students to dream up unusual names for their teams and assign numbers to team members.

On another occasion, use the sentence pairs to help children analyze the ways in which information in one sentence can be imbedded in a second. Students may be able to note that they sometimes use a group of words introduced by who, which, or that to imbed the information, that sometimes they convert the information of a sentence into a single word in a second sentence, and so forth. This type of analytical work is rather sophisticated, so you may wish to reserve it for the most cognitively mature youngsters, who may be able to discover for themselves that length alone does not indicate a "good" sentence; sometimes the best combinations are achieved with only a few words.

An easy way to combine sentences is to use the *-ing* form of one verb in an adverbial clause, i.e., Paddling as fast as they could, the canoeists escaped the currents of the rapids. This sentence pattern is particularly effective for describing two actions that occur almost simultaneously; it is, however, a relatively difficult pattern to master and requires considerable practice to perfect.

The baseball competition in the previous activity can be used as the framework for such practice. Each pitcher card now contains the outline of a sentence such as:

Galloping _____, the zebras _____.
Hollering _____, the pitchers _____.
Floating _____, the clouds _____.
Running _____, the football player _____.
Calculating _____, the pilots _____.
Rushing _____, many people _____.
Humming _____, the lawnmower _____.
Sleeping _____, my friend _____.
Swinging _____, the golfers _____.
Cleaning _____, the mechanic _____.
Dancing _____, the teacher _____.
Changing _____, the principal _____.
Clacking _____, the ducks _____.

Spinning _____,	the windmill _____.
Dumping _____,	the large trucks _____.
Building _____,	the construction worker _____.
Sawing _____,	the carpenter _____.
Crashing _____,	the elephant _____.
Spinning _____,	the tennis ball _____.
Talking _____,	my father _____.
Jumping _____,	the kangaroo _____.
Driving _____,	my sister _____.
Tilting _____,	the boat _____.
Writing _____,	I _____.
Speeding _____,	the police officer _____.
Wishing _____,	he _____.
Explaining _____,	the astronauts _____.
Dropping _____,	she _____.
Winning _____,	the two boys _____.
Collapsing _____,	they _____.
Falling _____,	the raindrops _____.

A pitcher draws a card and throws out the sentence to a batter from the opposing team. Working within the suggested sentence pattern, the batter must write a complete sentence on the manila sheet at home plate. Successive batters from the same team must complete the same sentence; drawing on different words, they write their sentences on first, second, or third bases.

Umpires must judge the validity of the sentences by asking, "Does the -*ing* phrase tell about the noun that is the subject of the sentence?" Write this question on a criterion chart posted by home plate to remind players that in this pattern the -*ing* part of their sentences tells about the subject or noun.

Before actually playing baseball, students may need some oral practice. If you think they have had little experience with this relatively complex pattern, encourage writing class sentences. Work with a sentence such as The crowd roared its approval. Supply a model by adding at the beginning Cheering wildly. Then ask the class to brainstorm other ways the crowd could show its approval. You can write their suggestions onto a transparency and immediately project them with an overhead projector. A transparency may begin to look like:

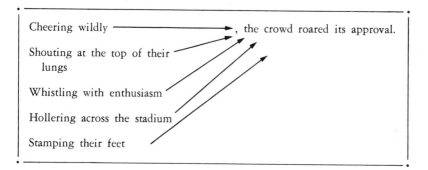

Do the same kind of thing with other sentence bases:

> The airplane took off down the runway.
> The car came to a fast stop.
> The astronauts climbed into their spaceship.
> The boys watched the lion walk away from them.
> The Minutemen faced the Redcoats.
> The robbers left the bank.
> The racers waited for the race to begin.

Just letter these sentences on a piece of transparency acetate, and ask youngsters to give exciting *-ing* phrases to attach on the front. The resulting sentences can be sources of ideas for a short story. Students select one version of a sentence and include it in an action episode.

COMBINING SENTENCE IDEAS   There are numbers of other ways to combine the ideas of two sentences that children may find easier to manage than using an introductory *-ing*. Two sentences can be built into one in the following ways:

Compound sentence. The mallards waddled toward us and The robins flew away can be transformed to The mallards waddled toward us, but the robins flew away. Words used as connectives in compound sentences are and, but, or, not, for, yet, and so.

Compound structure such as a compound subject, predicate, prepositional phrase, adjective or adverb group. John brought the sandwiches and He also brought the cake can be simplified to John brought both the sandwiches and cake. John brought cake and Bob brought cake too can be combined as Both John and Bob brought cake. The finches were turning over the leaves, The finches were searching the ground for seeds, and The finches were chirping loudly can be merged into The finches were turning over the leaves, searching the ground for seeds, and chirping loudly. The advantage of most of these compound sentences is that they eliminate unnecessary words.

Cluster of words following a principal noun. The man went to the party and He was fat can become The man who went to the party was fat. I saw the accident and It was gruesome can become The accident I saw was gruesome. Often clusters of words following nouns are introduced by who, whom, that, or which; however, these introductory words sometimes can be deleted to avoid wordiness.

Subordinative phrases introduced by words such as when, although, unless, if, since, while, as, because, whereas, or whenever. I was driving and I saw the accident, can be combined as While I was driving, I saw the accident. I didn't want to go and I went to the party can become Although I didn't want to go, I went to the party. Use of a subordinative phrase can clarify the relationship between two original sentences, suggesting perhaps a relationship of time, cause and effect, result, or condition.

To teach young people to write sentences that contain compound structures, try some of the following activities: Write the noun trees in the middle of a large chart, and ask students to brainstorm words that tell what trees do. They may supply single words or groups of words; write them in list fashion to the right. Then students suggest words that describe trees; write these words to the left as shown in the sample:

maple oak living	twist drop their leaves in fall
flowering graceful	become green in spring
weeping willow	burst into color
stately tall	sway in the breeze
growing branching	toss their branches
bending budding TREES	bend touch the ground
twenty green gold	tangle their branches
bamboo zombie-like	tilt tremble grow tall
	stand like wardens in the night
	reach toward the sky
	tumble to the ground

Place this chart in a sentence-building learning station, so that students can select words from it to build sentences with compound adjectives and verbs. Post the sentence pattern _____ and _____ trees _____, _____, and _____. at the station to help slower children with the construction. Repeat the class activity using at the center starter words such as friends, horses, rats, or football player.

Suggest that students write poetry-like pieces by drawing words from the charts. Compound adjectives and verbs can be strung out in several lines to produce results such as:

> Tall
> and
> stately maple trees
> tremble, twist, and
> touch their branches to the ground.

After writing poetry-like lines based on the charts, students can venture out on their own to write more string poems by using compound structures strung down and across a page.

> In the spring
> I
> run outside,
> open windows,
> hop about,
> and smell the smells of spring.

To stimulate the activity, read a poem such as Aileen Fisher's "When It Comes to Bugs" (*I Wonder How, I Wonder Why,* Abelard Schuman, 1962). Or use Mary O'Neill's "Sound of Fire" (*What Is That Sound!* Atheneum, 1966):

> The sound of fire is:
> A hiss,
> A sputter,
> A crackle,
> A flutter,
> A lick,
> A rumble,
> A roar,
> A grumble,
> A cry,
> A pop,
> A shift,
> A flop,
> A race,
> A sweep,
> A spit,
> A leap,
> A whoosh,
> A boom,
> A snap,
> A plume,
> A cackle,
> A crash,
> A fall,
> Of ash . . .

Besides hearing the poems, children should see them, so that they can get an idea of how string poems are placed on paper and how punctuation is used to separate components of a compound structure.

Play the listening-memory game in which each player adds another object to a growing alphabetical list of objects and repeats the entire list. Each youngster begins with a statement such as, "I went into the forest. When I came out, following me was/were . . ." or "I am getting ready to go on a trip and I am packing. . . ." When an item to go with each of the twenty-six letters of the alphabet has been identified, divide students into groups, give each group a flo-pen and large paper, and instruct each to produce a sentence that contains a similar list of items that are in, on, behind, under, above, or near something. The result must be a lengthy single sentence with items in a series separated by commas. Use these sentences as examples upon which to base a generalization about the use of commas in compound sentences.

Prepare learning center direction cards for writing sentences with compound structures:

In one sentence tell the sequence of actions you perform when you get up in the morning.

In one sentence tell the sequence of actions you perform when you pitch a ball.

In one sentence tell the sequence of actions you perform when you open a can with a can opener.

In one sentence tell the route you follow when you come to school.

In one sentence tell the names of the members of your family who live with you.

In one sentence tell the sequence of events from the time a car goes out of control until it strikes a telephone pole.

In one sentence tell the sequence of steps you perform to fold paper into an airplane.

In one sentence tell the sequence of steps in any task you do well.

In one sentence tell the order in which you take off your clothes when you undress at night.

Try one or two of the following activities to involve young people in writing sentences that contain a cluster of words following a principal noun.

Write at several locations on the board a model sentence such as, The boy who knows the answer will receive a reward. In groups students work at the board writing numerous word clusters to take the place of who knows the answer. Then suggest that they rewrite their sentences so that the information they have substituted will come at the end rather than within the sentence. Start by showing how the original sentence can be transformed into The boy who will receive a reward knows the answer. Repeat the activity using a sentence containing *that* rather than *who*, i.e.,

> The house that sits on a hill is for sale.
> The house that is for sale sits on a hill.

Arrange a game for students who have had some preliminary work with adjective clauses. Make three sets of cards containing words from the following list:

SET 1: my friend, her father, the secretary, the captain, that man, your teacher, the fire fighter, the police officer, the custodian, the engineer, the principal, your uncle, my aunt, their mother, the clerk, the actor, the ballplayer, the referee, the dentist.

SET 2: weary, bored, cheerful, witty, starved, friendly, mean, discontent, humble, shy, snobbish, bighearted, determined, calm, sober, self-satisfied, merry, patient, playful, delighted, inconsiderate, meek, tiny, nervous, thoughtful, lighthearted.

SET 3: owns a van, plays the banjo, is running in the marathon, knows all the answers, owns a sports car, likes to play practical jokes, carries a cane, is running for president, owns the First National Bank, sings in the shower, walks with a limp, has many friends, wants to become a doctor, flies a 747 jet, drives a red Datsun, forgets to go to work, enjoys football.

Make also many cards containing the words *who, is,* and *was,* and punctuation cards containing periods. Keep some additional blank cards in readiness. Write a model sentence on the board, i.e., The opera singer who is performing at the Met is from Russia. Divide the class into three teams. Each team sits in a circle on the floor with a working area in the center. A member from each team draws a card from each of the three sets. Using those words plus a *who* card, a period card, an *is* or *was* card, the player must put the pieces together to form a sentence that follows the pattern of the model. The person who puts together a sentence first earns a point for the team. Cards from the three sets are then returned to the boxes, and the next players on each team draw and build the words into sentences as quickly as possible.

For follow-up, place the card sets into pouches in a learning center. Students draw a card from each pouch, build them into a sentence, write the sentence on a large piece of oak tag mounted on the surface of the station, and return the cards to the pouches. They can also study the oak tag and write "flipped" versions of any of the sentences already recorded there; *Roni, who has yellow braids, is my sister* can be flipped into *Roni, who is my sister, has yellow braids.* You may suggest that students add original cards to the pouches to expand the word pool from which others draw as they add sentences onto the growing Flip-Flop Chart.

To teach young people to write sentences containing a subordinating structure, try some of the following activities:

Introduce the notion of subordinating structures with Match and Mix Cards. Have a student who needs handwriting practice prepare these word cards:

> when everyone is ready
> if there is time
> because it is raining
> although I want to finish the crossword puzzle
> while we are waiting
> after the rain stops
> since there are two of us here
> though the sun just came out
> unless he wants us to help
> I will stay in the house
> let's finish our homework

I will present the awards
we will go
we will play chess
let's drive to the shopping center
we will return home
I will do what you want
we will watch television

Distribute one or more cards to sentence builders seated around an open floor area. Retain one card introduced by a subordinating word for yourself. Keep in readiness a stack of comma and period cards, perhaps on a color different from the word cards.

Put out your card, placing your pen on top of the first letter to indicate it is capitalized and adding a comma after the phrase. Ask students to study their cards to determine if they hold a clause that could follow. Since these are multiple mix cards, almost any of the cards not introduced by a subordinator will work. Take the first card suggested, lay it out next to your card, and ask, "What will we need at the end to show that it is the end of the sentence?" Add a period card.

Other students will probably volunteer that they hold cards that will also conclude the sentence. Take a suggested card and substitute it for the original, slipping that one downward to leave an empty slot at the beginning:

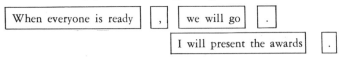

At this point students study their cards to find words that could fit into the slot in front of I will present the awards. Keep matching and mixing the cards until nine sentences are built on the floor, and then distribute strips of paper and encourage students to make cards that could be built into structurally similar sentences.

Finally, place a subordinating structure at the end of a

sentence and change the capitalization and punctuation to meet the needs of the new sentence:

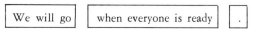

Have students switch the other sentences, and call to their attention that a comma is no longer necessary. Encourage thinking about any changes in meaning caused by the changes and development of a generalization about the punctuation of sentences similar to these.

Construct a simple follow-up learning station. Into a pouch put word cards that can introduce a subordinating phrase, i.e., when, if, because, since, although, while, though, unless, until, and after. Lay out a piece of large, colored construction paper and a flo-pen. A task card tells students to: 1) draw a word from the pouch; 2) compose a sentence starting with that word; 3) write the sentence on the colored construction paper; and 4) rewrite it by flipping the beginning part to the end. As more and more students add sentences to the sheet, a collage of sentences will result.

Build a writing activity on the Sentence Collage. Writers must select at least two sentences from it and include them in a short story. Drafts of the stories and the Sentence Collage can be posted on a bulletin board.

Once students have written many sentences containing subordinating structures, transfer the word cards to another, more difficult learning station. A student draws two word cards from the pouch and now must write a paragraph containing the two phrases.

PUTTING PARTS OF SPEECH TO USE

BUILDING SILLY SENTENCES   Young children in primary grades enjoy concocting sentences by selecting words from word pools and placing them in an order that is functionally acceptable but foolish in meaning. First help them

build word pools that will become the substance of their silly
sentences. Start by working with a simple pattern such as, *Fat
bananas ride on roller coasters.* This sentence is functionally
acceptable, that is, grammatical, although it is silly, because
bananas do not ride roller coasters whether they are thin
or fat.

Break the sentence into individual words, each of which
heads a column on a chart. Children add words to each
column that could substitute for the word that heads the
column. For example, hamburgers, alligators, whistles, ghosts,
and so forth can be substituted in the sentence for bananas,
while green, fast, rare, and so forth can be substituted for
fat. The chart shows other examples that youngsters might
build into their own charts:

Fat	*Bananas*	*Ride*	*On*	*Roller*	*Coasters.*
Green	hamburgers	sing	by	orange	boxes
Fast	whistles	sit	in	open	radios
Rare	goats	eat	through	rubber	rafts
Cozy	goblins	rush	into	purple	clouds
Wet	watermelons	play	under	loaded	bottles
Crazy	cucumbers	flow	above	broken	rivers
Dumb	alligators	run	with	stupid	crocodiles
Honest	peanuts	crash	beneath	phony	icicles
Watery	flowers	skate	to	empty	umbrellas

After children have built their own charts, they select a
word from each column to produce sentences that are fully
grammatical but also silly; i.e., "Crazy goats eat beneath
broken umbrellas" or "Wet hamburgers play beneath orange
clouds" or "Fast peanuts rush into broken bottles." Allow
sufficient time for sentence writing so that children in groups
can write sentences onto sheets of colored construction paper.
Groups can share their silly sentences with others.

Children can play in a similar way with other simple and more complex sentence patterns. Examples that can be broken apart to head columns for Word Pool Charts are:

> Some purple elephants eat turnips.
> Swaying chairs take aviators to the moon.
> Hungry horses are always silly on Sunday.
> Wishful lions are our friends.
> When wiggly witches fly, friendly goblins swim.

Write these sentences across the tops of large pieces of oak tag, draw lines to form columns, and attach a flo-pen with a long piece of string. Individuals can go to this sentence-building center to add functionally similar words in the columns, and later they can write silly sentences by choosing a word from each column. Sentences can be printed on strips of paper and mounted around the oak tag containing the word pools.

If students enjoy sentence-building play of this kind, you may want to extend the activity by including nonsense words at the head of some of the columns. Students can add more nonsense words to those given in the accompanying chart.

As	*ergels*	*whorpled*	*in*	*the*	*lopids,*
When	turpids	gerted	by	some	frebids
Since	jimbads	dreeped	through	many	bromiffs
While	patels	plened	into	five	glares
If	frebids	ploved	from	twenty	tenks
Though	talens	troned	under	my	marners

grehips	*hirtled*	*nearby*
sphines	froated	here
flemites	fleaked	away
phonels	honted	about
crisps	batted	within
floops	wated	by

Sentences built on nonsense words substituted for real nouns, verbs, adjectives, and adverbs can be rather humorous. They can be put together to form a Lewis Carroll–type poem:

> While turpids ploved under some glares, flemites honted by.
> As patels troned from twenty frebids, floops wated nearby.
> Though jimbads gerted into many tenks, phonels froated about.

Children can draw from nonsense charts containing nonsense words organized in different sentence patterns, such as:

> Her itsy bortroff at the tore trimbled beneath the rore.
> Some wallows and wates have pouded their firls.
> The arnts rimbly warded into topers of flots.
> The limsy gurter raned gosts to Flo.

Do also as Dr. John Savage of Boston College proposes in *Linguistics for Teachers* (Science Research Associates, 1973). Help youngsters identify the nonsense words in Carroll's "Jabberwocky," then scratch them out, and substitute real words to see if they can make sense from nonsense. The results, according to Dr. Savage, may resemble the following:

> 'Twas raining and the slippery eels
>   Did slither and slide in the mud.
> All chilly were the fishermen,
>   And the wise fish understood.

The authors of *Language and Thinking in the Elementary School* make a similar suggestion. Let young people analyze stories composed of English function words and of nonsense words substituted for nouns, verbs, adjectives, and adverbs. They study stories similar to the following and resubstitute real English words for the nonsense ones; this activity will allow them to see the structure of their language:

GLOOPY AND BLIT

Gloopy is a borp. Blit is a lof. Gloopy klums like Blit. Gloopy and Blit are floms.

 Ril had poved Blit to a jonfy. But Lo had not poved Gloopy. "The jonfy is for lofs," Blit bofd to Gloopy. "Rom are a borp." Gloopy was not klorpy. Then Blit was not klorpy.*

Students who have played with this story may wish to try their hand at writing similar nonsense episodes for their classmates to convert back to sense. It can be fun as well as an opportunity to learn about the way words work in English sentences.

UNDERSTANDING NOUN FUNCTIONS Work with nonsense words introduces youngsters to the ways in which words form sentences and is a first step in developing an understanding of how different parts of speech tend to pattern in sentences.

You may wish a more formal introduction to the parts of speech. If so, try the approach of the structural linguists who have devised test frames, sentences in which words of one part of speech are deleted. Students try to fit many different words into the blanks of the test frame. All words that can fit into the blanks of a noun test frame can function as nouns in that context as in these examples:

The _____ is there.
A _____ is a _____.
The _____ chased the _____.
The _____ on the _____ chased the _____†

*E. Brooks Smith, Kenneth S. Goodman, and Robert Meredith, *Language and Thinking in the Elementary School.* New York: Holt, Rinehart and Winston, 1970.

†Catherine Eisenhardt, *Applying Linguistics in the Teaching of Reading and the Language Arts.* Columbus, Ohio: Charles Merrill, 1972.

Print these noun test frames onto large charting paper and supply youngsters in teams with strips of paper. Working with each sentence in turn, they record on their strips as many words as they can think of that can fit the blank. Organize the activity as a race. The team writing down the largest number of words in a period of time receives a point. Repeat for each sentence. Students—especially those learning English as a second language—will begin to see how nouns function in English sentences.

Use the resulting words as a writing springboard. Cut up the strips of possible nouns students have identified and drop the slips into a box. Writers draw two word slips from the box and insert them into a title frame, i.e., The _____ and the _____. Working from this title, they write an encounter story—what happens when the word in blank one meets the word in blank two.

Middle-grade students who have brainstormed noun words to fit the test frames can return to analyze the frames. They can identify key words such as *the* and *a* that often signal that a noun is coming and other words that substitute for *a* and *the* such as one, two, twenty or words such as many, any, either, all, this, that, these, those, our, your, his, my, several, some, few, and no. All these words can function as determiners and indicate that a noun is about to follow.

Youngsters can devise additional sentences in which blanks take the place of nouns. They can be creative in building compound and complex patterns for frames such as: If his _____, and your _____, and my _____ eat twenty _____, then some green _____ will disappear into those _____. Other students can fill in the blanks to write preposterous sentences.

Return eventually to the test frames with which you began. Ask student linguists to change the frames so that all the words that can fit in the blanks are plurals. They must sub-

stitute words such as *these, those, some, many, few* for *the* and
a and must change *is* to *are*. They then take all the original
words and change them from singular to plural so that they
still are suitable in the test frames. In so doing, they gain the
concept that nouns are words that can be changed to mean
"more than one."

Nouns can also be identified by certain suffixes attached as
tails, i.e., *-age, -ance, -dom, -ment, -ism, -hood, -ship, -ness,
-ist, -ster, -tion,* and *-ity.* Youngsters in upper-elementary
grades can expand their concept of nouns by building word
charts containing words that end with a particular suffix. One
group might work with *-ment* and identify words such as
government, parliament, and advisement. Another group
might work with *-ness* and identify words such as hopefulness,
goodness, and sweetness. For fun, make the charts into the
shape of various animal tails and mount them on a bulletin
board called Noun Tails. Students can check the words they
record by testing them in noun test frames.

Test frames containing prepositional phrases are particularly fun to write and toy with; in fact, the writing and
toying reinforce the relationship between prepositions and
nouns. Remember that prepositions always are followed
shortly by nouns. In this respect, they, like determiners, are
noun indicators. One poetry-like frame that helps children to
see this relationship is:

> Let's just run as fast as we can run—
> across _____,
> over _____,
> around _____,
> under _____,
> through _____,
> up _____
> Until we're out of breath.

Another is:

> By the _____,
>   near the _____,
>   next to the _____,
>   opposite the _____,
>   beside the _____,
>   beneath the _____,
> I discovered a/an _____.

Students fill in the blanks with as many nouns as they can think of and compare their findings. They can continue to write their own creative sentences that contain strings of prepositional phrases in the manner of the test frames.

An easy activity for younger children and students learning English as a second language involves visualizing sentence meaning where a preposition communicates the key relationship. Youngsters draw a sketch to accompany each of the following sentences:

> The squirrel ran across the tree.
> The squirrel ran around the tree.
> The squirrel ran by the tree.
> The squirrel ran up the tree.
> The squirrel ran down the tree.

A second set to use as a follow-up for independent study is:

> A boy walked on the path.
> A boy walked near the path.
> A boy walked across the path.

Talk about word relationships is productive in this context. Students can identify the word that communicates the relationship between *squirrel* and *tree,* between *boy* and *path,* and demonstrate the relationships through pantomime

Incidentally, pantomime is a worthwhile activity for students studying prepositions. Young children can demonstrate meanings nonverbally and then identify the key word in the sentence that communicates the relationship. If you have a classroom rug, use sentences similar to the following:

> A student is walking across the rug.
> A student is walking on the rug.
> A student is walking next to the rug.
> A student is walking by the rug.

SUBSTITUTING PRONOUNS   Once young people have some understanding of the way nouns work in sentences, they are ready to learn the relationship between nouns and pronouns. Pronouns are words that can take the place of nouns and noun phrases; i.e., *she* can take the place of *the girl* in the sentence *The girl is my best friend.*

Young language students can play with the noun-pronoun relationship by substituting pronouns for nouns and noun phrases in sentences. On long strips of paper write such sentences as:

> The wolf awoke.
> The hungry boy ate his lunch.
> The hopeful girl awaited the news.
> Five giraffes were in the cage.
> Some boys ate a pizza pie.
> My father won the award.
> Your foot is swollen.
> Our car was stolen.
> His tongue was burned by the hot pizza.
> Her wish was granted by the genie.
> Their hands are in the pie.
> John and Rhoda opened the package.
> The girl won the race.
> Sandy sent the book to Jack and Bob.
> Marvin returned the book to Mary Lee.
> Some donkeys ate the grain.
> Mr. Warren saw the girl.
> Julie, Sue, and Butch gave Bruce a shirt.
> That dictionary is my book.

On individual word cards write the personal pronouns: I, me, mine, we, us, ours, you, yours, he, him, his, she, her, hers, it, its, them, and theirs. Each student holds a personal pronoun card. Place sentences one at a time on an open area of the floor. Participants try to substitute their pronouns for the nouns and noun phrases in each sentence. To involve holders of first-person pronouns repeat the activity with students thinking of themselves as one of the persons in the sentences.

For fun, students can try to write a short story without using any personal pronouns. By doing this, they will begin to see the important role of pronouns in preventing wordiness and needless repetition. Students who have written pronounless stories can exchange papers and rewrite classmates' stories substituting pronouns where appropriate.

Upper-grade students can substitute pronouns for nouns in sentences such as:

> The crow sat on a fence.
> The birds ate the seeds.
> The girls gave the boys three pizza pies.
> Dick sent Bob an invitation.
> Ruth called Sally to tell Sally the answer.
> Five camels were in the cages.
> The girls won the prizes.

Students will begin to see that pronouns can be so oversubstituted for nouns that the message ceases to be clear. Encourage children to think of ways to prevent this lack of clarity.

UNDERSTANDING VERB FUNCTIONS   Test frames for studying the way verbs work in sentences include:

> The girl _____.
> She _____ the machine.
> The story _____ interesting.
> The hardware store _____ there.

Youngsters can work in groups to think of words that make sense in the blanks and write workable verbs on slips of paper.

With younger students and those learning English as a second language, you may prefer to prepare word cards. Write some words that can fit in the blanks and some that cannot on individual cards. Words might include: runs, is, eats, seems, sad, silly, warm, hat, glove, slowly, quickly, jumps, works, operates, appears, sings, of, but, for, the, four, or yellow. Students test their words in the frames to see which ones can function as verbs.

Students who have participated in these types of activities may be ready to identify the special characteristics of verbs. One is their ability to indicate time relationships. To work with this characteristic, students add the word yesterday to each of the test frames, and then substitute tomorrow for yesterday. To change the sentences to the past and then to the future, students change the verbs on each of their cards; i.e., runs becomes ran, is becomes was, eats becomes ate. Then runs becomes will run, is becomes will be, and eats becomes will eat. Students can generalize from working with numbers of verbs that they change to indicate the time of action.

For reinforcement, students can write compositions that tell about things that happened in the past, things that are happening, and things that will happen. In their creative writing they use now, yesterday, tomorrow, last week, today, a week from now, Tuesday, and the like to communicate a sense of time; they also must use verbs in the appropriate tense.

A related characteristic of verbs is that they tend to employ an -*s* ending in the present tense when the subject word is a singular noun such as *a road, the machine,* or *she.* You may wish to help young people work with this characteristic by experimenting with nonsense words. Suggest that the nonsense word *florp* take the place of all nouns and verbs in the sentences with which students will be experimenting. It will change exactly as regular nouns and verbs do in English sentences. For example, The yellow florp florped in the florp is a perfectly grammatical English sentence. It is structurally similar to The yellow scarf flapped in the wind. Start out by giving students nonsense sentences written on large strips to analyze; they must figure out whether the sentences are possible in the English language. Students should hold a pad of paper and as you lay out sentence strips on the floor, they test their grammaticalness by writing down a real sentence that flows in the same way. Sentences to test for grammaticalness might be:

The florp florps. (The boy waves.)
The florps florps. (ungrammatical; "The boys waves.")
The florps florp. (The boys wave.)
The florp florp. (ungrammatical; "The boy wave.")
The florp will florp. (The duck will swim.)
The florp florped yesterday. (The machine worked yesterday.)
Twelve florps florped into the florp. (Twelve swimmers jumped into the pool.)
Do not florp your florps. (Do not wash your hands.)
Are you florping your florps? (Are you washing your hands?)

Remember that in this activity, students treat all nouns and verbs as normal functioning nouns and verbs. They do not consider nouns that form plurals in ways other than simply adding an *-s*, i.e., *children, men,* or *women.* They do not consider irregular verbs that form past tenses in ways other than simply adding an *-ed.*

Mature young people in upper grades who have begun to develop an analytical sense will enjoy working with such word puzzles. They will argue vehemently to support their contention that a particular sentence is or is not possible in English. They will write numerous sentences in which a nonsense word substitutes for all nouns and verbs, and in the process, they may develop the understanding that verbs change endings to agree with the nouns to which they relate. For less mature youngsters this type of work with words is difficult and best left until later years.

Just as determiners signal that nouns are coming in a sentence, auxiliaries signal verbs. Words that can function as auxiliaries include may and might, can and could, shall and should, will and would, must, the many forms of be, and has, had, and have. Upper-grade students can use these words to build sentence collages built around a single verb such as to push, to crash, or to collapse. A pushing collage would contain sentences such as, "I could push you into the lake." "Tom was pushing everyone around him." "The bodyguard will have pushed twenty people by Friday." Students who have constructed such collages can analyze their sentences by asking, "Where do we find words such as has, will, and must in sentences? In what way are these words associated with verbs?" They may be able to construct their own test frames for auxiliaries, such as:

The elephant _____ push the tree.
               (auxiliary)

The elephant _____ pushed the tree.
               (auxiliary)

The elephant _____ pushing the tree.
               (auxiliary)

Since certain affixes make words verbs, a study of prefixes and suffixes can be correlated with study of verbs. Verb suffixes include -ate, -en, -ify, -ish, and -ize; verb prefixes include be- and en-. Students can make mobiles for each of these, by identifying verbs that contain a particular suffix or prefix, writing them on slips of paper, and suspending the slips with string from a metal hanger. An -ify mobile, for example, could contain words such as signify, classify, clarify, and dignify.

MAKING ADJECTIVES WORK   Adjectives are words that are used with nouns; they appear in sentences in three major positions relative to nouns. The primary position is before the noun as in The feeble old man slipped on the muddy steps. Feeble, old, and muddy function as adjectives; they occupy the primary adjective position between determiner and noun.

A second adjective position is after the noun or before the determinater as in the sentences. The man, old and feeble, slipped on the steps. Old and feeble, the man slipped on the steps. and The man, fearful of what would happen, left the country. By changing adjectives from their typical position between determiner and noun, a speaker or writer heightens the importance of their meanings.

A third adjective position is in the predicate following a verb but still modifying a subject noun. Examples of adjectives used in this way are The man is very old, The story sounds strange, and The pizza tastes delicious. The predicate adjectives in these sentences are old, strange, and delicious.

Upper-grade youngsters who have done some previous work with nouns, determiners, and verbs may be able to discover for themselves these three characteristic adjective positions. Younger students and those learning English as a second language may be able to discover two positions, the one before the noun and in the predicate. To guide student discovery, prepare these individual word cards:

*the	eggs	taste	fell	on
your	carrots	smell	ran	by
my	tomatoes	are	rushed	to
some	oranges	seem	roared	under
many	children	appear	flipped	*into
this	bicycles		tossed	through
these	fence	mouse	carried	across

that	road	girl	pushed	
those	man	path	dropped	that
	river	robbers	ate	*and
	window	motorcycle	sat	*very
	rock	dog	stole	*
	boy	cat	crept	* ?

*Make many of these cards.

Prepare a second set of cards in a different shape, size, or color; cards in the shape of a parallelogram or words written with red ink make it easy to distinguish between the two sets. Words for set two are:

delicious	high	friendly	heavy	wicked
sour	thoughtless	happy	wide	large
bitter	fantastic	playful	muddy	tiny
sweet	yellow	open	slippery	ugly
rotten	purple	hungry	icy	noisy
sad	soft	deep	stony	funny
naughty	lonely	narrow	cruel	plentiful

First deal set-one cards to participants, who sit on the floor around an open area. Point at one youngster to place a card onto the floor. Ask other students whether they hold a card that could build onto the first word, either before or after. A student who thinks his or her word will begin to build a sentence adds the word card. Children keep adding (or even taking away) cards until a sentence is produced. Repeat the sentence building until there are several sentences on the floor. Students will still hold some word cards in their hands.

Then deal out set two. Ask if the children can add these new words to the sentences. Participants will probably position their words as adjectives between a determiner and noun. Since the adjective cards differ in appearance from the others, students may be able to generalize that the new words are all positioned between determiner and noun. Begin to call the new words adjectives, or with young children, describing words. See if they can construct a test frame for adjectives that will look something like, The _____ boy climbs up the _____ tree.

On another occasion redistribute cards from sets one and two. Ask students to construct several sentences with adjectives in the position previously identified. Then ask, "Is there another way we can build a sentence so that the adjective appears in a position other than between noun and determiner?" Students can try to build other sentences with their word cards. Those who hold cards bearing words such as taste and smell may concoct short sentences such as The eggs smell rotten or The tomatoes are soft. Encourage students to build more sentences similar to these. Ask them to identify the position of adjectives in these sentences and to construct a test frame for predicate adjectives that will look like this. The boy is very _____.

With upper-grade students, who are sophisticated about language, you may want to demonstrate another way to position adjectives. Use word cards and build a model sentence such as, Playful and friendly, the dog rushed to the children. Ask students to try to build another sentence or two using their words cards. They can produce sentences such as, Sad and lonely, the children sat by the window or Sweet and golden, the carrots are delicious. They may need words in addition to those on the cards, so keep some blanks handy on which participants can add words.

After students have put together a number of sentences in this pattern, ask if they can shift the adjectives to another location in the sentence. Remembering their previous work, they will most likely place the adjectives between the determiner and the noun. Move the adjective words there, and then ask them to identify still another location to which the adjectives can be shifted. Try the adjectives after the noun, set off by commas. Students may be able to produce a test frame to show both of these positions: _____ and _____, the girl ran away, and The girl, _____ and _____, ran away. Students may be able to conclude that these adjective positions are generally used when there is more than one adjective.

Encourage children to write lots of sentences with pairs of adjectives that either follow or precede the noun as in the test frames. Suggest that they add interesting adjectives to their sentences to produce striking descriptions. Ideas for sentences can be triggered by scattering set-two cards on the floor. Students write sentences built on these words and then share them with classmates.

To help youngsters understand the importance of adjectives in writing, you may wish to try an activity devised by Catherine Eisenhardt and described in *Applying Linguistics in the Teaching of Reading and the Language Arts* (Charles Merrill, 1972). Ms. Eisenhardt suggests giving youngsters a descriptive paragraph in which the adjectives have been deleted. They must add their own adjectives to give meaning to the paragraph. Later they can analyze the positions of adjectives and even the kinds of suffixes that characterize adjectives.

Also you may wish to give youngsters objects and pictures to describe. Ask them to write a paragraph describing a pencil, a dog, an ostrich, or an alligator. Display a picture and ask them to describe it to someone who has not seen it. Or ask students to describe a piece of lost clothing or an article they would like to buy. In the process of describing the items, they will use adjectives.

ADVERBING IT   Use the two sets of word cards again to teach young people about adverbs. Make a third set of cards of still a different shape, size, or color and include words that can function as adverbs of time, manner, and place. Notice that some appeared in set one, because some words do function both as prepositions and adverbs, others as both adjectives and adverbs:

when adverbs	*how adverbs*	*where adverbs*
yesterday	hard	there
then	loudly	in
soon	late	here
recently	sideways	outside
early	rapidly	up
tomorrow	amazingly	everywhere
now	gradually	somewhere
just	immediately	across
always	likewise	by
sometimes	backward	
recently	slowly	

First distribute sets one and two cards. Ask students to build short sentences, adhering to the pattern of:

Determiner   noun   verb   preposition   determiner   noun.

Students can construct sentences such as, The mouse crept by the window or Some children rushed across the road. Change to the pattern:

Determiner   noun   verb   determiner   noun.

Using this pattern, students build sentences such as, This boy threw the rock or The children ate the tomatoes. Encourage students to work with other patterns such as:

Determiner   noun   linking verb   adjective.

Students write sentences such as, The oranges are bitter or The eggs are fresh.

When students have built a pool of sentences, distribute cards of set three. Focus on one completed sentence, i.e., The boy threw the rock, and ask them to see if they can fit any set-three words into that sentence. They may add a word such as recently. Suggest that they try it in several locations in the sentence, at the beginning, between boy and threw, and at the end of the sentence. Urge them to see if other words can be moved into different spots in the sentence. Most adverbs can be shifted within a sentence and still make some sense; this movability is one of the characteristics that identifies adverbs. Help older students change adverbs to different sentence positions and talk about the differences in meaning achieved by locating an adverb in different positions. Try shifting adverbs in sentences of differing patterns.

Jean Malmstrom in *An Introduction to Modern Grammar* (Hayden, 1968, pp. 90–91) calls the end position the "favorite" adverb location and suggests that this position is the best for identifying adverbs. To discover this favorite adverb location for themselves, students can try the word backward in sentences similar to The boy threw the rock or She glanced; they can prepare a test frame for identifying adjectives:

Determiner   noun   verb   determiner   noun _____.
                                                  adverb

Middle-grade students can utilize the adverb cards of set three to develop classification skills and a beginning notion of the kinds of meanings communicated by adverbs. Adverbs communicate types of meanings—how, where, and when. Examples of adverbs that tell how something is done are *carefully, probably,* and *beautifully,* that tell where something is done are *there, up, near, across,* and that tell when something is done are *early, always,* and *then.*

Place all the cards of set three face up on an open area of floor where children group the words into the three categories. After all words have been sorted, participants suggest other words that could be added to the groups. They can pick words from set one that can also function as adverbs, first testing them (*in, across, before*) in the test frame. Then they categorize the words according to the meanings communicated.

Students who have played with both adjectives and adverbs can begin to construct sentences in which adjective-adverb markers preceed an adjective or adverb. Adjective-adverb markers, or intensifiers as they are also called, include words such as very, too, rather, really, more, most, somewhat, or quite when used in sentences such as: The horse ran very fast. The most wonderful thing happened! and I am somewhat concerned. These words, especially very, are good testers for the presence of adjectives and adverbs. To test whether a word is an adjective or adverb, try interjecting very before it in a sentence; if it sounds natural, then the word probably is an adjective or adverb.

To give students experience with intensifiers, prepare a fourth set of cards of still another shape, size, or color. These contain adjective-adverb markers identified in the preceding paragraph. Begin by having youngsters build sentences using cards from sets one, two, and three. Again, once students have put together a pool of sentences, distribute set-four cards, which students can add to the sentences. Since the adjective and adverb cards have a distinctive appearance, the fact that the intensifiers will all be positioned in front of them will become rather obvious. Encourage upper-grade students to prepare test frames that show typical positioning of intensifiers in sentences of different patterns.

Once students have constructed many kinds of sentences, place all the word sets in pouches at a learning station. Each day mount a sentence pattern on the backdrop of the center. Students go to the station in pairs to build sentences with the cards, following the suggested pattern. You may wish to write the pattern in a formula style using symbols to represent sentence components, using the following representational system:

  1 = noun (sometimes called Class 1 word or Form 1 word)
  2 = verb (sometimes called Class 2 word or Form 2 word)
  3 = adjective (sometimes called Class 3 word or Form 3 word)
  4 = adverb (sometimes called Class 4 word or Form 4 word)
  p = preposition
det = determiner
int = intensifier

An easy, beginning sentence formula is simply 1 2; a sentence fitting this pattern is Carrots smell. Other formulae with a sample sentence are:

det 1 2 det 1.	The robbers stole the fence.
det 3 1 2 int 3.	These sweet oranges are certainly delicious.
4 det 3 3 1 2 det 1.	Yesterday that thoughtless playful boy broke my window.
det int 3 1 4 2 p det 1.	Those very noisy children just rushed by the fence.

Students working at this sentence-building station may go on to write formulae for additional sentences. Other participants can test their validity by attempting to put together sentences that fulfill the requirements of the formulae. Students may also add more cards to the pouches as they attempt to build more and more sophisticated sentences. They may particularly want to make cards bearing auxiliaries so that they will be able to include them in their formulae. Remember that auxiliaries are verb markers.

CLASSIFYING SENTENCE PATTERNS

HANDLING SENTENCE PATTERNS   In several of the preceding activities basic sentence patterns have been mentioned; i.e., students write sentences following a particular order. Because most contemporary textbook language series stress sentence patterns, teachers may wish to focus directly on basic patterns so that young people can begin to understand the structures of their language.

Many linguists identify five sentence patterns that function in English:

Pattern 1	Noun verb	Lions roar.
Pattern 2	Noun verb noun	Ed likes ice cream.
Pattern 3	Noun verb noun noun	The bus driver gave Karen a ticket.
Pattern 4	Noun linking verb noun	Pat is my friend.
Pattern 5	Noun linking verb adjective	Lions are friendly.

Obviously each of these patterns can take on additional words when sentences are expanded with determiners, adjectives, adverbs, and prepositional phrases as well as auxiliaries and intensifiers. For example, The hungry lions were roaring ferociously in their cages is an expansion of pattern 1 (noun verb). Similarly, The tired bus driver hurriedly gave little Karen is a one-way ticket to Salem is an expansion of a pattern 3 sentence.

Teachers can introduce the concept of sentence patterns to students who already know something about nouns, verbs, and adjectives by working with a group of simple sentences written on large strips. Keep the sentences short so that student linguists can begin to make comparisons. Start with sentences from only two patterns, one and two:

The boys arrived.	Cats drink milk.
The telephone rang.	The fellow mowed the lawn.
Your friend called.	The man lost the election.
The book fell.	People like Tim.
Cats purr.	The girl sent a gift.
The umbrella opened.	Susan opened the package.

Spread cards containing sentences from the two pattern groups onto an easily visible surface. Select one, i.e., The boys arrived, and ask students to identify the parts of speech contained in it. After they identify the noun (or noun phrase) and verb sequence, cut the sentence into two parts and place *The boys* under a noun labeling card and the word *arrived* under a verb labeling card:

Ask students if they can choose from the remaining sentences another that could be analyzed in the same way. Students cut apart the sentence strips they select and place the words beneath the noun and verb labels.

If a student should select a sentence of pattern 2, cut it up too. However, when that student tries to place the two parts beneath the labels, ask her or him to identify the last word. Test it for nounness using the test frame described earlier. Develop the outline for this new pattern by placing a second group of labels on the working surface. Students can now categorize sentences either under the noun-verb labels or the new noun-verb-noun labels.

Encourage young people to write their own short sentences that adhere to either of the patterns. They can test their productions by slicing them into segments and placing each under the proper label. Encourage writing expansions of sentences already analyzed as well as writing original, expanded sentences in both patterns. The latter can become new material for other students to analyze after deleting all the expanded matter and then categorizing it as pattern 1 or 2.

Spend several sessions on patterns 1 and 2 before moving on to the others. To introduce a new pattern, lay out the label cards for the previous patterns and present new sentence cards. Students attempting to categorize them will find that they need to devise a new pattern. Again, after students have analyzed pattern 3 sentences, encourage writing expansions of the model sentences and/or original ones to fit the pattern requirements. For convenience in preparing cards, sentences for patterns 3, 4, and 5 are listed below:

Pattern 3	Pattern 4	Pattern 5
The girl sent her friend a gift.	An ant is an insect.	Those flowers are yellow.
My brother gave Miriam that book.	Janice is an engineer.	My dress is dirty.
The druggist handed me the bottle.	Paris is the capital.	That paper is cheap.
The lion showed me its teeth.	My friends are my guests.	This meat tastes terrible.
That visitor brought the invalid some candy.	The couch is a bed.	She looks sick.

For follow-up, students can play sentopoly in groups of two to four. A sentopoly board is shown in the accompanying diagram. In addition to the board, a stack of playing cards, a single die, and a token for each player are needed. To make a sentopoly board, simply obtain a large piece of cardboard—colored oak tag will serve nicely. Mark off blocks around the perimeter, list the sentence patterns, block off boxes for the playing cards, and add directions in some of the blocks along the perimeter. Use index cards for the playing cards. On the face of each, write out a sentence, and on the reverse, write the pattern to which it belongs. Place the cards face up on the playing board.

In sentopoly a turn consists of the following sequence:

1. Read the sentence on the top of the pack of cards.
2. Categorize its pattern; check the answer by turning over the card. If you are wrong, your turn is over.
3. Throw the die if you have answered correctly; move your token forward the number of spaces indicated on the die.
4. If you land on a spot that has special directions, follow those directions.

| Special spot: Draw a second card. If you get it right, move four more jumps. | | Joker: Jump back four jumps. | | Bonus: Take an extra turn. | | Starting Terminal |

SENTOPOLY

SENTENCE PATTERNS:
1. N v
2. N v N
3. N v N N
4. N lv N
5. N lv Adj.

Bonus: Take an extra turn.

Bonus: Jump 2 more jumps.

Place cards here face up.

Bonus: Jump 2 more jumps.

Joker: Miss your next turn.

Place completed cards here face down.

Bonus: Take an extra turn.

Bonus: Jump one more box.

Special spot: Write another sentence in the same pattern. Then jump three more jumps.

Joker: Jump back two.

Bonus: Jump four more jumps.

Joker: Jump back two.

The game is won by the player who returns to the starting terminal first.

Because you will need different cards to keep the game challenging, youngsters who have played the game can produce more cards by writing sentences on the front and indicating their patterns on the back. Preparing new cards can be an option for students who have won several games. They can prepare cards of two different colors—difficult cards with expanded sentences and easier cards with simple basic sentences. To make sure the answers are correct, teachers would probably be wise to check the cards before shuffling them into the deck.

HOPSCOTCHING WITH SENTENCES   English sentences have been classified into four groups—statements, questions, imperatives, and exclamations; this classification is used in most language arts textbooks. Teachers may wish to introduce the following activity to reinforce understanding of this facet of English sentence building.

In preparation, outline a full-sized hopscotch design on the floor and prepare cards containing sentences such as those below, but *without* final punctuation:

>I lost my scarf.
>The radio crackled during the storm.
>Small cars consume less gas.
>Seventeen dictionaries weigh a ton.
>It went crashing to the floor.
>Slippers keep your feet warm on cold days.
>Permanent press slacks need no ironing.
>Many pieces of chalk were broken.
>The spring popped out.
>The sidewalk is slippery.
>
>Put down your suitcases.
>Run as quickly as you can.
>Do not stop now.

Open your books to page 88.
Stop fooling around, everyone.
Turn on the radio for the news.
Do not believe everything you hear.
Read nothing unless I tell you.
Don't forget to take along a raincoat.

Are you coming to my party?
Where are the charade cards?
When are we going to play charades?
How many peanuts were in the dish?
Are your shoes dirty?
Why are the monkeys waving at us?
Is it time to go?
Does he want to win a lottery prize?
How are we going to get the job done?
Will you loan me fifty cents?

Help!
The Redcoats are coming!
Run for your lives!
A stupendous thing has happened!
That's enough now!
Fire! We're on fire!
Here come the engines!
Am I glad to see you!
Am I impatient to get started!

Spread all the cards face down on the floor in front of the hopscotch design. Divide the class into two, and give each team a token to mark progress through the hopscotch.

A player from team 1, perhaps called The Word Giants, picks up a card, reads the sentence, showing orally through intonation whether it is a statement, a question, an imperative, or an exclamation. He or she must classify the sentence into one of the four categories and tell the final punctuation required. Having successfully completed all three tasks, he or she places the team's token onto block 1 and puts the card face up beneath the appropriate category label.

In turn, a player from team 2, the Sentence Makers, picks a card to read, categorize, and punctuate. The player may select a card that is face down or face up. If the latter, he or she must read the sentence using an intonation pattern that makes the sentence express a meaning different from that given by a previous player. For example, *Are your shoes dirty?* may be read as a question with an upward rise of the voice at the end of the sentence or it may also be read as an exclamation *Are your shoes dirty!* indicated by a downward pitch. By similar changes in intonation a statement like *I lost my scarf,* can be converted to an exclamation; an exclamation, *The Redcoats are coming!* can be converted to a statement or a question; and an imperative, *Put down your suitcases* can be converted to an exclamation or even a question.

If the player correctly completes the task, he or she jumps the team token to block 2, since only one token can sit on a block at a time. If the player does not complete the task, the token does not move. Of course, players from both teams take turns analyzing cards and moving the team token. When it reaches block 7, it is moved in the reverse direction until it is jumped out of the hopscotch. The team that successfully jumps its token through the hopscotch and then out after a return trip wins the game.

HOPSCOTCH
PLAYING
BOARD

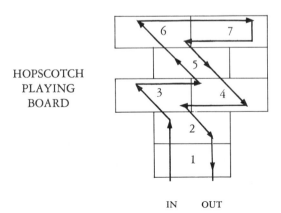

IN   OUT

SUMMING UP

An English sentence can be expanded and transformed in ways so diverse and numerous that it is impossible in a single chapter to provide activities for introducing young people to each and every variation. Some important elements of sentence structure have by necessity been left out—how to handle thought transitions, parenthetical expressions, apposition, and negative transformations, to name just a few. Teachers who must teach these elements, however, will find that the activities described—word cards, punctuation and labeling cards, non-sense words, test frames, string poems, word ladders, and sentence and word collages—can be rather easily modified for different contents. In games such as hopscotch, sentopoly, sentence baseball, and mix and match, other sentences and words can be substituted for those given to develop other skills and understandings.

One caution before ending! When working with the structure of language, it is easy to slip into the trap of over-stressing knowledge of terminology and ability to categorize words and sentences. Such knowledge and analytical ability are helpful in communicating with one another about language, but even more important is the skill in creating sentences that express ideas in a clear and interesting fashion. This skill is gradually acquired through much listening and speaking, reading and writing, not through systematic analysis of language. For this reason analytical study should be integrated closely with written and oral expression.

Thoughts shut up want air,
And spoil, like bales, unopen'd to the sun.

NIGHT THOUGHTS: NIGHT II, EDWARD YOUNG

6. OPENING UP THOUGHT:
Activities in Processing and Producing Language

Youngsters and oldsters alike find pleasure in the fantasy world of stories. There words create webs of make-believe in which animals sometimes speak, good often triumphs over evil, and dreams come true, perhaps with the aid of a fairy godmother. Listening to and reading the language of story, people easily fall under this spell of words and begin to acquire an understanding of the many patterns into which they can be woven. By producing one's own stories about things—both real and imaginary—and sharing them in oral or written form, children can begin to weave the spell of words themselves. In the process, their thoughts will open up and expand much as mushrooms do in the rain.

Thoughts can blossom too through encounters with the language of poetry. Through poetry everyday things can be viewed from unusual perspectives, and thoughts can be expressed in ways that actually clarify the thought itself. Words can be played with so that even ordinary ones take on new meanings. Sound, shape, and sense can blend together to form unique images.

The language of persuasion offers strikingly different kinds of experiences with words and things. Today's world is filled with objects—automobiles, detergents, perfumes, breakfast cereals—to be bought and sold. It is filled with people who wish to become mayor, senator, or president. Each year millions of words are written, spoken, heard, or read that endeavor to persuade people to buy a particular brand or vote for a particular candidate. Processing and trying to use words that carry persuasive messages require careful thought that, in turn, produces more perceptive consumers of the language of persuasion.

In the previous chapters elements of language such as word choice, creative use of words, the sound and shape of words, and the structure of sentences have been stressed. In this chapter the story, the poem, the advertisement, and the commercial—larger units through which thoughts are communicated—will be emphasized. Story, poem, and persuasion activities have been designed so that teachers can select individual ideas and integrate them into larger themes, modules, or units on-going in their classrooms.

THE LANGUAGE OF STORY

SPINNING WORD WEBS   Encourage students to listen to how words are used in stories. Upper-grade students can discover meanings for previously unfamiliar words, hear how these words function in sentences, and perceive creative ways of handling words to tell a story more effectively.

To begin a listening word hunt, read aloud a book such as *A Story A Story* by Gail E. Haley (Atheneum, 1970). Although a picture book, this 1971 Caldecott Award winner is useful as a word builder even in upper-elementary grades, particularly as an introduction to creative use of words in stories. Things students can hunt for in this story include:

UNFAMILIAR WORDS: In the sentence, "Next Ananse cut a frond from a banana tree and filled a calabash with water," what do *frond* and *calabash* mean? Students who hear this sentence as well as others containing these new words may be able to sketch a frond and a calabash. They can check the dictionary for the origin of these words.

NAMES ASSIGNED TO CHARACTERS: Osebo the leopard-of-the-terrible-teeth, Mmboror the hornet who-stings-like-fire, and Mmoatia the fairy whom-men-never-see.

SAYING WORDS: Chuckled, laughed, answered, cried, and hummed substitute for the less expressive *said*.

CREATIVE WAYS OF USING WORDS: *Mouth* becomes *crying place,* words and phrases are repeated for emphasis as in *binding binding game* and *by his foot, by his foot, by his foot,* and sounds become words. *Yiridi, yiridi, yiridi* is the sound of running; *tive, tive, tive* is the sound of laughing.

After reading this type of story, divide the class into four groups, and reread the story. Each group attends primarily to one of the four language features noted above. While listening a second time, they list examples of words or phrases in their assigned category and later talk together to compare notes while a group scribe reports the findings.

Particularly good for such purposeful listening are books such as Dr. Seuss's *Horton Hatches the Egg* (Random House, 1940), *The Lorax* (Random House, 1971), and *And to Think That I Saw It on Mulberry Street* (Hale, 1937), Ludwig Bemelmann's Madeline books (Viking Press), and Robert McCloskey's *Time of Wonder* (Viking, 1957) and *Lentil* (Viking, 1940). Things young people can hunt for in these volumes include good descriptive words, alliteration, effective rhyming lines, humorous use of language, creative comparisons, and deliberate repetition of words, phrases, and sentences.

Upper-elementary-grade students can pursue this activity independently as a reading rather than a listening adventure. Just stack a heap of picture books on a library cart along with construction paper and flo-pens. Young people read the books and design word webs on the construction paper. Webs consist of interlacing lines in the manner of a spider web that contain words, phrases, and sentences that pack a wallop in the story. Through this web of words the writer weaves his or her story. By working with webs, students will begin to see the relationship between words and story development; they will see how important it is to find the most effective word or phrase when they write their own stories.

The idea that storywriting is like weaving a web of words can be reinforced by reading the story *Anansi The Spider,* a folktale of the Ashanti of Ghana that has been adapted and illustrated by Gerald McDermott (Holt, 1972). McDermott tells how Anansi the Spider, or spinner of tales, placed the moon in the sky. Students can spin similar Anansi tales to tell how the universe came into being, how the sun began, how the big dipper was placed in its spot in the sky, or how the north star began to point the way. They can use some of the same linguistic devices that characterize the Anansi tales that are used by McDermott and by Haley.

A related crafts project is to collect actual spider webs. Sybil Harp in "Cones and Stones and Spider Webs" (*The New York Times,* August 3, 1975, section D) describes how to collect a web and spray an abandoned one with white paint. Carefully transfer the paint-covered web to a piece of black or colored construction paper by touching the paper to the wet web. After the paint has dried, spray both paper and adhering web with clear lacquer. The resulting design can serve as the cover of books of Anansi tales written by your students. If you are fortunate enough to have the use of a copying machine, the design can be duplicated many times. Students can print their stories on the reverse sides and they can be compiled into a spider book.

A WORD WEB*

*Based on Patricia Thomas's *"Stand Back," Said the Elephant, "I'm Going to Sneeze!"* (Lothrop, Lee & Shepard, 1971).

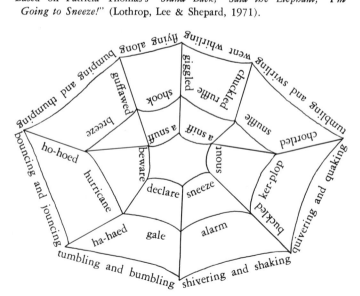

STORIES FROM PATTERNS   Another way to involve young people in the mechanics of storywriting is to introduce them to some of the traditional patterns writers have employed in the past. One of the easiest story patterns to develop is the accumulative story—a story in which the main events are repeated again and again as a major character encounters additional characters. Sometimes a line of conversation or description is also repeated as the event reoccurs.

This story pattern appears over and over in folk and fairy tales such as "Henny Penny," "The Gingerbread Boy," and in more modern stories such as Marjorie Flack's *Ask Mr. Bear* (Macmillan, 1958) and Fernando and Maria de la Luz Krahn's *The First Peko-Neko Bird* (Simon and Schuster, 1969).

You Look Ridiculous Said the Rhinoceros to the Hippopotamus by Bernard Waber (Houghton Mifflin, 1966) is my favorite for introducing students to the accumulative story. Since the Waber tale is a talking beast story, youngsters become familiar with this story form as well. In *You Look Ridiculous* a hippopotamus meets a succession of animals each of whom suggests a way to improve the hippo's appearance. She is given advice about her nose, her mane, her spots, and her ears until she finally wakes up to the fact that she would look ridiculous indeed if she could implement all the suggestions made by the other animals. Read the Waber or a similar story to your students, suggesting that they concentrate on the story's sequence.

Then try a class story following the Waber model. Place animal name cards on the floor in a spot visible to all participants. Cards might include Porcupine, Mouse, Blue Jay, Giraffe, Elephant, Mite, Duck, Ant, Pig, Donkey, Turtle, Dragon, Turkey, Hornet, or Toad. Ask students to select the animal that will be the major character. Talk about the kinds of problems this character could have and what the beast would say to himself or herself and to the other characters.

For example, if Dragon were chosen as the main character, its problem could be an inability to breathe fire, bad breath, a sore front tooth, or not being able to make friends. Once the class has decided on a problem, a scribe writes it on a long strip of paper and places it on the floor next to the dragon card. Next students choose the characters the dragon will encounter as it seeks a solution to the problem. Students can select characters from the cards on the floor or they can write cards for others they prefer. They arrange the cards on the floor in the order that Dragon will meet them.

Begin to work with dialogue, as students suggest the line or two that Dragon will speak to each character. The line should express the problem and sound catchy. The scribe writes this line on another strip of paper. Students then indicate the verbal response of each character and a nonverbal expression as well, and the scribe makes sentence strips for them.

When the groundwork has been taken care of, begin the story, starting with the words, "Once upon a time in the land of fiery dragons . . ." Using the strips of paper on the floor as cue cards, students one by one add lines, each in turn telling part of the story. Repeat the storytelling with different youngsters revising the lines at each telling. Do this several times until the class agrees on the best development. Then turn on a tape recorder and have several children record the class story.

A guided interactive session can be a springboard for independent writing of accumulative stories too. On a board list the characters students have brainstormed. In groups of two or three students go to the board to select a main character, invent a problem, select a sequence of characters to be encountered, devise lines of dialogue, plan an ending, and orally put together a story, which they then write down.

Schedule storytelling times so that they can share their tales with others. Compile all the written stories in a bound volume titled "Stories for Telling."

You may wish to set up a reading center where students can read other accumulative tales to learn how this kind of story is constructed. Include some traditional tales such as the Norwegian "The Ash Lad Who Had an Eating Match with the Troll" and "The Princess Who Always Had to Have the Last Word (*Norwegian Folk Tales from the Collection of Peter Christen Asbjornsen and Jorgen Moe* (Viking, 1960) and some of the modern picture books that follow the same pattern, i.e., *One Fine Day* by Nonny Hogrogian (Macmillan, 1971), *The Camel Who Took a Walk* by Jack Tworkov (Dutton, 1951), and *In the Forest* by Marie Ets (Viking, 1944). Although the latter books are intended for younger children, upper-grade students can analyze the stories to discover their patterns.

Once students have played with the cumulative tale, introduce other patterns. One commonly encountered in folktales and modern storybooks is the adventure-away-from-home. "Little Red Riding Hood" and "Hansel and Gretel" essentially follow this format—the character or characters venture away from the safety of home, have an adventure, and finally return to safety at the end. Maurice Sendak's *Where the Wild Things Are* (Harper & Row, 1963) and Marjorie Flack's *Story About Ping* (Viking, 1933) employ a similar format.

Again read a story to students that adheres to the pattern and talk together about its development. Then cooperatively build a story that adheres to the model. Decide on a main character or characters, talk about what kinds of adventures this character or characters could have, why the character would leave home, and how she or he will return home. Using notes recorded during the brainstorming, student participants tell the story. Follow up with independent story-writing or taping.

With young children you may prefer to try a story pattern that Barbara Grant has successfully used to trigger oral story construction. She begins with the simple book *Bears, Bears, Bears* by Ruth Krauss (Harper & Row, 1948; also in paper from Scholastic). This story is fundamentally a play with the sounds of words. Each page tells where one finds bears or what bears do, "on the stairs," "at fairs," "everywheres." Once children have discovered the device used—each activity or place rhymes with *bears*—they are on their way to creating their own versions.

Dr. Grant states that children have concocted wonderful stories starting with phrases such as Pigs, pigs, pigs (who, of course, can dance jigs, run in zags and zigs, like to eat funny figs . . .), Cows, cows, cows (who take bows, live with sows . . .), Giraffes, giraffes, giraffes, and Fleas, fleas, fleas. To start the activity, encourage youngsters to brainstorm words that rhyme with the plural animal name. Record each rhyming line on a different sheet and let students select the sheet they want to illustrate. Bind the sheets together to form a book.

There are many interesting kinds of books being marketed today that can provide a pattern for story building. One of the simplest is the nonverbal book in which there is little or no print. Brian Wildsmith's *Circus* (Franklin Watts, 1970), Noriko Ueno's *Elephant Buttons* (Harper & Row, 1973), John Hamberger's *A Sleepless Day* (Four Winds Press, 1973), and William Wondriska's *A Long Piece of String* (Holt, 1963) are cases in point. Having "read" books such as these, youngsters who find it difficult to relate stories through words can "write" their own nonverbal books in which pictures communicate the tale.

The format of an ABC book is likewise easy for youngsters to adapt. There are hundreds of ABC books on the market, any one of which can serve as introduction. One of my favorites is Bruno Munari's very creative *ABC* (World, 1960). In writing their own ABC stories, children simply write a few lines that go with each letter of the alphabet, draw an accompanying illustration for each letter, and compile the results alphabetically. This can be an individual activity or a total class experience with each youngster contributing an illustration and lines for one letter.

Day-of-the-week books are good models for storywriting as well. In these something different happens on each day, building up to a climax on the seventh day. *May I Bring a Friend?* by Beatrice De Regniers (Atheneum, 1964) and *The Preposterous Week* by George Keenen (Dial, 1971) are good examples of this type of story. Again group brainstorming identifies something that happens on each day of the children's imaginative week, student scribes write cue cards of each day's happening, and oral storytelling based on the recorded information follows.

A really unique book such as Arnold Adoff's *MA nDA LA* (Harper & Row, 1971) can trigger a very different kind of storywriting. In *MA nDA LA* Adoff uses resonant sounds repeated in varied patterns to produce a simple story-poem. MA is mother, DA is father, LA is singing, RA is cheering, NA is sighing, and AH is feeling good, according to the explanation on the book jacket. Students who have chanted the lines of the story-poem can make up words and sounds to continue the story, or they can invent their own sound-symbol system to build into their own story-poems.

VISUALIZING STORIES Visualizing relationships is a creative way of interpreting and designing stories. By depicting visually what is happening in a story, a youngster is forced to go beyond the details read, heard, or originally conceived to invent additional details required for a visual representation or storyboard.

Visualization can take many forms. One fun form is the story map. Stories such as Quentin Blake's *Patrick* (Walck, 1969) place characters in several locations. Patrick, the young fellow with the magical violin, wanders from his home, through the town full of stalls, to the stall kept by Mr. Onion, into the fields, near a pond, along the road, to an orchard of apple trees, by the cows, and finally back to town. A student who reads this picture book or listens to it on tape can translate the details into a map that includes Patrick's home, the town street with its many stalls, the road through the country, and the road back to town. Since there is no map in the book itself part of its accuracy depends on student invention.

The Funny Little Woman as retold by Arlene Mosel with pictures by Blair Lent (Dutton, 1972) is easy enough for even a first-grade student to hear and translate into a map. Locales to be plotted include the Little Woman's house, the hole from her house to the underworld region of the *oni,* the tunnel of statues, the river, and the house of the *oni.* In contrast *The Red Carpet* by Rex Parkin (Macmillan, 1948) is complex enough for sixth-grade students to outline as a map. In Parkin's story there are specific streets and geographical directions, and a map-knowledgeable student can add a directional symbol, a scale, and even hypothetical lines of longitude and latitude to his or her story map.

A flow chart is also fun to produce, especially when the story to be plotted is an accumulative one. A story flow chart is simply a series of diagrams each of which represents a major story happening. The student who uses this device to analyze a story sketches key events and connects each sketch to the next in the series to indicate the direction of story action. One story that primary-grade children can interpret in this way is Nonny Hogrogian's *One Fine Day* (Macmillan, 1971). Each step the fox takes to regain his clipped tail can be represented by a simple sketch; arrows connect the sketches to show the logical development of the tale.

Flow charts work particularly well for outlining books that describe procedures such as how-to-do-it books. Rather than verbally outlining the processes they have read about, students make a rough sketch of each step and connect them with arrows to indicate sequence.

A time line is a modification of the flow-chart idea. To outline a sequence of events using a time line, a student places a sketch representing each happening in its appropriate position on a line. Books such as Eth Clifford's *A Bear Before Breakfast* (Putnam, 1962) lend themselves rather easily to interpretation through a time line. In it two children react to figurative uses of language such as Charley horse, bear before breakfast, white elephant, out of the clear blue sky, monkey's uncle, and so forth. They encounter these expressions in a sequence that can be plotted chronologically on a time line. *May I Bring a Friend?* by Beatrice De Regniers (Atheneum, 1964) can be outlined in a similar fashion. Each new event and the friend taken to that event can be plotted sequentially on a line that has peaks and valleys to indicate excitement levels in the story. In plotting story development on this sophisticated kind of time line, older students can begin to substitute words for pictures.

Young people who have listened to or read stories and interpreted them visually can use their graphics to retell the tales to other students. Maps, flow charts, and time lines can become visual outlines that help a storyteller remember sequences of stories.

Once young people have made storyboards based on their listening and reading experiences, they can use the same devices as outlines for their own writing. They can map out the locales they will use, sketch story characters, or schematically represent the steps in a procedure they intend to describe verbally.

These visuals can serve a second purpose too. After writing stories based on their storyboards, young people use them as cue cards when orally sharing their tales with classmates.

Most storyboard activities—listening to stories recorded on tape, reading stories, preparing boards based on ideas heard or read, writing original tales based on original maps and time lines, recording stories on tape—can be pursued by students working independently at a classroom learning station. This is one of the major advantages of storyboard activity—through it students are enriching all their communication skills.

WRITING A STORY FROM A DIAGRAM   An article in the December 1972 *Scholastic Teacher* proposed that teachers give young children a diagram from which they write a story including all the things in the diagram in order. The things in the example are connected by a dotted line. Mount the diagram, which is really a story outline, on four pieces of cardboard fastened together with tape or twine, to produce

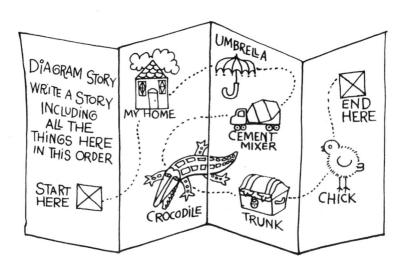

a zigzag book. After writing their versions of the story, children can mount a final copy directly on the back side of the zigzag book.

By the way, if you are working with bilingual children, you may wish to write each story incident twice on the diagram. Write it first in students' original language and again in the target language.

PUZZLING WITH WORDS   Cut one side of a file folder into six interlocking puzzle pieces. Label each piece with a word that represents a story ingredient: one with a character word, i.e., lifeguard, a second with another character word, i.e., swimmer, a third with a location, i.e., at the beach, a fourth with an action word, i.e., struggled, a fifth with a feeling word, i.e., worried, and a sixth with a time phrase, i.e., at high tide.

As a class, students fit the six pieces of the puzzle together and orally devise a story using the key ingredients named on the pieces. They brainstorm what could happen when a lifeguard encounters a swimmer. They assign names to the two characters, talk about how to begin and end their story, and propose various plot sequences. Finally, they orally put together sentences for a story.

Once students have enjoyed the experience of building a class puzzle story, you may find that they are eager to do one on their own. Make many puzzles so that each participant has an envelope with six pieces labeled with characters, location, time, feeling, and action.

To introduce youngsters to new words, try to include an unfamiliar word in each envelope that a youngster must dictionary check. For example, the action word in one envelope may be stalked, the character word in another may be luminescent cat, the location word in a third may be interplanetary space, the feeling word may be hostile, and so forth.

WORDS FOR PUZZLE STORIES

Character 1	Character 2	Action	Feeling	Location	Time or Occasion
luminescent cat	farmer	crept	excited	under the back porch	one dark night
hen	carpenter	dropped	famished	in the farm yard	early one morning
whirligig beetle	frog	revolved	dizzy	on the pond	at dawn
turtle	caterpillar	crashed	frustrated	on a bean leaf	after a rain shower
ironworker	crane operator	riveted	energetic	on the sky-scraper	a cold day
butcher	meat packer	chopped	trapped	in the meat freezer	a busy day
Stegosaurus	Tyranno-saurus	lunged	startled	in a marsh	Mesozoic times
peasant	pheasant	clawed	annoyed	rice field	noon
Rolls-Royce	Toyota	snubbed	haughty	parking lot	New Year's eve
chimney	chimney sweep	spewed	determined	old building	1980
peddler	woman	argued	hostile	by wagon of goods	Christmas eve
dappled horse	brown horse	trotted	tired	at the race track	in-the-stretch
kettle	pot	whistled	agitated	on the stove	just before lunch
hobo	tramp	ransacked	itchy	in a deserted house	yesterday
witch	goblin	careened	uncertain	on bald mountain	Halloween
snowplow	jeep	stuck	frozen	on a moun-tain road	in a snowstorm
bank teller	holdup person	stalked	daring	at the bank	noon

A MODEL PUZZLE SHAPE

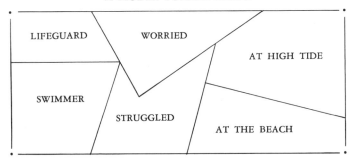

Story puzzles can reflect the time of year. During the pre-Christmas season, Ms. Patti Cifrodelli designed a holiday tree puzzle consisting of five pieces, which was easier for her younger elementary students to handle. Each piece was cut from different colored construction paper and bore a key story-making word. When put together, the pieces formed a tree shape. The words printed on the segments were Miami Beach, Santa Claus, mouse, exhausted, and crept. Ms. Cifrodelli divided her class into groups of five, and each member of a group received a puzzle piece. The groups first tried to fit their pieces together to form a tree, then stapled the pieces to construction paper, and finally orally composed a story using the words. A scribe printed the story of each group at the bottom of the construction paper.

As an independent follow-up, students in Ms. Cifrodelli's class could work at a station creating their own puzzle pieces to make into a story. They cut out five tree-shaped pieces and labeled each with a character, location, action, or feeling name. After mounting all the pieces to form a tree, they composed stories based on their labels.

Ms. Elaine Hunt used the winter season and the image of a snowman to help her students at Christopher Columbus School in Elizabeth, New Jersey, use words for description. She made a colored drawing of a snowman on blue oak tag and put snowman words around it. She then cut the picture into twenty-two large pieces, one for each third grader. She taped on the chalkboard a frame the size of the original oak tag. One at a time youngsters came up to tape their pieces in the appropriate place in the puzzle frame.

After completing the puzzle, they began to create a story from the word pieces. Each child remembered the word that had been written on his or her piece, and as Ms. Hunt signaled, he or she contributed a sentence containing the word. The story they composed together went like this:

Once upon a time there was a *snowman*. His *name* was Tony. Tony was built from *snow*. He lived in a *backyard* in *New York*.

The snowman had a blue *hat* and a *broom*. He wore bright green *gloves*. Tony's *scarf* was very pretty. It was red. Tony's *cheeks* were rosy and pink. He was *tall*. Tony was a very *happy* snowman.

Tony liked to play with the *children*. *Everyone* liked Tony. I *loved* to play with him.

One day it *rained* on the snowman's hat. Then it was *summer* and Tony *melted*. The children were *sad*. But the *next winter* Tony came back. He saw the children again. All the children were happy when *Santa Claus* came. Santa Claus gave Tony *presents* too.

Incidentally, this activity is an easy one to adapt for use with bilingual children. On each puzzle piece write the word twice, once in the child's first language, and once in the target

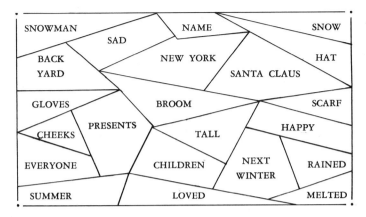

Ms. Hunt's Puzzle—
outline of snowman was drawn across the oaktag surface

language. The child tells his or her story orally in the first
language and then writes it in the target language.

SHAPING A STORY   In the February 1975 *Instructor,*
Joanne Gillespie described a story-sharing activity that she
uses successfully with fifth graders. She cuts different-colored
and different-sized shapes—circles, ovals, triangles—from construction paper. Each shape represents either a character or
action in a story she intends to tell. As she shares the story,
she places the colored shapes on a white sheet of paper, setting
up a grouping of shapes for each major episode.

Students create original stories to share in a rather similar
way. First, they work out a story line and divide it into a
number of episodes. For each episode they cut out a grouping
of shapes, each of which represents a character. They paste
each grouping of shapes sequentially on a sheet or strip of
paper and beneath each grouping they print a sentence or
two that tells the story action occurring during that episode
of the story. Students use their sheets or strips as visuals during
story-sharing time.

Describing students' reaction to shaping a story in this way, Ms. Gillespie wrote: "Enthusiasm was so high that before the stories were entirely assembled, pupils were sharing them with their classmates."

If you have a flannel board in your classroom, you can adapt Ms. Gillespie's technique into an easy way to tell a flannel-board story. Just cut colored shapes from construction paper and stick a strip of self-adhering flannel tape to the back. The tape is available from most school-supply companies. Working with a variety of colors and shapes, both youngsters and you can share read or created stories by moving pieces on the flannel board.

An even easier technique is to use the pre-cut flannel pieces that are generally used to teach the concept of mathematical sets. Numbers of stars, birds, rectangles, and so forth are packaged together and sold for under five dollars by the supply houses. If you have a set, encourage children to invent stories and to post the shapes on a flannel board during story sharing.

THE LANGUAGE OF POETRY

AN ODYSSEY: WRITING WITH WORD PICTURES
David Lyons finds that modern folk songs stimulate students in his fourth-grade class to produce their own word pictures. A folk song he considers most useful is "City of New Orleans," which describes one man's journey down the Mississippi and his encounters with various people and happenings; it is popularly associated with Arlo Guthrie. Mr. Lyons says, "The 'City of New Orleans' carries an inspiring melody for a group sing-along plus an image-packed story. Its music and its poetry provide an excellent stimulus for the children's own ideas for odyssey stories and poems." Music and lyrics by Steve Goodman are available in sheet-music form.

Mr. Lyons introduced "The City of New Orleans" by singing it to the class as he projected the words with an overhead projector. The fourth graders joined in first on the chorus and then on the whole song. Students located places mentioned on a wall map of the United States and traced the itinerary of the singer's trip down the Mississippi. They talked about words and phrases through which the folk writer communicated word pictures. They considered the meaning of the word *odyssey* in the song and discussed the ways words were used to express feelings.

Their teacher then introduced the idea of embarking on their own odyssey or adventure. Children suggested various means of transportation such as cars, buses, planes, boats, rockets, horses, motorcycles, and feet. The class divided into groups, and each group brainstormed word pictures it associated with one of these forms of transportation. Each recorded its words on index cards, which were posted at a follow-up writing center. Students went individually to the station to select a form of transportation about which to write their own odysseys. They could also incorporate some of the brainstormed words from the cards into their stories or poems.

Reporting on the students' reaction to the odyssey, Mr. Lyons stated: "The use of a folk or pop song that the children identify with and enjoy turned out to be very effective in causing them to appreciate the ways in which words are manipulated in poetry. There was no difficulty in their comprehending the song. For example, in the chorus the writer addresses America in the form of a greeting, 'Good morning, America, how are you? Don't you know me, I'm your native son?' The children seemed to absorb the enthusiasm the song writer displays in greeting the country he loves. They had no difficulty understanding the kind of abstract language represented in the greeting. They had no difficulty either in picking out all the word pictures in the song."

Students created word pictures that were rather good. For example, phrases brainstormed about cars included "gray highways," "fuming factories," "sticky tar" and about horses "grassy meadows," "trotting slowly," "all alone." Working at the Odyssey station, one boy wrote:

ON THE HIGHWAY
On the highway On the road
Many a truck with heavy load.
Long long tar without end.
Scary turn. Scary bend
So many cars roaring fast
On the highway At last At last.

A girl wrote a horse odyssey:

Trit, trot, trit, trot
I see the meadow bay.
Trit, trot, trit, trot
The rain came down and blocked the sun.
Trit, trot, trit, trot
There will be another day.
Trit, trot, trit, trot
When we can see the meadow bay.

If you have trouble locating songs that will involve children in word pictures as Mr. Lyons did, encourage youngsters to bring in their own recordings or sheet music of folk and pop songs. Working from one of these songs, you may be able to introduce poetry in a form that will turn on youngsters who have been turned off by conventional forms of poetry.

If you cannot locate the music for "The City of New Orleans," use instead Peter Spier's illustrated version of the familiar *Erie Canal* (Doubleday, 1970). Both words and music are included in the book, and Spier's illustrations translate the word pictures into detailed visual images depicting life during the 1800s.

SINGING AND SEEING COLORS   Lyrics to a popular song liltingly ask listeners to "sing a rainbow." The answers to this command are the names of the colors of the spectrum.

What makes this song so unique is that in everyday life people do not normally sing rainbows, they *see* rainbows. Similarly we do not sing apartment houses, zoos, traffic, storms, or sunny days, yet it is possible to sing a sunny day by thinking of a string of sunny words and putting them into a two- or three-note pattern. Traffic can be sung by juxtaposing the sounds, sights, and smells of a traffic jam.

Before beginning to create "songs," students individually search for words that fit their topic. Actual songwriting is a group activity in which participants discuss their words and decide which ones paint the clearest picture of the subject in question. Beat the rhythm of "Sing a Rainbow" on a drum, and as students order their words, they attempt to tie the words to the beat. Once a sequence of words has been selected, students try singing them by alternating two or three notes. Another song that can be used in much the same way is "My Favorite Things."

It is possible to buy collections of songs in book form that give full piano parts, lyrics, and chords as well as pictures. A good source is Peer-Southern Publications (1740 Broadway, New York, NY 10019), which distributes collections of country and folk such as the 128-page folio of sixty-one songs called *The Best of Folk*. It is divided into five sections: This Land Is Your Land, Gotta Travel On, Those Were the Days, Hammer of Justice, and Bell of Freedom. In addition, Peer-Southern sells popular personality collections such as Cat Stevens anthologies, songs of Don McLean, Jim Croce hits, and Richie Havens anthologies. Upper-grade students can study songs in these or similar collections to see how popular songwriters build word pictures, sounds, and action into their lyrics.

A number of years ago Lee Bennett Hopkins, author of *Pass the Poetry, Please* (Citation Press, 1972), introduced me to an extremely easy but tremendously striking device for stimulating young people to devise the word pictures that are the heart of poetic expression.

Just pour some water into a glass pie plate, and place the plate on the platform of an overhead projector. Turn on the projector light and turn off the classroom lights. Focus the projector and shake the plate gently. A swirling, shimmering reflection of rainbow-filled water appears on the screen and ceiling. By setting up two projectors, pointing in opposite directions, the classroom becomes a fishbowl with students and teacher suspended somewhere inside.

Students brainstorm word pictures that come to mind as the water swirls. To encourage imaginative thinking, put the projector slightly out of focus so that the Pyrex label on most glass pie plates is distorted. Try adding blobs of food coloring —reds, greens, blues—to the dancing water to produce a psychedelic effect. Try putting a few drops of water directly on the projector platform before placing the pie plate there; big bubbles will be projected on the screen. You will be amazed at the numbers and kinds of words and phrases students will dream up in response to these visual images. I have been!

Working from these words, groups or individuals can build delightful haikus and cinquains. Haikus are three lines of unrhymed verse that follow a 5-7-5 syllable pattern. Cinquains are five lines of unrhymed verse that follow a 2-4-6-8-2 syllable pattern. In both haikus and cinquains, words create a picture or feeling as in the following piece written by a group of students who had brainstormed together.

> Kaleidoscope of
> My rainbow's changing colors.
> Reds, blue, greens, yellows.

Students in upper grades who have had a little practice with calligraphy may wish to extend the experience as Lou Ann Kennelly's students have done. In Ms. Kennelly's class, students enscribe their haikus and cinquains on transparent acetate sheets, using circles and flourishes to decorate the letters. Later they share their poems by projecting the sheets with the overhead projector on which a glass pie plate of colored water is mounted. The shimmering water forms an effective backdrop for the words of the poems.

Other students may wish to borrow a storywriting technique from Bruno Munari. In his popular *The Circus in the Mist* (World, 1968), Munari draws words and pictures on semi-transparent, vellum-like paper that gives a misty gray effect, blending with the theme of the book. Students can make similar transparencies to use in telling their stories. They can even go on to adapt Munari's technique of cutting holes in the pages of his book to achieve a peekaboo effect that is quite delightful.

CREATING PATCHWORK POEMS   In the March 1975 *Instructor,* Lorraine Ellis Harr describes an "exciting approach to poetic composition"—the patchwork poem. To create a patchwork poem, a "poet" browses through discarded magazines and newspapers, clipping words, phrases, and small pictures that strike his or her fancy, organizes them into themes, and then looks for additional words and phrases that seem to fit with ideas already clipped. The composer arranges related words, phrases, and pictures on a large sheet of construction paper, eliminating some, adding others, and experimenting with various designs. When sounds, shapes, and meanings blend in a pleasing way, the "poet" pastes the pieces to the sheet of paper. Not just one, but several poems might be designed, each on a separate sheet.

Ms. Harr suggests that browsing for words "can benefit reading skills" and that students gain "knowledge of the value of the right word for the expression of an idea" as well as "a much better concept of what it takes to make a poem." Since patchwork poems can be haikus, cinquains, or free verses, students gain greater understanding of the kinds of messages that can be communicated through different forms of poetry as well as skill in working with those different forms.

Try variations of patchwork poems with students who have had experience with the technique. One variation is to mount clipped words and phrases onto full-page illustrations from a magazine or newspaper or painted by the poet, making a collage poem in which the words complement the illustration.

Poems can also be pasted on pieces torn from brown paper bags or they can be written in calligraphy. The bags can be hung outdoors where sun, wind, and rain can work upon the surface to produce additional effects. According to Ms. Harr, this treatment has been called a "weathergram." If you do not want to wait for nature to do its work, try dipping poems mounted on white paper into a dark solution of tea. Remember to rip the edges a bit before dipping to give a weathered appearance. Some ideas for patchwork poems are:

The travel section of Sunday newspapers and travel magazines is chock full of interesting words about places and things. Encourage children to bring such magazines and newspapers to class as well as magazines that have many advertisements in which words are used creatively. Don't forget your old copies of *Instructor*, *Teacher*, *Early Years*, or *Learning*, if you feel you can part with them.

Stack the source materials at a Patchwork Poem Composing Corner in the classroom, along with scissors, paste, and paper, so that students can browse and create independently by themselves or in pairs.

Try a few class patchwork poems so that children will get the idea that they should browse for really interesting words and phrases. A good way to do a class patchwork poem is to begin with a multi-colored, large picture such as those found on calendars. Armed with scissors and a magazine, each student clips words that fit the picture. Later the class chooses words from all those clipped and assembles them on the picture in a way that helps communicate its message. As the class searches for words, remind them that they can also clip letters from the middle of words. For example, *a*, *an*, or *I* can be clipped out of another word; *s* can be similarly clipped to add to the end of words to make plurals. If a particular word is absolutely necessary to complete a thought and it cannot be found, it can be patched together from letters clipped from other words.

BUGGING IT ‸Devising and designing word bugs is another activity that combines the verbal with the visual; at the same time it helps young people understand the concept of symmetry. Making word bugs intrigues upper-elementary students and is easy enough for primary youngsters to try.

To make a word bug, students fold a piece of construction paper lengthwise down the middle. They write a word along the fold so that it extends down its full length as shown in the accompanying example. With the paper still folded, they cut along the outer edges formed by the letters, making sure not to cut the fold itself. Opening up the folded paper, they will find a symmetrical "bug" formed by the letters of the word they wrote.

A bug shape can stimulate a poem about the word on which it is based. If, for example, the word forming the pattern is toadstool, the thought is about toadstools; if the word is action, as in the example, the thought is about action. Any kind of word can form the pattern—one's own name, an object, or a feeling work particularly well. Likewise, the thought can be written in any form, such as an acrostic in which the letters of the word are the beginning letters for each line, nature puffs, free verse, concrete poems in which the words are also arranged in the shape of the object, haikus, and so on.

You may wish to borrow an idea from mathematics—the tangram—to spruce up your language program. A tangram is a Chinese puzzle consisting of a square made up of five triangles, a square, and a rhomboid. These seven pieces can be combined to form a variety of other figures and shapes. By working with them, young people can learn something of geometric shapes.

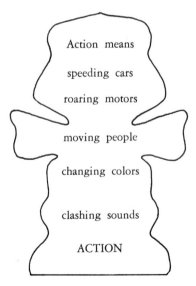

Action means

speeding cars

roaring motors

moving people

changing colors

clashing sounds

ACTION

In addition, youngsters can combine the seven pieces into artistic patterns and mount them on pieces of construction paper. Working from the idea inspired from the pattern, a student composes a thought expressed in seven lines. Each line is written on one of the mounted shapes, or all seven lines are enscribed on an open area of the paper.

Diamond-shaped thoughts sometimes are fun to do in conjunction with tangram patterns. A diamond-shaped thought consists of seven lines with:

> One word in the first line,
> Two words in the second line,
> Three words in the third line,
> Four words in the fourth line,
> Three words in the fifth line,
> Two words in the sixth line, and
> One word in the seventh line.

In "Exploring Poetry Patterns," *Elementary English* (December 1970) Iris Tiedt explores the intricacies of the diamante, as she has developed it, and suggests that:

Line 1 consist of a subject noun,
Line 2 consist of adjectives about the subject noun,
Line 3 consist of participles that refer to the subject noun,
Line 4 consist of nouns that relate to the subject,
Line 5 consist of participles that refer to a noun-opposite of the subject,
Line 6 consist of adjectives that tell about the noun-opposite,
Line 7 consist of the noun-opposite of the subject.

This diamante is an ideal form to use with a tangram pattern. Both tangram and diamante have seven parts; both have a geometric flavor. Designing the seven pieces into a shape that communicates a message reinforcing the verbal message of the seven lines of the diamante is a real challenge for upper-elementary students.

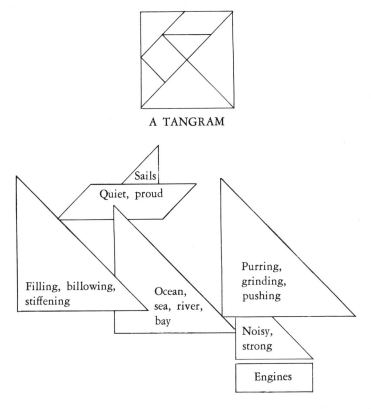

A TANGRAM

Sails
Quiet, proud

Filling, billowing, stiffening

Ocean, sea, river, bay

Purring, grinding, pushing

Noisy, strong

Engines

WISHING AND LYING Two books are absolute musts for teachers wishing to introduce young people to the word pictures of poetry: Kenneth Koch's *Wishes, Lies, and Dreams* and his more recent *Rose, Where Did You Get That Red?* (Chelsea House–Random House, 1970, 1973). These volumes provide many "Ideas for poems," patterns that should stimulate children to produce the language of poetry.

Perhaps the best known of Koch's "Ideas for poems" is the wish-poem. To write a wish-poem, one begins every line with "I wish. . . ." Another is the lie-poem or the ridiculous exaggeration piece in which one begins each line with a similar phrase, such as "I saw . . . ," and each line must contain a wild exaggeration, really a hyperbole of sorts. This technique was used by a sixth-grade girl who wrote:

LIES

Once I saw a fish that lived on land.
Once I saw a rabbit eat a tiger.
Once I saw a man with no head.
Once I saw money grow on trees.
Once I saw a pig doing a jig.
And once I saw The End.

Still another pattern is the comparison poem. Every line must contain the words *as* _____ *as* i.e., "Snow is as white as the sunshine," or "The sky is as blue as a waterfall."

Once a beginning poet becomes familiar with Koch's ideas, he or she can devise original patterns. Students may find it easy to write pieces in which every line begins "Suppose that . . ." or "I remember when . . ." or "Don't forget. . . ." They may enjoy playing with pairs of opposites in which one line begins "I like . . ." and the next begins "I dislike . . ."; these continue alternating throughout the piece. Other pairs of opposites that work well are A mountain is . . . /A valley is . . . , Silence is . . . /Noise is. . . .

In *Rose, Where Did You Get That Red?* Koch turns to the great poetry of the past and identifies some of the patterns that poets have created. Students can use these patterns to produce their own original pieces. One pattern is the communication-with-object poem. A good example is William Blake's "The Lamb," in which Blake directly addresses the lamb:

Little Lamb, who made thee?
Dost thou know who made thee;
Gave thee life and bid thee feed
By the stream and o'er the mead; . . .

Blake, a master of this kind of direct address, does the same in "The Fly":

Little Fly,
Thy summer's play
My thoughtless hand
Has brushed away.

in "The Tyger":

> Tyger! Tyger! burning bright
> In the forests of the night,
> What immortal hand or eye
> Could frame thy fearful symmetry?

and in "The Sunflower":

> Ah, Sunflower! weary of time,
> Who countest the steps of the Sun....

It was this pattern that the youngster who wrote Koch's title, *Rose, Where Did You Get That Red?* was following when she wrote her own communication-with-object poem.

If you find that students begin to produce really effective word pictures using these patterns, get your own copy of the Koch books. They are jammed with ideas that start children writing the language of poetry.

THE LANGUAGE OF PERSUASION

NAMING PRODUCTS Encourage youngsters to analyze the language of advertising by setting up a learning station with these instructions:

WHAT'S IN A NAME?

TASK: To figure out why products are named the way they are.

DIRECTIONS:

1. Browse through the magazines and newspapers you find on the table. Study the advertisements.
2. Locate an advertisement for a product that has been given a particularly interesting name. Write the product name on an index card.
3. Try to figure out why the product was given that name. Write your explanation on the card. You may refer to some other part of the advertisement that gives a hint as to why the name was chosen.
4. Put your card with your name printed in the lower right-hand corner into the Finished Card pouch.
5. Fill in several cards, each for a different kind of product.

After several young people have visited the station, schedule an analytical talk time. Distribute completed cards to students who wrote them. They report their findings orally to the class, while one student keeps notes on a large wall chart that looks like this:

Product Name	Possible Reasons Product Was Given That Name

After compiling the group chart, students may be able to generalize about product names. They may realize that some products have been given scientific-sounding names so that people will have more faith in them; for instance, Kellogg's Product 19, Preparation H, and Kaopectate were probably deliberately named to make the products appear scientifically sound.

Students may generalize that some products have names that allude to one of its particular features. Was the Dodge Dart so named to communicate the notion of a fast pickup? Were the Lincoln Continental and Cadillac Sedan de Ville named for their snob appeal? Probably so.

Other reasons students might propose include: the product names themselves are catchy and not likely to be forgotten, they are alliterative or simply sound pleasant, they are acronyms or they allude to people, places, or things about which most people have positive feelings.

Once students have suggested reasons why products have been given their names, you may want to reverse this exercise to see if students can identify product names based on their generalizations. To do this, mount sheets of 8½ x 11 inch construction paper on the backdrop of a learning station. Print one naming generalization at the top of each paper. Stack magazines and newspapers nearby. Students working at this easily prepared station browse for product names and list them under the applicable generalization.

Naming hypothetical goods or services is a natural follow-up activity that is both productive and fun. To begin, brainstorm as a group with an item such as a new candy bar. "What are some of the characteristics of this bar? its shape? size? composition? Who are the most likely consumers? What names could communicate to this consumer group? What names could communicate some key feature of the bar?" Questions like these guide students as they think about their new product.

Divide the class into three-person teams; since this activity is basically a brainstorming one, it is more successful when there is student interaction. Give each team a guide sheet to talk about and complete. It suggests a new product and its characteristics. Students brainstorm possible names and reasons to support them and record the names and reasons on the guide sheet. Allow the groups time to share their findings with one another.

Students who find this task challenging may wish to invent names for products for which they determine the key characteristics. You may suggest that they name a new antacid, a detergent, deodorant, cold remedy, breakfast food, or rock group and give reasons for the name chosen.

A SEARCH FOR A PRODUCT NAME

PRODUCT: Small car with sporty lines; loud colors available; inexpensive to operate; probable market—18 to 40 age group.

POSSIBLE NAMES   REASONS FOR SELECTING THAT NAME

PRODUCT: Plant magazine about gardening and growing things; a monthly publication of about 60–80 pages an issue; probable market— 35 to 75 age group, middle class, average readers.

POSSIBLE NAMES   REASONS FOR SELECTING THAT NAME

PRODUCT: Perfume for men; packaged to have a he-man look; probable market—wealthy men-about-town.

POSSIBLE NAMES   REASONS FOR SELECTING THAT NAME

PRODUCT: Large expensive car with many plush features; probable market —people with a lot of money for whom buying gas is no problem.

POSSIBLE NAMES   REASONS FOR SELECTING THAT NAME

PRODUCT:

POSSIBLE NAMES   REASONS FOR SELECTING THAT NAME

SPOTTING WORD TRAPS Encourage upper-grade students to browse through magazine and newspaper advertisements and to listen to TV commercials to find examples showing different ways words are purposefully manipulated to persuade a consumer to buy. One kind of word trap that is easy to spot is the glittering generality, a statement so general in its description that it adds little or no relevant information about the product advertised and may possibly not be true. For example, a gasoline company brags that it "not only keeps your car going but keeps you going"—whatever that means. A resort hotel claims that it has "more of everything." Can that be true? A department store announces a menswear clearance sale by offering, "Men, here's your chance to look like a millionaire and save enough to live like one." In the same vein, an ad for a humidifier claims, "This machine can do wonders for your throat, your nose, your furniture, your plants, and even your wallet." Statements similar to these gross exaggerations abound in advertisements. Browsing and clipping, students can easily fill a piece of large construction paper with their own examples.

A related form of puffery is use of glamour words, words that people tend to react to in a positive way. A student search of ads found in just ten pages of a well-respected newspaper uncovered the following examples: magnificent, incredible, award-winning, stunning, exquisite, unusual, super, ultimate, Olympic-sized, miracle, purebred, extraordinary, and fantastic. Superlatives included greatest, finest, newest, and most celebrated as well as superlative-like phrases such as unequaled luxury and in a class by itself. With the glamour words students found high-pressure sales words that push consumers into making an immediate and perhaps unnecessary purchase, words such as last chance, only this week, just arrived, now, huge savings, final offer, today, and fantastic opportunity.

Prepare a sheet to guide beginning ad investigators in their search. It contains a checklist of glamour and high-pressure sales words commonly found in newspaper advertisements. As student investigators browse through newspapers at home or at school, they place a check next to a word each time they encounter it in an ad. Students who find other words repeated over and over may add those to their checklists.

SPOTTING THE TRAPS	
The Word Traps	*Tallies*
great	
save or savings	
new	
super	
today	
now	
better or best	
improved	
special	
just arrived	
offer	

The purpose of advertising testimonials is to cloak a product in glamour, or give it a positive aura. Joe Namath endorses a line of cosmetics for men and is quoted extolling their virtues. George Plimpton plugs an ocean liner's cruise to the South Pacific, describing the pleasures in store for the traveler. Redd Foxx's picture and words are the substance of an ad for a well-known brand of scotch. This is the glamour-personality trap, one of the easiest for a beginning consumer specialist to spot. As young people find examples of testimonials, they clip and mount them on colored construction paper for later posting on a bulletin board. Encourage them to answer the question, "Why do celebrities endorse products?"

Sometimes advertisers try to build a positive feeling about their products by associating them with well-known and liked things such as objects, book titles, lines of successful poems or songs, or personalities living or dead. An ad for a Swiss liqueur asks, "And you thought the Swiss only made cuckoo clocks?" associating the liqueur with the familiar cuckoo clock. A whiskey ad is captioned, "The taste of success. How sweet it is," an allusion to Jackie Gleason's familiar lines. Another competing ad declares, "Tasting is believing," alluding to the familiar saying, "Seeing is believing." Perceiving allusions is considerably more difficult for young investigators who must be familiar with the referent to recognize the allusion. Elementary-grade students probably will lack the background necessary to comprehend the points being made.

On the other hand, elementary-grade students will have no trouble recognizing advertising statements that base their appeal on the sounds of words, sound traps. Alliteration, rhyming, repetition of prefixes and suffixes are all used to make readers remember. For example, Bermuda is described as, "unspoiled, unhurried, and uncommon." Investments are said to, "grow in need and deed." A fertilizer ad states, "Glorion Grows It Greener—Guaranteed to Grow a Great Lawn!" Korea Oil begins an ad with the words, "Partners in Prosperity," and a champagne ad starts, "Pop goes the Piper." In hard-sell advertisements and commercials, hard consonant sounds seem to reappear, *p, b*, hard *g*, and *k*. These sounds produce a clanging, attention-getting effect. Softer sounds are used to describe products that soothe. Keep a large chart posted on a classroom bulletin board so that word investigators can record the examples they encounter on TV commercials and in magazine and newspapers advertisements.

Once students have compiled lists of examples of generalizations, glamour words, high-pressure sales words, testimonials, and sound traps, they are ready to create advertisements of their own. Use a Search for a Product Name sheet given earlier to get things started. Students select a product from the sheet and write advertising copy to describe it, "lifting" words and phrases from the lists they have compiled from actual advertisements and commercials if they wish. Set aside time for writers to share their advertisements orally. Since students will tend to exaggerate even more than professional copywriters, oral sharing can be fun.

Some sources you may wish to check before introducing students to word manipulation in advertising are:

Ivan L. Preston. *The Great American Blow-Up: Puffery in Advertising and Selling* (University of Wisconsin Press, 1975). An examination of puffery, concentrating on deceptive use of words in advertising.

Hugh Rank, editor. *Language and Public Policy* (National Council of Teachers of English and Citation Press, 1974). Articles discussing the need to build young people's skills in interpreting the language of persuasion.

Hugh Rank. "The Worldly Wise," *Instructor,* December 1974. An excerpt from Mr. Rank's conclusion to *Language and Public Policy.*

Consumer Reports, a monthly publication of Consumers Union that summarizes consumer news and rates products tested. (P.O. Box 1000, Orangeburg, NY 10962).

HITTING HARD WITH SLOGANS A fundamental component of most advertising campaigns is the slogan, a short phrase or sentence that is particularly catchy and that consumers will remember and come to associate with the product. The slogan appears in most advertisements and commercials for the product.

Slogans that have been around a long time are remembered even though they have been changed or even dropped, as was the case with Dupont's "Better things for better living through chemistry," General Electric's "Progress is our most important product," General Motors' "See the USA in your Chevrolet," Birds Eye's "Better buy Birds Eye," Greyhound's "Go Greyhound," and Pepsi-Cola's "Join the Pepsi generation." More recent additions to the slogan pool include "Never underestimate the power of an Opel" (a takeoff on the familiar saying about the power of a woman), "TR7: The shape of things to come," and Eastern's "You gotta believe!"

Upper-elementary-grade students enjoy seeing if they can name the products associated with specific slogans. Prepare a sheet of slogans for a station titled Can You Recognize These Slogans? Students begin by filling in the blanks with product names. Make the exercise self-checking by tucking answers into an answer pouch at the center. Keep on hand a pack of small index cards. After finishing the introductory sheet, students write a real slogan they remember on the front of a card and the product on the reverse side. As more students visit the station, they not only complete the sheet and write slogan cards but they test themselves with the cards previous students have completed.

CAN YOU RECOGNIZE THESE SLOGANS?

Fill in the name of the product on the blank line. Then check your answers by referring to the list in the answer pouch.

1. _____ is ready when you are.
2. Mr. Whipple, please don't squeeze the _____.
3. We're number two. We try harder. _____.
4. _____, the wings of man.
5. Come to where the flavor is. Come to _____ country.
6. Do you suffer from tired blood? Then take _____.
7. Use all-temperature _____.
8. I feel clean. I smell clean with _____.
9. I'm Barbara. Fly me! _____.
10. Join the _____ generation.
11. Let your fingers do the walking through the _____.
12. Progress for People _____.
13. You deserve a break today at _____.
14. _____ refreshes you best.
15. Put a tiger in your tank. _____

ANSWERS FOR ANSWER POUCH

1. Delta   2. Charmin   3. Avis   4. Eastern
5. Marlboro   6. Geritol   7. Cheer   8. Lifebuoy
9. National   10. Pepsi   11. Yellow Pages   12. General Electric
13. McDonald's   14. Coca-Cola   15. Exxon

This sheet is only a model. You will need to revise it to reflect slogans popular in your own area.

Having paired slogans with products, upper graders will be eager to compose their own slogans for popular products such as Coca-Cola, Alka-Seltzer, Bufferin, the Volkswagen Rabbit or Bug, Dial Soap, Kellogg's Rice Krispies, Trans World Airlines, Dash, and so on. Each student can compile a small booklet of original slogans. Schedule a class sharing time when all students present their best ones. This session can be organized as a contest with the class selecting the best two or three slogans of the day. By the way, encourage students to send their best slogans to the company that produces that particular item. Obtain the address from the package or from a local library's directory of companies such as *Standard and Poor's Register, Moody's Industrial Manual*, or *Thomas's Register*.

It is fun to compose slogans for hypothetical products too—detergent, candy bar, insect repellent, hair spray, chewing gum, house paint, car, airline, or soup. Even more fun is to concoct what Hugh Rank calls "counter commercials"—slogans that twist the wording of well-known ones. He gives as an example the playful "You deserve a stroke today! Pimples today! Coronary tomorrow!" Such takeoffs on actual commercials are relatively easy to devise. For instance, a slogan appearing in magazine ads reads, "Our cigarette is More. . . ." A plausible counter commercial is, "Our cigarette is More Deadly!" Another company introduced a new version of an item with, "Tops all of ours and all of theirs too." A counter commercial version is, "Flops—all of ours and all of theirs too!" One suggestion—the easiest way to devise counter commercials is to browse through magazines studying the ads, so keep a variety of magazines available just for that purpose. Students can clip an original slogan, mount it, and print their own counter version beneath.

An integral element of radio and TV advertising is the jingle, short poetry-like lines set to a catchy tune. Since most jingles rhyme, composing one is no easy task, especially since the rhythm of the words must follow the rhythm of the music. However, some students seem to have a natural bent for rhythm and rhyme, and they may opt to try their hand at jingle writing. If some of them are successful, allow them time to coach others on how to sing and physically interpret the jingle. Then schedule a general sharing time.

GOING BEYOND WORDS

Take students beyond the verbal components of the language of persuasion so they can consider the visual components—the illustrations, trademark, print, type, and color—that are also designed to communicate an advertiser's message. These visual elements are chosen and arranged as purposefully as the related words and are just as significant as the words.

Even younger elementary students can make a collection of product trademarks by clipping them from magazines and newspapers and mounting these firsthand data on construction paper. They ask themselves as they clip and mount, "What message is the designer trying to put across with the graphics of the trademark? What determines the content of a particular trademark?" Some marks incorporate the name of the producing company, the initials of the company, or the product name itself. Letters may be intertwined or superimposed; the design may be sharp and angular or smooth and flowing. Encourage young people to compare and contrast the design, content, and message of different trademarks.

A fun follow-up is to design a mark for oneself. Students can use their own initials, nickname, or last name, and their design should communicate some characteristic they associate with themselves. For example, Bob, who plays baseball, may build a bat into the *B* of his name and a baseball into the *O*. Trademarks may be lettered in ink or cut from construction paper. Other related projects include designing a trademark for the school, school team, community, or a local industry.

Students will have to decide what kind of letters or type to use. Those who have written patchwork poems by utilizing words and phrases from magazines and newspapers will have discovered that type differs in size, darkness, and style, and young investigators of advertising techniques will also learn the relationship between message and print.

A search and spot expedition conducted by a group, each of whom inspects a magazine or newspaper, can help students think more directly about the message being communicated by print itself. Each student locates one ad and uses aspects of its type to answer the following questions: "What features of the print are particularly eye catching? What are the key words in the ad? How does type communicate the importance of those words? What is the relationship between print, empty space, and the message? Does the print form a picture or design? Why was this done? What feeling is communicated by the print and its layout on the page?" Individuals then share their chosen advertisements with the group and describe how print affects the message being communicated.

During talk time, help students to focus on details of the print in ads they are sharing. Ask, "Do the letters have tails? no tails? Do the letters vary in thickness?" Letters with tails and parts of different thickness are printed in *serif* type. Letters without tails and with all parts of equal thickness are printed in *sans serif* type. Ask further, "Are the letters all upper case? all lower case? a combination of the two? Are letters shaded to give a three-dimensional effect? Are letters connected to give the appearance of script? Are some letters in italic type (with extra slant)? bold type (with extra thick lines)? light type (with extra thin lines)? extended type (with extra space between letters)? condensed type (with less space between letters)? Have the letters been decorated in some unique way, i.e., series of parallel lines, dots, swirls, flowers?"

These lead into the why question, "Why have these techniques been used? What message is the graphic designer trying to communicate nonverbally?"

Set up a center for graphic designing sometime during the study of advertising where students can design a name sign for a store, industrial company, newspaper, or magazine. The sign must relate to the product being sold. For example, Tom selected The Platters, a record shop, and designed this sign for it.

THE
PLATTERS

Other names students may enjoy working with are:

    The Rose, a flower shop
    The Bike Seat, a bicycle shop
    The Stables, a horse farm
    The Pie Plate, a bakery
    Mod, a boutique
    Animal World, a pet shop
    Flash, a new chain of fast-food restaurants
    The Milk Bottle, a dairy shop
    The Crown, a London pub
    Anchor Savings Bank, a bank
    Welcome Inn, a restaurant for expensive dining
    The Hammer and Nail, a hardware store

Post suggestions such as these in a graphic designing center. Students may either select from the suggestions or work from their own creative ideas.

A second activity to include in the center is Laying Out a Slogan. Post a series of slogans such as the following on a backdrop:

Fly Into the Sun
Leapfrog into the Future
Stop, Look, and Listen at _____
You'll Feel Like Royalty With _____
Big Oaks from Little Acorns Grow
Stop Thinking Big! Think Small!
A Little Bit Goes a Long Way
Slow Down and Live
Hard as Nails
Soft as Silk

These slogans imply a product, but students must decide what particular product relates to the slogan they select. In addition, include a list of slogans where a specific product is named such as:

An Apple a Day Keeps the Doctor Away—Eat Apples
Come to the Florida Sunshine State
See *Jaws*
Put Your Legs in L'Eggs

Students select from the suggested slogans or create an original one for a real or hypothetical product. They then lay out the slogan across a blank piece of paper, drawing on their understanding of print to communicate a forceful message. Some of the best results have been produced by printing with black India ink on white paper or oak tag, using a quill pen or a Leroy lettering pen. Younger children may simply use black flo-pens that have a fine point.

Adding color and a picture is a natural next step. With a slogan such as "An apple a day . . ." a student designer will almost always want to add a bit of red and green and an apple or two to the design. As students begin to enhance their designs, encourage them to search for and clip advertisements where picture or color makes a strong impact. Add to the collection yourself by contributing examples that show how picture and print can produce an integrated effect. A recent Union Carbide ad in *Science,* which considered food problems, was captioned, "We're expecting a few extra people for dinner tonight." The picture showed a newly plowed field across which was set a long table with white cloth, silver, crystal, and red carnations; the table stretched non-stop across the field and disappeared into the distance. The caption was a fine example of understatement, while the picture juxtaposed two elements—earthy soil and elegant dining—that are intimately related but usually not associated together. Post on the bulletin board a few striking ads such as this to prime the pump. Encourage students to add their own discoveries of striking pictorial messages used in advertisements.

The developing bulletin board can trigger talk during transitional moments in the classroom when students are waiting for the arrival of a specialist or for a bell to ring. They can hypothesize together why a particular picture was chosen for a particular product ad and can translate the visual message into words.

Incidentally, as students add pictures and colors to their layouts, they can use pictures from out-of-date calendars and magazines, paste materials collage-fashion onto a page, strike a potato or woodblock print, or overlay strips of colored paper. Students with drawing skill can sketch cartoon figures, and those with painting ability can work with watercolors or pastels.

Besides helping students to understand the kinds of techniques used by advertisers, work with the visual components of the language of persuasion carries a secondary benefit—introduction to a profession that students tend to know little about and that is gaining in importance. The graphics designer plays an important role in advertising, television, and book, magazine, and newspaper production. Some of your students may discover an ability and an interest in working in this growing field.

PREPARING A HARD SELL   Once upper-grade students have had some introduction to the verbal and visual elements of the language of persuasion, they may want to organize themselves into an ad agency that has four or five major products to sell. They divide into groups, each of which works on a particular product of its choice; probably a hypothetical one will allow the greatest creativity. The group decides the characteristics of the product, creates a name for it, originates a series of slogans and perhaps a jingle, writes advertising copy, produces a trademark, lays out advertisements, produces the graphics, and so forth. Within groups, individual students take on different tasks, with some students performing as graphics specialists and others as writers.

When both verbal and visual materials have been produced, the group presents its ideas and materials to a board of executives who represent the manufacturing company, bank, or other organization paying for the advertising campaign. The executives—other students in the class—ask questions to see whether the agency has done its job well.

An alternative project can be to conduct an advertising campaign for a country or part of the United States to persuade travelers to vacation there. This activity works especially well at the end of a series of social studies explorations into different countries of the world or regions of the United States, and is a natural way of integrating both social science and language understanding. Each advertising group selects a country or region and produces advertising brochures, magazine and newspaper layouts, and television and radio commercials. To do an adequate job, participants must know something about both advertising and the country or region being advertised.

A second alternative project is to conduct an advertising campaign for a candidate running for elective office. The candidate and the office may be hypothetical, they may be part of an actual election in progress, or they may be part of school or classroom elections. Students design slogans, posters, billboards, brochures, and fliers and write and tape speeches outlining points of view. One way to handle a political campaign project it to pick at random from class members four competing candidates for a national or state office such as senator or governor. Other members of the class divide into four groups, each attached to a candidate and responsible for producing campaign materials, which later are presented to the entire class.

Do not overlook social issues as bases for advertising campaigns. Publicizing issues related to health, safety, conservation of resources, preservation of the environment, honesty in government, or truth in advertising are worthwhile endeavors. They are even more worthwhile and meaningful if students use the information they gather to write persuasive brochures, invent slogans, and design awareness buttons and posters.

SUMMARIZING, EXPRESSING, AND INTERPRETING ACTIVITIES

This chapter has focused on activities through which young people can enrich their skills in processing and producing the languages of story, poetry, and persuasion. These areas were chosen because of their natural appeal to students in elementary grades and because of their relevance today.

There are other ways, of course, that people use language. Language can describe, state opinions, judge, and explain. Language is verbal as in a paragraph describing the appearance of someone or in an editorial stating a viewpoint on an issue. Communication is visual as well; a painting can describe appearance perhaps more clearly than a paragraph, and a cartoon can state a viewpoint perhaps more explicitly than an editorial. Then there is the whole range of ways by which people communicate their thoughts and feelings nonverbally through gestures, posture, movements, intonations, and facial expressions (see author's *Smiles, Nods, and Pauses,* Citation Press, 1974). Encounters with all these forms of expression have their place in the curriculum of elementary schools.

Such encounters take place almost spontaneously in classrooms where young people are involved in things going on in their community and in the world. Reading newspapers and talking about what they read, experimenting with things around them and explaining what they have done, viewing art and translating impressions into words, and looking at the world and describing what they see are some of the ways young people develop skill in processing and producing language in a variety of forms. Perhaps "the name of the game" is involvement. From involvement come thoughts and words to express those thoughts.

Sumer is icumen in;
 Lhude sing cuccu!
Groweth sed, and bloweth med,
 And spriggeth the wude nu.
 Sing cuccu!

7. LHUDE SING CUCCU!
Activities
in Language Origins

It is believed that the joyful "Cuccu Song," which opens this chapter, was composed about 1240 during what has been called the Middle English period. About 150 years later Chaucer wrote the famed *Canterbury Tales* that began with the lines:

> Whan that Aprille with his shoures sote
> The droghte of Marche hath perced to the rote,
> And bathed every veyne in swich licour,
> Of which vertu engendred is the flour; . . .
> Than longen folk to goon on pilgrimages
> (And palmers for to seken straunge strondes)
> To ferne halwes couthe in sondry londes;
> And specially from every shires ende
> Of Engelond, to Caunterbury they wende,
> The holy blisful martir for to seke,
> That hem hath holpen, whan that they were seke.

Both "Cuccu Song" and *The Canterbury Tales* were written in an English considerably different from that spoken and written today. Even by 1596 when Spenser penned *Prothalamion,* substantial differences in the English were evident although it had changed extensively from Chaucer's times and can be read with much less difficulty:

> Calme was the day, and through the trembling ayre
> Sweete breathing Zephyrus did softly play
> A gentle spirit, that lightly did delay
> Hot Titans beames, which then did glyster fayre:

Comparing English selections written during the last 750 years makes clear to students and teachers alike that language changes. It has changed in the past, is changing now, and will continue to change in the future as it reflects the needs of society and forces at work within society.

Young people in upper-elementary school can begin to understand how language has developed and changed. They can compare words in related languages, trace the etymology of specific words, study the structure of words, analyze maps for clues on language development, identify words recently coined or borrowed, propose reasons for these coinages and borrowings, and analyze current slang expressions. As they work, young language investigators may begin to perceive language as a dynamic reflection of changing life-styles and needs. As they hypothesize about interrelationships based on their comparative linguistic studies, they will actually employ research procedures utilized by linguists, and they may begin to perceive how linguists develop generalizations about language. As junior linguists, they can develop skill in handling references, especially the dictionary, and possibly discover the wealth of information contained within dictionaries. In so doing, they may begin to find that verbal language is a fascinating area to investigate.

NAMING

WORD WATCHING   Nighthawk. Green kingfisher. Chimney swift. Meadowlark. Brown creeper. These are just a few of the many names that are sure to intrigue bird watchers. They are names that can intrigue word watchers as well and can be a base upon which young people can develop generalizations about the reasons some objects bear the names they do.

To begin, select a bird and bird name with which most students are familiar and whose name identifies some characteristic of that bird. Perhaps a robin redbreast or a cardinal will be a productive opener. Ask, "Why do you think this bird was given its name?" Help youngsters hypothesize that some birds acquired their names because of a characteristic color.

Then divide the class into three-person work teams and

distribute a sheet of bird names with space for listing reasons why each bird bears the name it does.

IT'S NAMING DAY

There are many reasons why objects have the names they do. Let us look at a few of these reasons. Study the following list of bird names. Next to each name, write down the reason you believe that name was given to the bird. Because you are really only making a guess, we will call your reason a hypothesis.

Name	*Hypothesis (reason for name)*
1. Hummingbird	
2. Blackbird	
3. Snowbird	
4. Whippoorwill	
5. Woodpecker	
6. Nighthawk	
7. Meadowlark	
8. Brown creeper	
9. Roadrunner	
10. Chimney swift	
11. Green kingfisher	
12. Flycatcher	
13. Gnatcatcher	
14. Bobwhite	
15. Bluejay	
16. Sandpiper	
17. Screech owl	
18. Mockingbird	
19. Tufted titmouse	
20. Robin redbreast	

Can you now summarize the reasons why some objects are called by the names they are? Complete this sentence:

Objects are sometimes named because of

Students who have hypothesized that birds' names are often derived from their size, color, feeding habits, living habits, place of origin, sound, movements, general appearance, and so forth can test their hypotheses by investigating the names acquired by other creatures. They can study the names given to insects, fish, breeds of dogs and cats, fruits, trees, and shrubs and again project reasons for specific names. Particularly good insect names upon which students can build generalizations are grasshopper, horsefly, mite, bumblebee, bedbug, katydid, cricket, dragonfly, water bug, and water strider.

Useful references in making such word investigations are standard field guides or handbooks. They typically supply names of each species and a concise description, which often gives a clue as to why it bears the name it does. The "Golden Nature Guides" to birds, trees, seashores, and fish (Golden Press) and "The Peterson Field Guide" series on birds, insects, wildflowers, and trees and shrubs (Houghton-Mifflin) are particularly helpful; their illustrations also give clues to the possible relationships between physical characteristics and names.

Student investigators can prepare word origin cards for each being about which they read in a guide. The card contains the name and a probable reason why it was acquired. Students orally share their word cards during group or class sessions, and then the cards are posted on a word-origins bulletin board.

MAPPING WORDS   Objects have been named after places with which they have been associated, places have been named after people and other places, and places have been named from historical or geographical relationships. Thus map study is a profitable way to help students develop generalizations about the ways names may be acquired.

Even young students can be involved in this type of study.

Print on slips of paper names of objects and the places from which they get their name, such as:

hamburgers/ Hamburg, Germany	tuxedo/ Tuxedo Park, New York
cologne/ Cologne, Germany	port wine/ Oporto, Portugal
Great Dane/ Denmark	turkey/ Turkey
Persian cat/ Persia	cashmere/ Kasmir
jersey/ Jersey Islands	a Danish/ Denmark
frankfurter/ Frankfort, Germany	wiener/ Wien, Austria
champagne/ Champagne, France	oxfords/ Oxford, England
china/ China	panama hat/ Panama
Swiss cheese/ Switzerland	Dalmatian dog/ Dalmatia, Yugoslavia
damask/ Damascus	munster cheese/ Münster, Germany
parmesan cheese/ Parma, Italy	Gouda cheese/ Gouda, Holland
	Persian rug/ Persia

If you attach a little roll of masking tape to the back of each slip, participants can stick them to the appropriate places on a globe or an outline map of the world that they trace onto a bulletin board. As they develop the map with product names, they can simultaneously be developing the understanding that products sometimes acquire their names from their places of origin.

Give older students only the product names and an outline map of the world. Working with a dictionary and an atlas, teams race one another to figure out and locate on the map places of origin of their words. The first team to finish explains to the class the hypothesized origins of their words.

Comparing maps of the United States with maps of Europe can produce other generalizations about the origin of place names. Start with your own geographical region of the United States and use your knowledge of patterns of immigration into that region to focus students' attention on appropriate portions of the map of Europe. Students in New England compare names found on their regional maps with areas in

England; Exeter, Portsmouth, Plymouth, Yarmouth, Wey-
mouth, Cambridge, Dartmouth, Newport, and Boston have
their origins in English towns or cities. The term New England itself is the most obvious example. Students in the middle
Atlantic states may find familiar place names on a map of
Germany and the Netherlands as well as of the British Isles,
i.e., Harlem, Bergen, Amsterdam, Kinderhook, Jersey, Sussex,
Oxford, and Orange. Spanish place names are common on
maps of the South and Southwest; German and Scandinavian
names are found in the Middle West. See if your students can
hypothesize why this is so.

Once students have begun to investigate names on maps,
their eyes will begin to pick up other interesting names that
reflect a geographical feature in the region. They may find
Wind Gap, Pennsylvania; Clearwater, Florida; Redlands,
California; Boulder, Colorado; Hot Springs, Arkansas; Sweet
Water, Alabama; Black River Falls, Wisconsin; and High
Hill, Missouri. Each student can concentrate on one or two
states and search for names that describe a geographical
feature. Each can sketch an outline map of his or her state
and print the place names on it. Allow time in a class program
for sharing of interesting names; this type of sharing of research findings makes a worthwhile discussion session.

Study of some areas of the United States will produce place
names that have Indian origins. Young people searching maps
may uncover Pawnee City and Tecumseh, Nebraska; Hia-
watha and Seneca, Kansas; Sioux City, Iowa; Tallahassee,
Florida; and Susquehanna River, Pennsylvania. A team of
students may undertake this type of investigation as an independent study project and compile their data on a map of
the United States.

Similar projects can focus on place names derived from
the names of famous, and not so famous, people. Some of the
most obvious examples to start students off are Washington,
D.C.; Jefferson City, Missouri; Lincoln, Nebraska; Bismark,

North Dakota; Cody, Wyoming; Edison, New Jersey; Houston, Texas; Boone, North Carolina; Van Buren, Arkansas; Sutter Creek, California; and Astoria, Oregon. Students may wish to begin close to home and identify streets, schools, and geographical features named after local celebrities. They can study local area maps to uncover other less well-known names.

This investigation may lead to consideration of names such as Johnston, Youngsboro, Allentown, Susanville, or Harrisburg. These names may trigger questions such as, "Why are towns, cities, roads, and so forth named after every Tom, Dick, or Harry? Why are there endings such as *ton, burg, boro,* and *ville* on the ends of place names?" To answer, students check the dictionary for the meaning of *burg, burgh,* and *borough* and relate *ton* to *town* and *ville* to *village*. They begin to think about who Tom, Dick, or Harry may have been.

Another project for individual or team investigation is a study of names having religious significance. A map of eastern Pennsylvania shows towns called Damascus, Bethlehem, Nazareth, and Quakertown. A map of the Southwest and South shows St. Augustine, St. Petersburg, St. Louis, San Antonio, San Bernardino, San Francisco, St. Mary, and St. Joseph. A map of Quebec will supply a student investigator with numbers of names that are derived from saints. Suggest to students they check the index of an atlas under *Santa, San,* and *St.* for hundreds of other place names derived from religious personages.

If you can obtain road maps of western sections of the United States, a student group can search for names that have particular significance in terms of the western migration and the gold rush and mining days, such as Last Chance, Dead Man's Gulch, Goodsprings, Glory Hole, End-of-the-Trail, and Lookout Point.

As teams of investigators share their data, generalizations about how place names originate will begin to surface. Students may arrive at the following conclusions:

Settlers to an area often brought place names from their homeland and attached them to the new home; place names can be a clue to the past history of an area.

Settlers named new towns and cities after themselves and famous people; suffixes such as *ton, town, burg, boro,* and *ville* were added to the name.

Settlers named places to reflect geographical features, especially features related to water and mineral deposits.

Settlers named places to reflect their religious beliefs.

TRACING OUR OWN NAMES   Students who have played with place names will find it easy to hypothesize possible origins of surnames. Start with surnames such as Armstrong, Ford, Johnson, Carpenter, and Scott. Ask students to suggest, "Why was the first Armstrong called *Armstrong?* Where did the first Mr. Ford live? From what country did Mr. Scott come? Who was Johnson's father? What kind of work did Mr. Carpenter do?" Working with a few examples that are rather obvious, students can propose a hypothesis similar to the following: "Originally some surnames designated characteristics of the person, i.e., strong arms; the kind of work performed by the person, i.e., carpentry; the place a person lived, i.e., near a ford; a person's father, i.e., son of John; and a person's country, i.e., Scotland."

Students can support their statements by searching for additional examples. One important clue to use in conducting a name search is that the following suffixes mean *son of:* -*ez* (Lopez—son of Lope), -*vich* (Ivanovich—son of Ivan), -*vicz* (Pietreivicz—son of Peter), -*ski* or *sky* (Adamski—son of Adam), -*sson* (Ericksson—son of Erick), -*s* (Hennings—son of Henning), -*sen* (Andersen—son of Ander), -*witz* (Jandrowitz—son of John) as do these prefixes: *Mac*- (MacGregor—son of Gregor), *Mc*- (McInnes—son of Innes), *Fitz*- (Fitzpatrick—son of Patrick), *O'*- (O'Malley—son of Malley), and

B- (Bowen—son of Owen). The prefix or suffix carried by patronymic names such as these is also a clue to the national origin of the name.

In conducting a surname search, students must stretch their imaginations to perceive existing relationships among words. For example, Miller, Taylor, Smith, Weaver, and Farmer are obvious examples of names that had their origins in occupational pursuits; less obvious are Sawyer (carpenter) and Naylor (nail maker). Davidson, Zavatsky, and Gomez clearly are patronymic names; less clear are Nixon, son of Nick, and Robson, son of Robert.

Students also must search into other languages as well as English. Some surnames come directly from other languages; i.e., Kovaks is a common name among Hungarian-Americans and means smith. Fleischer translates directly from the German as butcher, Steinberg from the German as stone mountain, and Castillo from the Spanish as castle. Parents who speak other languages may be able to contribute similar names whose origins student investigators can categorize. These words can be added to word charts as examples to support hypotheses being developed.

Two references that will be helpful to students are Helene and Charlton Laird's *The Tree of Language* (World Publishing, 1975) and H. L. Mencken's *The American Language* (Alfred A. Knopf, 1963). *The Tree of Language* is very readable and describes in a clear style how surnames developed; it contains a substantial listing of surnames derived from occupations, personal characteristics, places, nationality, and fathers' names. *The American Language* is considerably more technical. It explains the origins of surnames derived from the French, Dutch, German, Spanish, Slavic, and Scandinavian as well as many other languages. It details how surnames have changed and been changed, how American blacks acquired surnames, and lists the most common American names.

Use *The American Language* to help students trace the

origin of their own surnames. Investigators question parents about the area of the world from which their ancestors and name came and trace how the surname has changed or has become Americanized. They print surname cards showing their names as they exist today and indicating derivations. Finally they compile a class map of surnames on which surname cards are affixed to a world map at probable points of origin.

An interesting follow-up activity is an investigation of how family names are indicated in other countries. Students who have Spanish surnames such as Garcia and Rodriguez may want to investigate the way names are assigned in Spanish-speaking countries. Students with Chinese or Japanese surnames can investigate naming in China or Japan. Parents and friends are a ready source of information for such studies.

A natural next step is to study given names. Many dictionaries contain a list of common first names indicating the meanings and probable origins. Using this type of dictionary, youngsters can find the meaning of their own names. George will discover that his name means landowner, Barbara will find that her name means foreigner, Peter will discover that his name means rock, and Lucy will find that her name means light.

Upper-grade youngsters can complete a more systematic investigation. Researchers go to each class in the school and collect the names of all students. They then tally the names to discover which are the most common among boys and girls in their age group. In 1950 a survey of this type was conducted nationally by Eldson Smith, which indicated that the most popular name for girls was Mary, followed by Elizabeth, Barbara, Dorothy, Helen, Margaret, Ruth, and Virginia and that the most popular name for boys was John, followed by William, Charles, James, George, Robert, Thomas, and Henry. Student investigators can compare their results with those compiled in 1950 and propose reasons why some of the old-time favorites are no longer as popular as they were.

NAMING THE MONTHS AND DAYS   From a comprehensive dictionary you and your students can draw information about the origins of month names to build an understanding of the prevalence of Latin derivatives in the English language. Divide your class into twelve groups. Each group looks up a month name in several dictionaries to determine its origin. Student reporters share group findings, which can be compiled into a chart for posting:

Name	*Origin*
January	Janus, an ancient Italian diety regarded by the Romans as presiding over doors and gates and over beginnings and endings; commonly represented with two faces looking in opposite directions.
February	Februarius, the Roman festival of purification; celebrated February 15.
March	Mars, the ancient Roman god of war; Romans generally did not make war until March when the weather became milder.
April	Origin uncertain, perhaps from the Latin *apero* meaning second; in the early Roman calendar, April was the second month of the year. Or perhaps from *Aphro,* a pet name for Aphrodite, the Greek goddess of love; spring is the time of love.
May	Maia, the Roman goddess of increase; May is the time when everything begins to grow plentifully.
June	Junius, a gens or group of families in ancient Rome who claimed descent from a common ancestor and were united by a common name and common religious rites.
July	Julius Caesar, ruler of Rome, who was born in this month.

August   Augustus Caesar, first emperor of Rome.

September   From the Latin *septem,* meaning seven; September was
             originally the seventh month in the early Roman
             calendar.

October   From the Latin *octo,* meaning eight; October was orig-
             inally the eighth month in the early Roman calendar.

November   From the Latin *novem,* meaning nine; November was
             originally the ninth month in the early Roman calendar.

December   From the Latin *decem,* meaning ten; December was
             originally the tenth month in the early Roman calendar.

Young people analyze the derivations to see if they can perceive a feature common to all the derivations—that each has come from Latin. The reason can be traced to the establishment of the Julian calendar by Julius Caesar in 46 B.C. It consisted of 365 days (366 in leap years) divided into 12 units or months. Many related language groups adopting this calendar also adopted names similar to those the Romans assigned to the monthly units.

Month names are similar within the Indo-European language family. Upper-grade investigators can make that discovery by comparing names in German, French, Spanish, Italian, Portuguese, and Norwegian. For contrast, they can look at the month names in Japanese, as transliterated in the Roman alphabet.

Students who speak one of these languages as their first language can be responsible for writing down and then describing the similarities between the month names. If your class is totally English-speaking, students can divide into language groups, each of which can find and write down month names in a different language. A simple phrase book or pocket dictionary of the type carried by travelers will supply the information.

Compile the results of team or individual investigation on a comparative language chart:

English	German	French	Spanish
January	Januar	Janvier	Enero
February	Februar	Fevrier	Febrero
March	Marz	Mars	Marzo
April	April	Avril	Abril
May	Mai	Mai	Mayo
June	Juni	Juin	Junio
July	Juli	Juillet	Julio
August	August	Août	Agosto
September	September	Septembre	Septiembre
October	Oktober	Octobre	Octobre
November	November	Novembre	Noviembre
December	Dezember	Decembre	Diciembre

Norwegian	Japanese	Italian
Januar	ichigatsu	gennaio
Februar	ai-gatsu	febbraio
Mars	sangatsu	marzo
April	shigatsu	aprile
Mai	gogatsu	maggio
Juni	rokugatsu	giugno
Juli	schichigatsu	luglio
August	hachigatsu	agosto
September	kugatsu	settembre
Oktober	jugatsu	ottobre
November	juichi-gatsu	novembre
Desember	ju-ni-gatsu	dicembre

From this activity language researchers can hypothesize that when a group of people borrows an idea from another language group, it often borrows the names associated with the idea as well and that a group borrowing names from another group often changes them to utilize sounds more common in its own language.

For contrast, upper-grade investigators can study the names of days of the week. Again a dictionary will supply researchers with the following type of information:

Day Name	Origin
Sunday	From the Latin *dies solis,* sun's day; in Old English called *sunnandaeg.*
Monday	From the Latin *lunae dies,* moon's day; in Old English called *monandaeg.*
Tuesday	From the Old English *Tiwesdaeg,* Tiw's day; Tiw was an Anglo-Saxon god of war, son of Woden.
Wednesday	From the Old English *Wodnesdaeg,* Woden's day; Woden was the most important Anglo-Saxon god and was the father of Tiw.
Thursday	From the Old English *Thunresdaeg,* Thunor's day; Thunor was the Anglo-Saxon god of thunder and a son of Woden.
Friday	From the Old English *Frigedaeg,* Frig's day; Frig was an Anglo-Saxon goddess and the wife of Woden.
Saturday	From the Latin *Saturni dies,* Saturn's day; in Old English called *Saeternesdaeg;* Saturn was the Roman god of Agriculture.

Ask young people who have investigated these origins to think about why only three days of the week are named from the Latin sources and the other four named for Anglo-Saxon gods. In contrast, all the month names were borrowed from the Latin. Young people may hypothesize that the days of the week were a more significant part of living patterns and, as a result, people developed their own terms based upon their own religious beliefs. On the other hand, the structure of the calendar was borrowed almost directly from the Julian calendar and its words were absorbed in the process.

Students can test their hypotheses by comparing day names in related languages. They can predict that in French, Italian, and Spanish the days named in English after the Anglo-Saxon gods will differ considerably. They may predict that some of those same Anglo-Saxon words may pop up in German, since the Old Germans worshiped some of the same gods as did the Old English. A comparison chart of day names is given below:

English	*French*	*Spanish*	*Italian*	*German*
Sunday	dimanche	domingo	domenica	Sontag
Monday	lundi	lunes	lunedi	Montag
Tuesday	mardi	martes	martedi	Dienstag
Wednesday	mercredi	miercoles	mercoledi	Mittwoch
Thursday	jeudi	jueves	giovedi	Donnerstag
Friday	vendredi	viernes	venerdi	Freitag
Saturday	samedi	sabado	sabato	Samstag

Language comparison activities of the type just discussed are particularly profitable in bilingual classrooms. Young people do not need to go to foreign-language dictionaries to uncover words to compare, for all students can write down the same words in their own languages. Composite charts are drawn up, i.e., charts of English and Spanish words for the same events or objects, so comparisons of word forms can easily be made.

INTERPRETING LANGUAGE CHANGES OF THE PAST

ANALYZING OUR LANGUAGE FAMILY Comparison activities are a way for upper-grade elementary students to discover relationships among the Indo-European language family and to identify "close" and "distant relations" of English.

To establish the concept of a family of related languages, start with the notion of a family tree. Students can diagram their own family trees. In situations where this might prove painful to children whose families have experienced dislocations, use several children and their families as examples with which all students work.

Students fill in the names of relatives on a chart similar to the accompanying one. They must modify it depending on the number of brothers, sisters, cousins, aunts, and uncles in their families. Follow up with discussion triggered by questions such as, "Who are your closest relatives? Why do we say that one is related to people one calls aunt and uncle? How are you related to your cousins? Are you more closely related to your father and mother or to your uncles and aunts? Are you more closely related to your cousins or to brothers and sisters? Have any of your cousins married and had children? If so, what are these cousins called? Are people more closely related to their cousins or their second cousins? Who are your parents' parents? If you have brothers and sisters, in what way do you resemble them? Do you more closely resemble your brothers and sisters or your cousins?"

Suggest that student investigators compare their family-tree charts to those of other members of the class. Are some families larger than others? Do some families have more members?

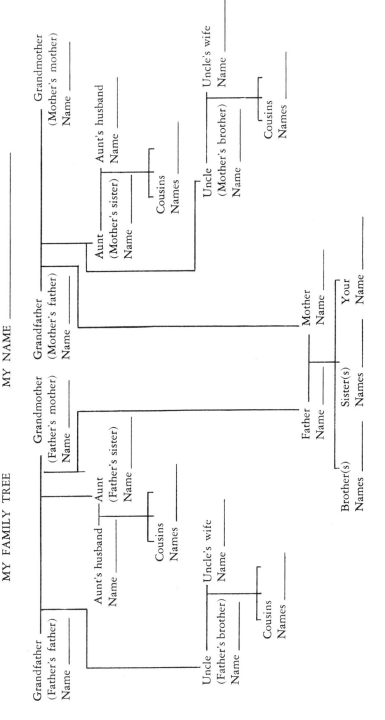

MY FAMILY TREE   MY NAME ———

Grandfather
(Father's father)
Name ———

Grandmother
(Father's mother)
Name ———

Grandfather
(Mother's father)
Name ———

Grandmother
(Mother's mother)
Name ———

Uncle
(Father's brother)
Name ———

Uncle's wife
Name ———

Cousins
Names ———

Aunt's husband
Name ———

Aunt
(Father's sister)
Name ———

Cousins
Names ———

Aunt
(Mother's sister)
Name ———

Aunt's husband
Name ———

Cousins
Names ———

Uncle
(Mother's brother)
Name ———

Uncle's wife
Name ———

Cousins
Names ———

Father
Name ———

Mother
Name ———

Brother(s)
Names ———

Sister(s)
Names ———

Your
Name ———

DIRECTIONS: Fill in the names of your brothers, sisters, father, mother, grandparents, uncles, aunts, and cousins.

Apply students' growing understanding of relationships and resemblances among members of a family to an interpretation of words in languages belonging to the Indo-European family and those belonging to other language families. Use these data as a basis for a linguistic comparison activity. Ask students to study the words to identify:

Words that resemble one another in most of the languages shown, i.e., tobacco;

A language or languages that only rarely resemble any of the other languages, i.e., Japanese, Finnish;

Groups of languages that very often have words that resemble one another, i.e., English, Dutch, and German and Latin, French, Spanish, and Italian;

Languages that sometimes have words that resemble one another, i.e., French and English.

Once students have identified words or languages that fall into categories, help them attach labels. Languages that bear some resemblances to one another are relatives or members of the same language family; they trace their ancestry back to a common beginning. Languages that share numerous resemblances are close relatives or members of the same group within a language family; they share a more recent common ancestor. Languages that bear almost no resemblances belong to different language families.

If you have bilingual children in your class, use their skills to develop your own word or phrase comparison charts. Give an English word or phrase and ask students with bilingual abilities to give the comparable word or phrase in their own first language. For example, a youngster who speaks German may supply the equivalent of "Good morning, father," in German *Guten Morgen, Vater*. A speaker of Spanish may supply *Buenos días, Padre*. Use the German and Spanish equivalents of the phrase to begin a language comparison chart.

COMPARISON OF WORDS IN DIFFERENT LANGUAGES

English	Dutch	German	Swedish	Danish	Norwegian	Finnish	Latin	French	Spanish	Italian	Japanese
winter	winter	Winter	vinter	vinter	vinter	talvi	hiems	hiver	invierno	inverno	fuyú
mother	moeder	Mutter	moder	moder	mor	äiti	mater	mère	madre	madre	okāsan
bread	brood	Brot	bröd	brød	brød	leipä	panis	pain	pan	pane	pan
egg	ei	Ei	ägg	æg	egg	muna	ovum	oeuf	huevo	uovo	tamágo
apple	appel	Apfel	äpple	æble	eple	omena	malum	pomme	manzana	mela	ringó
six	zes	sechs	sex	seks	seks	kuusi	sex	six	seis	sei	muttsú
God	God	Gott	Gud	Gud	Gud	Jumala	Deus	Dieu	Dios	Dio	Kámi
boat	boot	Boot	båt	båd	båt	vene	linter	bateau	barca or bote	battello / barca	bôto
cow	koe	Kuh	ko	ko	ku	lehmä	vacca	vache	vaca	vacca	me-ushí
little	klein	klein	liten	lille	liten	pieni	parvus	petit	pequeño	piccolo	chiisái
milk	melk	Milch	mjölk	mælk	melk	maito	lac	lait	leche	latte	gyūnyū
tobacco	tabak	Tabak	tobak	tobak	tobakk	tupakka	—	tabac	tabaco	tabacco	tabakó
fish	vis	Fisch	fisk	fisk	fisk	kala	piscis	poisson	pez or pescado	pesce	sakaná
two	twee	zwei	två	to	to	kaksi	duo	deux	dos	due	fütatsú
hen	hen	Henne	höna	høne	høne	kana	gallina	poule	gallina	gallina	mendorí
air	lucht	Luft	luft	luft	luft	ilma	aer	air	aire	aria	kūki
coffee	koffie	Kaffee	kaffe	kaffe	kaffe	kahvi	—	café	café	caffè	kōhi
flower	bloem	Blume	blomma	blomst	blomster	kukka	flos	fleur	flor	fiore	haná

Excellent aids to help students compile language comparison charts are the pocket conversion dictionaries and phrase books used by travelers to foreign countries. Conversion dictionaries usually give an English word and its equivalent in the other language and are available for almost every language you may wish to handle. Phrase books supply common expressions first in English, then in the other language, expressions such as "Hello," "Good morning," "What time is it?" Ask students to check at home to see if they have one or more of these references or check your local library. With the aid of phrase books, students can expand their Good Morning, Father chart to include:

> God morgon, Fader. (Swedish)
> God morgen, Far. (Norwegian)
> Guten Morgen, Vater. (German)
> Goeden morgan, Vader. (Dutch)
> Buenos dias, Padre. (Spanish)
> Bonjour, Père. (French)
> Buon giorno, Padre. (Italian)
> Dziendobry, Tatus. (Polish)

They can use the chart to hypothesize relationships among the languages included.

If you can locate a number of foreign-language dictionaries, you can extend this activity. Distribute the dictionaries and appoint several students who do not hold dictionaries as scribes. Call out specific words such as *husband, summer, sister, honey, day, friend, chocolates, television, dog,* or *night* for dictionary holders to look up. In columns labeled by language, recorders list the foreign-language equivalents of the English term, producing a chart that gradually begins to resemble the one given. Again students analyze their charts to identify languages in which some words bear a strong resemblance to one another and others in which there is almost no resemblance.

Based on their investigations, budding linguists can group related languages schematically. They can use a branch-like configuration and plot specific words given on the column chart or noted on their own language comparison charts. The schema may look something like the branches on which the word *mother* has been plotted. Incidentally, you may find it helpful to reproduce this chart, deleting the word *mother* and its equivalent in the other languages. Students can add specific words to mimeographed copies of the chart as they develop an understanding of two major groups within the Indo-European family—Germanic and Italic.

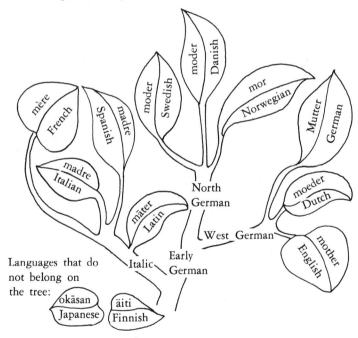

After working with family trees and similar configurations using specific words, young people are probably ready to interpret a full-grown language tree depicting relationships within the Indo-European language family. Reproduce the following schema and place a stack in a learning station pouch. Make multiple copies also of the task-card instructions and add them to the center. Individually or in groups students go to the center to develop relationships based on analysis of the tree.

TASK: To figure out relationships within the Indo-European language family.

DIRECTIONS: First, examine the family language tree and complete the coloring activity described below. Then answer the questions by writing directly on this sheet.

ACTIVITY: On your copy of the Indo-European family tree, color the branch representing the Celtic group blue, the branch representing the Italic group brown, the branch representing the Germanic group green, the branch representing the Hellenic group yellow, the branch representing the Albanian group black, the branch representing the Indo-Iranian group red, the branch representing the Balto-Slavic orange, and the branch representing the Armenian group purple. You may like to color sub-branches of each language group shades of these colors.

QUESTIONS:

1. What language is a really close relative of:

English _____ Danish _____ Polish _____

Ukranian _____ Bengali _____ French _____

Welsh _____ Lithuanian _____ Bulgarian _____

2. What language was the parent of:

Irish _____ White Russian _____ Hindustani _____

Latin _____ Spanish _____ Lettish _____

3. What are the two major subdivisions of the Indo-European family?

_____   _____

4. What are the two major subdivisions of the Germanic group?

_____   _____

5. What are the two major subdivisions of the Indo-Iranian group?

_____   _____

6. What are the two major subdivisions of the Balto-Slavic group?

_____   _____

7. Thinking question: How do the languages on the outer fringes of the tree generally differ from those closer to the main trunk?

_____   _____

THE FAMILY OF INDO-EUROPEAN LANGUAGES

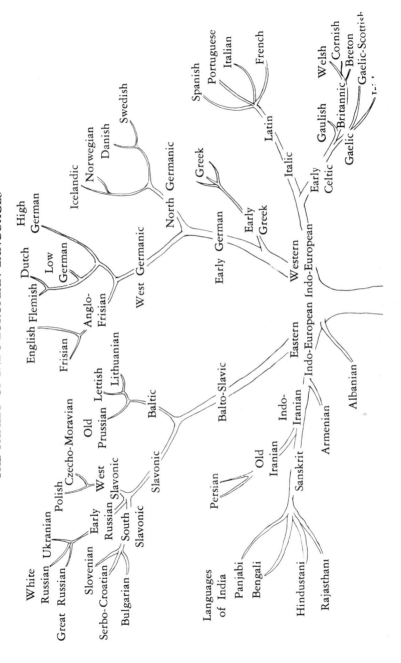

PLOTTING LANGUAGE MIGRATIONS   A map plotting activity can help young people perceive that often languages in the same group are spoken in areas geographically adjacent to one another—with exceptions, of course.

In preparation, ask one student to copy the following charts onto a large piece of heavy charting paper so that the information is visible to all linguistic geographers working on the project, or duplicate copies of the charts for each student. Also distribute an outline map of Europe and western Asia to groups of students who will work together.

Students mark in different colors the areas where single language groups are spoken today. Most of the British Isles, most of Scandinavia, Germany, and the Netherlands can be colored green to show that a Germanic language is spoken there today; portions of Wales, Brittany, and the west coasts of Ireland and Scotland are colored blue to indicate Celtic language areas. Students develop their maps by referring to the charts and by checking standard maps to locate countries noted on the charts.

Suggest that the young people examine their maps to see if they can generalize about where languages in a related group often are spoken. A quick glance can produce the easy generalization that related languages are spoken in adjacent areas. More involved study can develop the understanding that languages are not always confined to the borders of a single country and that political borders change faster than language boundaries.

INDO-EUROPEAN LANGUAGE FAMILY

Family Group	Languages Within the Group and Countries Where Spoken Today
Indo-Iranian (color: red)	Persian (Iran); Hindustani, Bengali, Rajasthani (India)
Hellenic (color: yellow)	Greek (Greece)

Italic (color: brown)	Italian (Italy, southern Switzerland); French (France, Belgium, western Switzerland); Spanish (Spain); Portuguese (Portugal); Romanian (Romania)
Celtic (color: blue)	Welsh (Wales); Breton (Brittany, France); Gaelic (northern Scotland), Irish (west coast of Ireland)
Balto-Slavic (color: orange)	Lettish (Latvia, now Russia); Lithuanian (Lithuania, now Russia); Great Russian (Russia); White Russian (Russia); Ukranian (Russia); Polish (Poland); Czecho-Moravian (Czechoslovakia); Bulgarian (Bulgaria); Slovenian and Serbo-Croatian (Yugoslavia)
Albanian (color: black)	Albanian (Albania)
Armenian (color: purple)	Armenian (Armenia)
Germanic (color: green)	German (Germany, northern Switzerland, Austria), Danish (Denmark), Swedish (southern and central Sweden), Norwegian (Norway), Dutch (Netherlands), Icelandic (Iceland), Flemish (Belgium and Netherlands), Frisian (islands off Netherlands), English (British Islands)

URAL-ALTAIC
FAMILY

Finno-Ugrian	Finnish (southern and central Finland), Lappish (northern Finland and Sweden), Livonian (Estonia, now Russia), Magyar or Hungarian (Hungary)
Samoyedic	Samoyedic (USSR, north of the Arctic Circle)
Turkish-Tataric	Turkish and lesser tongues (Turkey); Tataric (Crimea)
Mongolian	Kalmuckian (area between Black and Caspian seas)

SEMITIC

Arabic	Arabic (northern Africa to Baghdad)
Maltese	Maltese (island of Malta, below Sicily)
Syrian	Syrian (eastern coast of the Mediterranean)

BASQUE

Basque	Basque (France and Spain on the border, south of the Bay of Biscay)

You can expand this activity by having students plot approximate locations where other language families are found, i.e., the Ural-Altaic, the Semitic, and the Basque, which has only one group comprised of one family.

A reference such as *Goode's School Atlas* (Rand McNally), which includes a detailed language map of Europe, western Asia, and northern Africa, is helpful in putting together language maps. Such a detailed map can be projected against a large bulletin board with an opaque projector. The outline can be traced on the board surface, and language families and groups labeled to produce a large map that can be used to hypothesize language beginnings.

To this map or small outline maps prepared by students and based on the information given in the accompanying charts, add arrows to show the migration paths of the ancient tribes who spoke the language that was the parent tongue of all the groups in the Indo-European language family. Start by explaining that all Indo-European languages have been traced back to a common linguistic ancestor, a tongue spoken by nomadic tribes living some 4,500 years ago somewhere in eastern Europe or western Asia. About 2500 B.C. these speakers of what is called Proto-Indo-European began to expand in numbers, to move out from where they were living, and to migrate into distant regions of Europe and Asia. What caused these tribes to migrate has never been fully resolved, but language scholars have proposed a number of hypotheses.

Your students may be able to hypothesize their own explanations, such as there was not enough food for the growing population; there was a climate change that brought drought, flooding, or extreme cold; there were numbers of tribal leaders each of whom wanted to be boss and each led a group of followers from the area, and other stronger tribes came into the area, pushing out the speakers of Proto-Indo-European.

Students place a large circle on their maps somewhere in western Europe to represent an approximate location of this parent language. They draw arrows out from this center to show the hypothesized paths of the migrant groups into Europe and Asia, or they overlay their maps with curved arrows cut from colored paper to represent the movement of a nomadic tribe from which one of the eight Indo-European language groups developed. For example, the arrow swinging down across Persia into India represents the migration of the Indo-Iranian group, while a second slopes down toward Greece to indicate the movement of Indo-European speakers into that area. The map given indicates the general directions of arrows for each of the groups. Keep this map in mind as you guide young people in constructing their own maps.

MIGRATIONS: From parent language—Proto-Indo-European

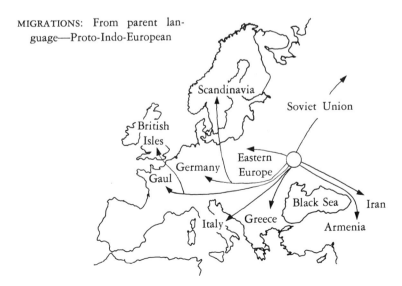

TRACING THE HISTORY OF AMERICAN ENGLISH
Plotting on a time line the major historical events that have
influenced the development of American English is a way to
summarize visually the history of the language used in the
United States.

Older students can gather data to present on a time line
from a number of excellent references that describe language
developments. James Ludovici's *Origins of Language* (Putnam,
1965) contains a chapter that traces the history of English
from the fifth-century invasion of England by the Germanic
tribes, the Angles, the Saxons, and Jutes, through the invasions
of England by the Vikings in the ninth century and by the
Normans in the eleventh century. Helene and Charlton Laird's
The Tree of Language (World Publishing, 1957) describes
the Anglo-Saxon, the Viking, the French, and the Latin contributions as well as the contributions of the North American
Indians, the Chinese, the Romance languages, and many more.
Both books are very readable by upper-elementary students.
More detailed but still easy to understand is Paul Robert's
Understanding English (Harper & Row, 1958), which also
describes events that have had a major influence on the
English language.

Based on sources such as these, you and your students can
compile a time line plotting historical events and their influence on the changing English language. A two-column time
line is perhaps the easiest to work with, one column listing
historical events, the other language happenings and especially
sources from which words were borrowed during the period.
An example of a time line containing the most important
data is given; use it as a guide for building a classroom time
line.

A striking time line can be put together by stretching a wire
or cord across the classroom and suspending from it cards
marked with dates, events, and words. Students first prepare
time-interval cards, i.e., A.D. 400, A.D. 600, A.D. 800, and so

A TIME LINE OF IMPORTANT LINGUISTIC EVENTS
IN THE HISTORY OF ENGLISH

Old English		Angles, Saxons, and Jutes wandered in northern Europe.	Ancient English borrowed words from Latin.
	A.D. 449	Angles, Saxons, and Jutes moved into Britain, pushing the Celts into Wales and portions of Ireland and Scotland.	English borrowed words from Celtic.
	A.D. 597	Anglo-Saxons were converted to Christianity by Latin-speaking missionaries and learned the Latin alphabet.	English borrowed words from Latin.
	A.D. 866	Anglo-Saxons opposed the invading Vikings from the North.	English borrowed words from Vikings.
Middle English	1066	Normans (French) invaded, conquered, ruled Britain, and gradually became English.	English borrowed words from Old French.
		English people began to make contact with peoples speaking other languages.	English began to borrow words from a multitude of languages.
	1500	English people rediscovered the classical languages, Latin and Greek.	English borrowed words from Latin and Greek.
		English people brought their language to North America (as well as to India, Australia, New Zealand, South Africa).	English borrowed heavily from other languages: American Indian, Dutch, German, French, Portuguese, Spanish, Japanese, Chinese, Hebrew, Malay, and so forth.
Modern English	1700		

forth, and suspend them at equal distances across the wire. Then they prepare cards of a different color on which they note key events, add these cards to the wire at the appropriate locations, make paper rings to mark off the divisions between Old and Middle English and between Middle and Modern English, and slip the rings onto the wire time line. Finally they prepare cards in another color on which they write sources of borrowed words such as Celtic or Viking and add these to the line. They may also attach to each source card slips of paper bearing the names of actual words that entered the language from this source. Construction of the time line can become an extended class project in which young people search books for information to include and systematically add that data to their growing time line.

Simultaneously you may wish to involve the class in an etymological study of specific words. Students can check word origins as detailed in the entries of dictionaries such as the *Random House College Dictionary*. Students will need to know how to translate the abbreviations employed by the particular dictionary they are using. They can relate the abbreviations to the concepts they are working with as they construct their time lines. *OE* means that the word was in use during the Old English period, *ME* means that the word was in use during the Middle English period, *t* stands for taken from, which simply means borrowed from, *m* stands for modified, which means that the word has changed somewhat since it began to be used, *der* means derived from, *c* stands for cognate, a word in another language that comes from the same source, and *g* means going back to.

With this background information, young language investigators can interpret the entry for a word such as *defend:* "ME defende(n), t. OF: m. defendre, g. L dēfendere, ward off." This entry reveals that defend has been in the English language since Middle English times and was probably borrowed from the Old French at the time of the Norman conquest. The

French word of that day was *defendre,* which goes back to the Latin word *dēfendre,* meaning to ward off. Investigators who have traced the origin of defend may wish to prepare a "defend" word card to hang on the time line.

Some fascinating words to trace in this way are coffee (borrowed from the Turkish *quahveh,* which in turn was borrowed from the Arabic *qahwa),* tea (borrowed from the Chinese *t'e),* bamboo (borrowed from the Dutch *bamboes,* which in turn was borrowed from the Malay *bambu),* or banana (borrowed from a Portuguese word, which in turn was borrowed from an African word from the Congo district). Other interesting words to trace are those that appear to be the original language spoken by the Anglo-Saxons upon their arrival in England, words such as eat, ox, lamb, boat, and thunder; these are called native words.

Students can summarize information about the origin and development of particular words on word trees such as the following:

SALAD
▲
SALADE (in Middle English)
↑ borrowed from
SALADE (Old French)
↑ borrowed from
SALADA (Old Provencal)
↑ derived from
SALAR (meaning *to salt*)
↑ derived from
SAL (Latin, meaning salt)

NOON
▲
NONE (in Middle English)

↑
NON (in Old English)
↑ taken from
NONA (Latin, meaning ninth
    hour)

These charts make explicit how words have changed and how many sources have been tapped in building the language that today has become English.

A few adventuresome language investigators may wish to explore the *Oxford English Dictionary* to search out even more detailed information about the origin of chosen words.

Most dictionaries tell the language(s) from which a word has been borrowed, but the *Oxford English Dictionary* goes further and gives a multitude of cognates and the dates of the first known use of the word in written English. Just looking at the twelve volumes will make an investigator realize how extensively the English language has been studied.

IDENTIFYING THE ORIGINS OF WORDS   Here is an activity through which upper-grade students who have learned to interpret the etymologies found in a college-level dictionary can apply their newly developed skills. They now attempt to identify the common origin of a group of related words.

In preparation, cut a large circle from a piece of colored oak tag and divide it into seven pie-shaped pieces. In each print a group of related words brought into modern English from the American Indian, Spanish, Italian, French, Dutch, German, or African languages. Print a task card with directions and mount it at the hub of the circle:

TASK: To use dictionary etymology entries to trace the origin of English words borrowed in modern times.

DIRECTIONS: Take a piece of paper from the paper pouch.

Select a group of words from the piece of pie in which there are the fewest number of check marks. Look up these words in the dictionary we use to trace etymologies.

Write each word in the group on your paper and next to it write its origin.

Then answer the following questions on your paper.

1. From what language or languages are these words borrowed?
2. Can you think of other words that are borrowed from the same source? If so, write them on your paper. Check them in the dictionary.
3. What kinds of words tend to be borrowed from this source? Why did English speakers find it necessary to borrow these kinds of words?

When you have tried to answer all the questions, put your name on your paper and place it in Pouch 2. Then put a check mark in the pie piece you have just completed.

Your pie-shaped tabletop learning station will look like this:

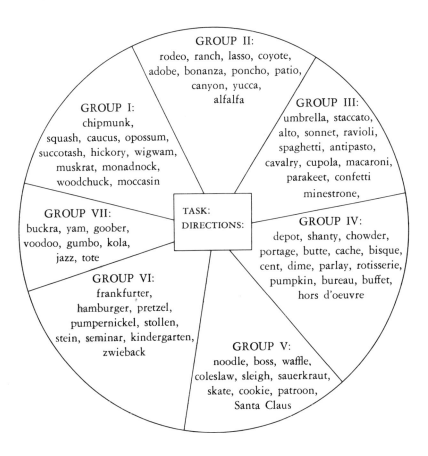

GROUP II:
rodeo, ranch, lasso, coyote, adobe, bonanza, poncho, patio, canyon, yucca, alfalfa

GROUP I:
chipmunk, squash, caucus, opossum, succotash, hickory, wigwam, muskrat, monadnock, woodchuck, moccasin

GROUP III:
umbrella, staccato, alto, sonnet, ravioli, spaghetti, antipasto, cavalry, cupola, macaroni, parakeet, confetti minestrone,

GROUP VII:
buckra, yam, goober, voodoo, gumbo, kola, jazz, tote

TASK: DIRECTIONS:

GROUP IV:
depot, shanty, chowder, portage, butte, cache, bisque, cent, dime, parlay, rotisserie, pumpkin, bureau, buffet, hors d'oeuvre

GROUP VI:
frankfurter, hamburger, pretzel, pumpernickel, stollen, stein, seminar, kindergarten, zwieback

GROUP V:
noodle, boss, waffle, coleslaw, sleigh, sauerkraut, skate, cookie, patroon, Santa Claus

Using a similar direction task card, develop a second table-top learning station that focuses on words taken from Arabic, Persian, Japanese, and Chinese:

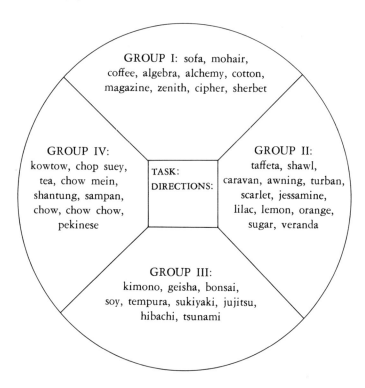

GROUP I: sofa, mohair, coffee, algebra, alchemy, cotton, magazine, zenith, cipher, sherbet

GROUP IV: kowtow, chop suey, tea, chow mein, shantung, sampan, chow, chow chow, pekinese

TASK: DIRECTIONS:

GROUP II: taffeta, shawl, caravan, awning, turban, scarlet, jessamine, lilac, lemon, orange, sugar, veranda

GROUP III: kimono, geisha, bonsai, soy, tempura, sukiyaki, jujitsu, hibachi, tsunami

Again students work with a dictionary that gives etymologies of words. This time, however, you may wish to make the activity self-correctional. On the reverse side of the card, coinciding with the word groups on the front, write the languages of origin and categories of words borrowed. Leave room for student researchers to add other words taken from these sources. Include a Sign Here sheet on which students sign their names to indicate they have completed the task.

Reverse side of circle chart:

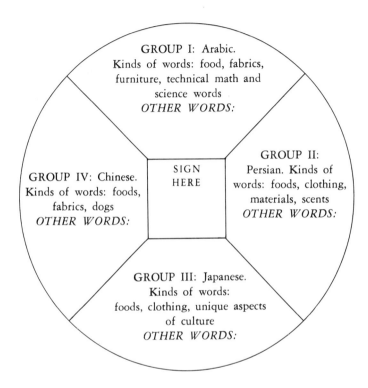

You may wish to make other tabletop learning centers containing specific words for students to trace. Print individual words around the circumference of the circle chart cut from heavy grade colored oak tag. Then prepare narrow slips of paper on which you (or a student assistant) print the originating language for each of the words selected. For example, if the word *fjord* is included on your chart, prepare a slip marked From Norwegian. Tape these slim slips to a spring-type clothespin.

Steps on a direction card read:

1. Check the origin of each word shown on the circumference of the circle by referring to the etymological entry in the dictionary on the table.

2. In the envelope, you will find clothespins bearing languages from which English words have been borrowed. Locate a pin with the language from which a word on the circumference has been borrowed.

3. Clip the pin onto the circle chart next to the word to which the language is related.

4. When you have paired all the clips with all the words, turn over the circle and check your answers against the answers shown there.

5. Then sign your name on the Sign Here sheet.

You will probably find it impractical to include more than ten words on the circumference of the chart and, of course, there should be no more than ten language pins in the envelope. The activity is easier for young people to complete if you select words of very diverse origins. The chart titled Words to Trace provides more than thirty-five words all borrowed from different languages of the world. From it you can make several clothespin-circle task cards. As students work with these cards, they will begin to appreciate the variety of language sources from which English has developed.

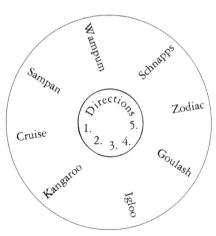

WORDS TO TRACE

fjord	from Norwegian	kauri	from Maori
shampoo	from Hindustani	wampum	from Algonquian
zodiac	from Greek		Indian
turban	from Persian	zombi	from West African
molasses	from Portuguese	zebra	from Congolese
lei	from Hawaiian	goulash	from Hungarian
berserk	from Icelandic	khan	from Turkish
balloon	from Italian	koodoo	from Hottentot
smorgasbord	from Swedish	batik	from Javanese
kibosh	from Yiddish	curry	from Tamil
parka	from Russian	schnapps	from German
sarong	from Malay	tomato	from Mexican
dandelion	from French		through Spanish
cruise	from Dutch	banana	from Congolese
cube	from Latin		through
bother	origin unknown		Portuguese
armadillo	from Spanish	monsoon	from Arabic
shamrock	from Irish		through Dutch
sauna	from Finnish	bayou	from Choctaw
sampan	from Chinese		through
kangaroo	from native		Louisiana
	Australian		French
kava	from Polynesian	potato	from Haitian
igloo	from Eskimo		through Spanish
toboggan	from French	babka	from Polish
	Canadian		

Most of the words on these task cards are relatively recent additions to the English language and are usually the easiest to trace because they have generally been borrowed from a language still spoken today or from a language that has borrowed it from another. If you are working with sophisticated young people, you may be interested in guiding them into an investigation of words borrowed during earlier periods of linguistic history. Prepare six slips of yellow paper, each containing one of the following phrases: Borrowed from Latin before the Anglo-Saxon migration to Britain, Borrowed from early Celtic, Borrowed from the Vikings, Borrowed from the

Latin after Anglo-Saxon conversion to Christianity, Borrowed from the Norman French, or Borrowed from Latin during the English Renaissance. Then prepare a hexagonally-shaped task card cut from colored oak tag. Along the edges write six words selected from the list below, one from each of the major borrowings, and at the hub mount these directions:

TASK: To identify the origins of words that have been in the English language a long time.

DIRECTIONS:

1. Check the origin of each of the words written on the edge of the chart by referring to the etymological entry for the word in the dictionary on the table.

2. Using the paper clips on the table, clip one of the slips of yellow paper bearing an origin label to each of the words on the edge. When you finish, each clip should be next to the word it describes.

3. Turn over the chart and check your answers against the answer sheet taped to the back. Sign your name to indicate that you have completed the task.

Be sure to include only one word from each category on the chart at any one time. Of course, you can change the words periodically so that a student investigator can trace down numbers of words and begin to appreciate our debt to each of these English-language sources. Of course, too, students may uncover words of similar origins to include on charts they themselves make.

MORE WORDS TO TRACE

Category I: Early Latin		*Category II: Celtic*	
kettle	cheap	cradle	bard
wine	monument	breeches	glen
cheese	butter	crag	bald
church	bishop	-don as in London	

Category III: Latin
After Conversion

angel	priest
martyr	purple
school	radish
oyster	plant

Category IV: Viking

sky	law
outlaw	egg
leg	ugly
scowl	they

Category V: Norman

parliament	tax
majesty	government
crucifix	beef
cream	music
poet	story
surgeon	romance
dance	conversation
jelly	incense

Category VI: Latin
During the Renaissance

pedestrian	paragraph
anatomy	benefit
bonus	inspire

BORROWING IN REVERSE   Word borrowing has not been a one-way street. The English language has helped itself quite lavishly to words from other languages, but these languages, in turn, have borrowed from English. *Radio, television, telephone,* and *baseball* are words that have moved from English into many other languages. Perhaps students will be able to hypothesize why words such as these have been adopted so rapidly throughout the world.

If some students are bilingual, they may be able to supply other specific examples of words that their first language has borrowed from English. The most probable words are those that specify things or processes developed in the United States. Even names for commercial products, i.e., *Coke, Kleenex,* and *Pepsi,* are names known to speakers of different languages all over the world.

Suggest to bilingual students that they build map charts showing the outlines of the nation where their first language is spoken and that of the United States. On the United States map, they print words borrowed by English from their first language; on the map of the other nation, they print words their first language has borrowed from English. Adding arrows to and from both maps will emphasize the cross-borrowing.

Bilingual students may also be able to add a spark to your class's language study by indicating areas where their first language and English are different rather than similar. One area to play with is imitative words that mimic the sound associated with a happennng, i.e., *whoose, buzz,* and *zing.* According to Nino LoBello in Not with a BANG but a TOCK-TOCK," (*The New York Times Book Review,* March 30, 1975), the words used in different languages to imitate the same sound are completely different. She asks, "How explain that in Finland an explosion goes POOF, whereas the same explosion in Denmark comes out BAR-ROOM? How explain that in France a cat purrs RON-RON, whereas the same cat in Germany purrs SCHNURR?" The answer, of course, has to do with the sounds important in a particular language. Bilingual students may be able to give an answer and produce other examples. Ask them to think about the sound used in their first language to mimic a cow, a duck, or a rooster. Ask them for the equivalent of squeak, buzz, whiz, or bang in their first language. They can prepare language comparison charts of imitative words in two or even more languages.

WORKING WITH TODAY'S LANGUAGE CHANGES

COINING WORDS   Give students a "quiz" to introduce them to the idea that words and word meanings are still changing today. Ask them to divide a piece of 8½ x 11 inch drawing paper into six equal-sized blocks. In each block they complete one of the following tasks, which you can dictate or prepare in written form:

1. Draw a picture of a snowmobile.	2. Draw a picture of a compact.	3. Draw a picture of a cassette tape recorder.
4. Draw a picture of a trash compactor.	5. Draw a picture showing what a rinse or an Afro is.	6. Write your ZIP code.

When all have completed the "quiz," schedule a class talk-time where students describe the meanings their pictures communicate. As they show their pictures and talk about them, have one student check each word in a dictionary—not just any dictionary but one that is at least twenty-five years old. You should be able to find a dictionary published in the 1950s from a teacher who went through college then. The checker will find that words such as ZIP code, snowmobile and Afro are not in that dictionary, that words such as rinse are in that dictionary but that their common meaning today (a hair coloring) is not given, or that words such as compact are included but the most common meaning today (small car) is given only incidental coverage. Ask youngsters to think about why such words as snowmobile and cassette are not in this dictionary. Then ask them to think about when and why the words most likely came into usage.

Through talking about these specific words, students may be able to generalize that new words are continually being incorporated into the language, that old words may acquire new meanings, and that changes occur as new products, ideas, and even organizations appear and as people·need words to talk about them.

Students can test their generalizations by thinking of other innovations that have been introduced in their own lifetimes. Words associated with these can be checked out in the older dictionary and then in a more recent edition. Pursuing their investigation in slightly more depth, students can interview parents and grandparents, asking for examples of words that were introduced during their lifetimes, have changed meaning, or have disappeared from common usage. One good example to suggest is the substitution of the word refrigerator for ice box as technology changed the design of the old box. Another example is the more recent substitution of record player for the older word phonograph and the even more recent substitution of the words stereo or hi-fi.

A natural next step is for students to investigate how new words develop. An easy beginning is to consider the manner in which new words are made by combining existing words. Start with the word snowmobile and ask, "Why do you think the first snowmobiles were called this name?" Move on to such familiar compound words and expressions as surfboard, playground, parkway, sidewalk, doghouse, doorbell, notebook, briefcase, hatbox, houseboat, bathroom, and high rise, and ask students to consider how some of these words originated. Encourage them to think of other door words: doorknob, doorjamb, doorman; other house words: housekeeper, householder, housemaid; other dog words: dog-eared, dogwood, dogtrot. Print the words on a large piece of either white or colored oak tag. During independent study times students can add to the collage other words that have formed in the same way.

Students can make similar visuals of words formed by adding suffixes and prefixes to existing words. An interesting prefix to start with is *mini-,* which is beginning to be attached almost indiscriminately to other words, i.e., mini-skirts, mini-computers, mini-calculators, and mini-bikes. Start students thinking by giving them one mini-word such as mini-computer. On a mini-card (just half of a small index card) students print other mini-words they have actually heard and then go on to coin their own mini-words that could conceivably come into usage. They print these words in a different colored ink to differentiate between real and hypothetical ones.

Similar word building units (or bound morphemes) for students to play with include *maxi-, multi-, super-, uni-, semi-, mega-, tri-, bi-, near-, eco-, and tele-.* Suggest that the visual on which words are recorded should communicate the meaning associated with the word-building unit being investigated. For example, maxi-words could be printed on an over-sized chart, bi-words on a two-pronged chart, multi-words on a many-pronged chart, and eco-words on a tree-shaped chart.

Word-building units affixed to the ends of words are just as much fun to play with, especially if you include endings used extravagantly today. One well-used ending is *-er* as in teen-ager, name dropper, draft dodger, and moonlighter. Another is *-caster* as in newscaster, sportscaster, telecaster, and broadcaster. Let students suggest other *-er* and *-caster* words, both in current vogue and invented words. In addition, let them build suffix mobiles, large cutouts, containing words built on a single suffix that can be hung from a ceiling projection. Suffix mobiles can be based on *-tion, -able, -ment, -like, -ster, -orium, -ette, -ee, -ade, -ic, -ile,* or *-tive.*

Do not forget about portmanteau words. They fit well into any study of how words are coined. A portmanteau word, such as squawk, or twiddle, is formed by combining the sounds of two or more words to form a new word that retains some of the meaning communicated by the old words. Squall and croak combined for squawk; twitch and fiddle for twiddle. Other portmanteau words, or blends, are smog, brunch, jounce, smaze, squash, and one coined recently by the economist Paul Samuelson, stagflation.

There are many activities to involve students with word blends. Prepare a sheet listing activities students can work on independently, and stack copies in an independent learning center pouch.

SMASHING WORDS TOGETHER

DIRECTIONS: Write ideas directly on this sheet.

A. Can you figure out what words have been blended together to form each of these words? Next to each word write your guess. Then check in the dictionary to see if you are right.

1. smog =   +   .
2. brunch =   +   .
3. splurge =   +   .
4. dumfound =   +   .
5. snoopervize =   +   .
6. jounce =   +   .
7. slanguage =   +   .
8. squish =   +   .
9. smaze =   +   .

B. Now coin some portmanteau words. Some previous inventions given by Perrin in *Writer's Guide and Index to English* (Scott, Foresman, 1965) are "posilutely," "absotively," "solemncholy," and "absogosh-darnlutely." Smash the following words together to form a new word. Then use your new word in a sentence to show its new meaning.

1. whistle + cackle =   6. cry + wail =

2. carmel + delicious =   7. chocolate + luscious =

3. twitch + turn =   8. circle + ripple =

4. gossip + whisper =   9. window + door =

5. lunch + supper =   10. Chevrolet + Pontiac =

C. Can you invent your own portmanteau words? Try blending two or more words together to form a new word. When you think you have created an interesting new word, prepare a definition and write several model sentences using the word. Be ready to share your invented word with the rest of the class.

Lewis Carroll, of course, was the master of the portmanteau word. In a piece called "Sylvie and Bruno Concluded," he coined smirkle from smirk and smile. In "Jabberwocky" he coined chortle from chuckle and snort, galumphing from galloping and triumphant, and frumious from frumpish and gloomy. Share "Jabberwocky" with students and see if they can figure out the meanings Carroll was communicating through his invented words.

Really creative students may wish to try their hand at writing similar lines containing their own word inventions *à la* Lewis Carroll or lines in which a concocted word or two help establish a mood. A poem to share with students beginning to write this type of material is e. e. cummings's "In Just—." In it cummings plays with *mud-luscious* and *puddle-wonderful,* delightful words that are really compounds rather than blends, but fun to listen to nonetheless.

SLAPPING SLANG AROUND

> Bill is a real ding-a-ling.
> Diane totaled the car.
> Booze was illegal during prohibition.
> Stan took hush money.
> Rich put on his duds.
> Doris knew how to turn a fast buck.

Ding-a-ling, totaled, booze, hush money, duds, and *turn a fast buck* are all part of our colloquial speech; they are words that are considered below the standard of educated speech but are used because they fill a communication need. As with most slang expressions, these words are rather colorful and slightly ingenious, and some have been around a long time. According to H. L. Mencken, "Booze has never got into standard English, but it was used as slang as early as the fourteenth century." Duds can be traced back to 1567, and hush money dates to 1709. Some of the other expressions are of more recent vintage; totaled meaning destroyed has appeared in the last ten years.

In discussing slang, Mencken argues its validity. He writes, "It [slang] is, in fact, the most powerful of all the stimulants that keep language alive and growing, and some of the most pungent and valuable words and phrases in English, and especially in American English, have arisen out of its bilge" (*American Language,* Knopf, 1963, p. 706). Particularly picturesque expressions Mencken identifies are rubberneck, piker, stooge, tightwad, nuts, O.K., phony, and double-cross.

If slang plays such an important role in language, rather than criticizing young people's use of it, perhaps teachers should encourage them to analyze expressions in current vogue. Such analysis will bring them into direct contact with language as it continues to change.

Prepare a sheet of sentence pairs in which a word is first presented with its accepted standard English meaning and then in a sentence with its recently popularized meaning. The sheet may resemble the following one, but be sure that it includes some sentences containing the most popular slang expressions students are actually using in your part of the country. Update the sheet as words go out of style.

SLAPPING SLANG AROUND

What is the meaning of the underlined words as used in each column? Beneath each word that is underlined, write its meaning.

John rapped his fist on the table.	Art took the rap and ended in jail.
	They stood on the street corner and rapped.
Imelda slipped and put her hip out of joint.	Unless you use some slang, you're not hip.
We buy bread in a bakery.	I need some bread—the green kind.
Elaine totaled my bill.	Sam totaled the car.
I sew with different colored threads.	Put on your threads; we're going out.
That food is bad for you.	That's a bad car he has.
On my trip I went to Poland.	That girl is a trip.
The box is heavy.	Mike is heavy in math.
Julie was sad when her dog died.	That dress is really sad.
I use rags for dusting.	Put on your glad rags.

In three-person teams young people analyze the pairs, drawing on the way words are used in the sentences, their own language experiences, and dictionary definitions for standard usage. Follow up with talk about the two meanings assigned each word and let students brainstorm other words that have a standard and a slang meaning. They can build sentence pairs modeled after those on the Slapping Slang Around sheet.

Continue with related activities such as:

Writing a story using at least five of the words previously studied and working with the standard meaning; then writing a second story using the same five words but this time working with the slang meaning.

Making a dictionary of common slang words. Student lexicographers write a dictionary entry for each slang word they can identify and include the meaning they think the nonstandard expression now carries.

Searching for slang expressions such as "with it," "turned on," and "tuned out." Students can write sentence cards for each phrase to show how it typically is used.

Checking dictionaries of slang to identify words that have been in existence a long time, words that once were slang and have now gained acceptance, and words that have fallen out of use. Students may hypothesize why some slang usages have become standard and why others have not.

Identifying slang words and expressions they themselves formerly used but which have already become passé or changed meaning.

Introduce students also to clipping, the process by which people delete portions of words. Through clipping, new words are coined that often bear a kinship to slang in that they are below the level of standard English. Coca-Cola has been clipped to Coke, bicycle into bike, microphone into mike, graduate into grad, penitentiary into pen, doctor into doc, and gasoline into gas. Divide your class into teams that work for ten minutes thinking of other clipped words. At the end of the time, teams count words to discover which has identified the most.

Making a filmstrip of slang expressions is a way for students to summarize their work with slang. On each frame of a strip of U-film available from Scholastic (Englewood Cliffs, NJ 07632), students print a single slang expression, add bright colors to the frames, and make an audio-taped accompaniment. The tape includes a description of each word and perhaps a musical selection to set the mood. A recording of Scott Joplin's piano rags playing softly behind the verbal script would be a good mood setter for this kind of "with-it" production.

RECENT ADDITIONS TO THE LANGUAGE   "What is the difference between the letters I am placing in the first column and the letters I am placing in the second?" is a question to guide older students toward a discovery of acronyms. Acronyms are words formed from the initial letters of other words, i.e., SCUBA and RADAR. Scuba stands for self-contained underwater breathing apparatus; radar comes from radio detecting and ranging.

As you ask your question, record CORE in the first column and USA in the second. Keep adding acronyms to the first column and abbreviations to the second until a student thinks he or she perceives the difference between the two listings. Instead of asking this student to explain the difference, ask her or him to add another example to one of the columns. As other students begin to catch on, they too can try to add examples. Acronyms and abbreviations to begin with include:

Acronyms	Abbreviations
CORE	USA
NASA	UN
NOW	TWA
WAC	NJ
HOPE	NAACP

After a number of students have given examples, encourage generalization. Some abbreviations are treated as words, and instead of pronouncing each letter in the abbreviation, people pronounce the letters in syllables. Label the columns Acronyms and Abbreviations. Suggest that students search out acronyms that are just coming into vogue as new organizations gain popularity.

A fun follow-up is inventing names for fictitious organizations and societies that convert easily to acronyms. Students in the past dreamed up STOP (Society to Overcome Pollution, US (Useless Society), and SOAP (Student Organization Against Phosphates).

After inventing original acronyms, students can go on to invent other kinds of names, adhering to principles of naming generally in use. Set up an activity through which students hypothesize some of these principles. First duplicate a list of words of diverse origins, and ask students in teams to run a dictionary check to determine these origins.

TASK: To find out where these words came from.

DIRECTIONS: Check each of the underlined words in the dictionary. Note the origin next to each word on the sheet.

1. Pasteurize
2. Polonium
3. Sandwich
4. Apollo space mission
5. Dahlia
6. Television
7. Astronaut
8. Insulin
9. Cell (in organisms)
10. Jumbo

By analyzing specific examples such as these, students can begin to hypothesize common methods of naming. New things are named after:

People who played a part in the development or discovery of the
  thing; i.e., pasteurization was named for Louis Pasteur, sandwich
  for the Earl of Sandwich.
Place; i.e., Marie Curie named the new element polonium after her
  native country.
Appearance; i.e., the first cell viewed under a microscope looked
  like a jail cell to its viewer.
Latin and Greek roots, i.e., television and astronaut.
Mythical characters and names of ancient gods and goddesses; i.e.,
  Apollo was the Greek god of light.

Once students have identified these naming methods, encourage a search for additional examples to fit each category.
The space program provides additional names taken from
gods of the past. Many flowers have been named after their
developer or discoverer, even the gardenia. Many science-
related words come from Latin and/or Greek. Again students
can record word finds on charts that indicate both word and
name origin.

Ask investigators who have studied naming methods to
make some hypothetical words of their own by naming a
new kind of telephone on which one can see the person to
whom one is talking, a bright purple variety of tulip, the next
space mission or the next spaceship to be launched, your own
invention, or a machine that makes you invisible, an original
way to cook oysters, or a new sandwich.

IDENTIFYING THE PURPOSE

The English language is full of fascinating words derived
from a variety of sources. Words have been traced back to
the language spoken by the early Anglo-Saxon people, such
as ox, night, mother, and man. Words have been traced to
other languages from which English people liberally helped
themselves, such as kangaroo, sauna, noodle, and legion.
Words have been coined by combining other words as in
whirlwind, by adding affixes as in superpower, by condensing

words together as in stagflation, and by imitating the sound of a phenomenon as in buzz. The continued influx of new words paralleled by the disuse of existing words and changes in meaning have produced an English language far different from that spoken by the Anglo-Saxons about a thousand years ago. It is so different that special training is required if one wishes to read an epic written in that day, *Beowulf*.

The investigations of words as described in this chapter can lead student linguists toward an expanded conception of the nature of language and communication. They can begin to understand that words do not have meaning in and of themselves but rather are symbols invented by humans to describe, name, and explain components of the world. Students begin to comprehend that language is not static but changes in response to changes in the society in which it exists.

Investigation of specific words also enables students to see how knowledge about language development and change has been compiled by language scholars. When students compare the words from several languages that name the same thing, they are making simple linguistic comparison studies similar to those pursued by linguists. When they generalize about a number of specific words, they are putting the pieces of our language heritage together much in the manner of linguists.

In these language investigations, teachers should not intend that elementary school students know such facts as the dates of the major periods in English-language history or the etymology of specific words. Such knowledge is short lived and relatively useless. Rather our purpose is to give young people a framework or a way of looking at words they encounter. They will begin to think of words as puzzles to be figured out and solved and the dictionary as a tool for discovering word relationships. By seeing relationships among words, students may grow in their facility to choose the appropriate word, to spell structurally related words, and even to invent words when the occasion demands.

Why, then the world's mine oyster,
Which I with sword will open.

THE MERRY WIVES OF WINDSOR, WILLIAM SHAKESPEARE

BEFORE ENDING:
A Story or Two

Every country has its share of folk tales that poke fun at the silly things people do when they come in contact with something new. Just as Americans enjoy jokes about hicks and hayseeds and the English chuckle at tales about yokels and bumpkins, the Danes have for generations been telling stories about the country folk of Mols, people living in the Ebeltoft region of Jutland. Many of the Mols tales tell what happens when the simply living Molbos encounter some of the conveniences of modern living. The Mols, who are a humor-loving people, have become proud of the old stories, and today it is in Ebeltoft where most of the stories have been collected for others to enjoy.

One story in the collection, "The White Bread," dates from 1780; and because it makes a particularly significant point with which to close *Words, Sounds, and Thoughts,* let me share the tale with you:

> Once a rather venturesome Molbo found a piece of white bread someone had dropped along the road near Ebeltoft. The Molbo had never seen any white bread before because black ryebread was what his family ate at home. At first, therefore, he was in doubt as to what to do with it. Eventually though, when it didn't move, the Molbo decided it looked safe enough and picked it up.
>
> After studying it rather warily for a time, he decided to risk a bite since it certainly did look like food. Amazed he discovered that it really tasted very good! Turning to his friend who stood near by, the Molbo remarked: "If only I had some bread to eat with it, I would eat this white thing I have found."*

Sometimes people in education speak much like the Molbo in this old tale. When we encounter an idea for a classroom activity for the first time, we pass it by because we do not have

---

*Adapted from "The White Bread" in *Old Stories from Denmark* (Ebeltoft: Elles Boghandel).

the exact materials to go with it or because we are not accustomed to doing things that way in our classrooms. For example, after hearing of Ms. Russell's diverse activities based on the story *Mushroom in the Rain*, teachers may discard her ideas because they do not have that book on hand.

The intent in most of the activities outlined in *Words, Sounds, and Thoughts* is not for readers necessarily to use particular materials or to design sessions exactly like those described, but rather, to show enjoyable ways of enriching children's language experiences. As you try the suggested activities in your classroom, it will, of course, be expected that you will draw on other available materials and revise procedures to meet the unique requirements of your situation. So, decide with the venturesome Molbo to risk a bite and nibble at an activity, or two or three.

The Mols people have a second story, "The Lazy Sundial":

Once the people of Mols bought a beautiful sundial as a gift for their town council so that the members of the council would know the time. They set it up opposite the Town Hall in Ebeltoft, which is the tiniest town hall in all of Denmark.

Even as they were putting it up, however, the rain came. Fearful that the shining metal dial would be spoiled, they covered it up and had a conference to decide what to do. Finally they all agreed that the thing to do was to put a little roof over the dial to protect it from the weather.

This they immediately did; and the little roof they built succeeded in keeping the dial bright and beautiful. To the disgust of the people of Mols, however, after they had taken all this trouble, the sundial never told the time again.*

Sometimes educators behave much like the people of Mols. Children often come to school brimming with natural curiosity about things, an impulse to share their questions and ideas, joyous pleasure in word play and discovery, and an innate

---

*Adapted from "The Lazy Sundial," in *Old Stories from Denmark*, (Ebeltoft: Elles Boghandel).

bent for fantasy and manipulation. In the manner of the Mols, we cover this bright and beautiful sundial with a little roof. The metaphorical roof is the standard textbook-centered curriculum that may foster little independence or creative thinking; it is the traditional requirements of school life that place energetic children on hard chairs most of the day and forbid normal talk or conversation.

To develop language facility (and dislike?), teachers often assign lists of words for students to look up in the dictionary, write down definitions, and write into sentences. To develop language understanding (and misunderstanding?), we frequently give priority to memorization of parts of speech and to exercises in which children identify parts of speech as they occur in sentences. We assign book reports to encourage (discourage?) reading, oral reports to encourage (discourage?) speaking, and a composition a week to encourage (discourage?) writing. We systematically lead whole classes of youngsters through the pages of a language development workbook or series, assigning each activity in turn after the children have read in round-robin fashion the introduction of each exercise.

Then we wonder, with the people of Mols, why our sundials never quite work the way we had intended. The children gradually lose their spontaneity of expression and some stop communicating in school almost completely. They wait to be told what to do rather than taking the initiative in their own learning. They think what they think teachers want them to think rather than striving for the original and new. And when we ask them to rate the curriculum areas they prefer, they typically give low marks to language study and English.

The people of Mols had a simple solution available—take the roof off the dial. We in education have the same solution, but in our case, the application is not quite so simple. We must begin by identifying the overarching goals of language programs and specifying objectives to be achieved at each level of language development. When selecting a language arts text or series, we are essentially involved in identifying goals and objectives as well as sequencing those objectives, for most series indicate clearly what the texts are trying to achieve and describe the particular goals to be developed at each level.

The selection of a language arts series is, therefore, an important decision. We must take care that the series strives primarily toward communication goals, that it will help children:

Grow in ability to express themselves. Children develop a functional repertoire of words upon which to draw; they use those words with facility and creativity in speaking and writing. They have control over a variety of sentence patterns, selecting those that best express the meanings they are trying to communicate. They have control over associated writing and speaking skills; they have control over a variety of forms of expression; they enjoy speaking and writing.

Grow in ability to react to communications directed toward them. Children interpret word meanings in terms of the context in which used; they are able to interpret instances where language is being used to persuade or distort meaning. They can read and listen for a variety of purposes; they vary their listening and reading according to purpose; they enjoy listening and reading.

Begin to enjoy working with word relationships and acquire rudimentary understanding of those relationships that contribute to increased communication skill.

Language arts series that stress in-depth analysis of literary selections and sophisticated sentence patterns at the expense of communication skills and that emphasize the terminology for describing language would have little place in a school seeking to take the roof off its language program.

In selecting a series, educators must take care that the activities suggested are ones that open up rather than close in thoughts. We must ask, "Will the activities arouse children's interest in language? Do they encourage children to think for themselves? Can I use them to spring into other activities that occur in the classroom? Can other classroom activities incorporate the ideas in the series? Does the format lend itself to creative adaptation? Are there ideas for interactive as well as independent activities?"

Selecting a language series that stresses communication and includes opportunities for creative learning is only the first step in taking the roof off language programs. The second and more important step is how teachers use the material in the texts. Do we view them as gospel to be followed line by line and page by page? If we do, the roof stays on. If, on the other hand, we view the books as a source of ideas and possible activities, we can use them as helpful supports to curriculum planning. We identify weaknesses in children's growth in language facility, and devise creative sessions to overcome them and to work toward greater facility. We do this by inventing activities, both interactive and independent, by taking from source books ideas that involve children in language and by building on ideas provided in the language arts series. We start with activities that involve children in thinking and doing with language. We turn to the language arts books to reinforce concepts and skills already beginning to bloom, not to introduce those concepts and skills.

In such an on-going program approach, rarely would all children sit down to write or read the same assignment at the same time. Actual writing goes on at writing stations, while some children are working with the teacher in a small-group guided reading activity, others are playing a sentence-building game together, others are in the library researching a social science problem, and still others are reading by themselves. Teachers prepare for independent work in the guided interactive sessions. Through group interactions, they build supportive skills and understandings and clarify directions so that young people know what to do and how to do it.

The kinds of activities children pursue independently and in guided interactive sessions move from the rote to the creative. Young people brainstorm ideas together and play with word and thought relationships. They write about all manner of things in a variety of styles and forms. They talk and listen together, making contact with many kinds of thoughts. They conceptualize and relate the often unrelatable, going beyond the ordinary as they look at things around them. They take the initiative and at times grope their own way.

In such an open environment where there is a blend of guided and independent activities and where children encounter the language arts as the process of communicating, children come to know the pleasures inherent in language and ideas. David Lyons, the teacher who guided fourth graders on an odyssey down the Mississippi (see chapter 6), recounts the reaction of the young people to this experience when he announced that it was time to go home and the class would have to put away their English materials. Several students asked, "Was this English, Mr. Lyons? It couldn't be 'cause English's boring." For them experiencing language on a Mississippi odyssey was far from dull. Then they popped the questions that thrill all teachers, "This was great! Can we stay and finish?" and "Can we do this another time?"

What a delight to teach children when they respond to what we do in this excited and involved way. As many teachers have discovered when they have substituted an on-going, integrated activity approach for the mundane follow-the-book technique, schools can be marvelously stimulating places for both teachers and students.

*Now, here, you see, it takes all the
running you can do, to keep in the same
place. If you want to get somewhere
else, you must run at least twice as fast as that!*

THROUGH THE LOOKING GLASS, LEWIS CARROLL

RUNNING TO KEEP
IN THE SAME PLACE:
*An Annotated Resource
Bibliography*

Faced with the burgeoning supply of materials helpful in enriching children's communication skills, teachers often feel as if they have slipped through the looking glass into that strange land where it takes all the running one can do just to remain in the same place. To keep abreast of all that is new in educational materials and related technology, teachers "must run at least twice as fast as that!"

In the following section, I want to share with readers some materials I have found particularly helpful in building an integrated language arts program in which guided interactive sessions set the stage for independent study activities. Although many goodies are not included because of the vast quantities on the market, weaker materials have been intentionally excluded. The result is a list that may provide some clues for incorporating some of the newer materials into a language arts program without getting out of breath from running "twice as fast."

RECORDS AND CASSETTES

A record or tape, perhaps accompanied by a companion book, can provide the content for an independent learning station activity or can be the springboard for group brainstorming. Here are titles of a few of the many recordings available on disk or tape cassettes. The producers issue catalogs describing their complete offerings.

- CAEDMON RECORDS
  505 Eighth Avenue
  New York, NY 10018

Catch a Little Rhyme: Poems for Activity Time. Record or cassette.
  A collection of Eve Merriam's poems that stimulate children to react verbally and nonverbally. Elementary and junior high.
Edward Lear's Nonsense Stories and Poems. Record or cassette.
  Stories "that illustrate the right words used wrongly and short

words used longly." Several youngsters can listen to this recording, narrated by Claire Bloom, and then together write their own nonsense story or poem. Elementary and junior high.

Miracles: Poems Written by Children. Record or cassette. A collection of poems written by children all over the world and organized according to themes such as morning, spring, and so on. Children can follow listening with reciting their own poems. Upper-elementary grades.

Ogden Nash's Reflections on a Wicked World. Record. A collection of some of Nash's best reflections that you can introduce to upper-grade elementary students as examples of creative manipulation of language. Use also a second collection, *Ogden Nash's Parents Keep Out.*

Tongue Twisters. Record or cassette. A collection of tongue twisters narrated by George S. Irving. A good introduction to the way children can play with sounds and have fun.

- FOLKWAYS RECORDS
  43 West 61st Street
  New York, NY 10023

Sound, Rhythm, Rhyme and Mime for Children. Record. A fine context for improvising rhythms, chants, and movements following patterns established on the recording. Primary grades.

You'll Sing a Song and I'll Sing a Song. Record. A collection of songs that lead children to create their own call and response patterns. Use to stimulate simple, repetitive songwriting by youngsters. Grades K–3.

- SCHOLASTIC AV CENTER
  904 Sylvan Avenue
  Englewood Cliffs, NJ 07632

Favorite Rhymes from a Rocket in My Pocket/Teeny Tiny Woman. Record with two companion books. Side one, rhymes, riddles, and tongue twisters; side two, the English folktale about that tiny woman. Use this one as an introduction to the importance of sound in communication. Elementary.

Folk Songs for Young People. Record. Folk music sung by Pete Seeger. Use to encourage young people to find word pictures in the poetry of song. Elementary.

Sounds of the Sea. Record. Sounds of surf, ships, lighthouse, and sea birds. Use to stimulate writing of words that imitate sounds. Middle elementary.

Sound Patterns. Record. A collection of man-made and natural sounds that children can express as words on paper. Use also a second collection from Scholastic, *Sounds of a Tropical Rain Forest in America.* Grade 2 and up.

This Is Rhythm. Record or cassette. An opportunity to hear rhythm in everyday sounds. Use with Langston Hughes's *The First Book of Rhythms* (Franklin Watts, 1954), which describes the rhythms in nature, rhythms in music, rhythms in daily life. Elementary.

- SPOKEN ARTS, INC.
  310 North Avenue
  New Rochelle, NY 10810

Wishes, Lies, and Dreams: parts 1 and 2 (Teaching Children to Write Poetry). Cassette. An introduction to some patterns of poetry identified by Kenneth Koch: wish poems, comparison poems, color poems, lie poems, poems using Spanish words, dream poems, snow poems. Intended for teachers but also useful with upper-elementary students.

FILM LOOPS

Silent film loops are an especially practical material for young people to view independently in learning stations. After reading a short book on a topic, a student simply slips a film loop into a projector, flips a switch, and sees a short visual presentation on the same topic in the seclusion of a carrel-type booth. This is possible because the film loop is already loaded in a cartridge and never needs rewinding for projection.

Silent film loops are also useful as one part of a multimedia adventure in which a loop has been carefully correlated with a story, chart, and/or musical selection in the manner outlined in chapter 1. A loop can extend the feelings and ideas developing through listening to a story; it can trigger additional feelings and ideas.

Numerous companies market Technicolor loops with nature themes that are most helpful in extending appreciation of a story enjoyed in a class group. A complete catalog of titles, *Technicolor Silent Film Loop Source Directory*, is available from Technicolor, Commercial and Educational Division, 299 Kalmus Drive, Costa

Mesa, CA 92627, at minimal cost. It lists well over seventy-five distributors of film loops and titles available from each. In addition, you may write for individual catalogs from specific distributors.

Doubleday Multimedia, 277 Park Avenue, New York, NY 10017

Ealing Corporation, 2225 Massachusetts Avenue, Cambridge, MA 02140

Encyclopedia Britannica Educational Corp., 425 North Michigan Avenue, Chicago, IL 60611

Eye-Gate House, 146-01 Archer Avenue, Jamaica, NY 11435

International Visual Aids Center, 691 Chausee de Mons, Brussels 7, Belgium

Thorne Films, Inc., 1229 University Avenue, Boulder, CO 80302

Troll Associates, Rt. 17, Mahwah, NJ 07430

FILMS

Some really creative films are being produced today that can stimulate children to think, talk, and write. The following is a listing of sources of films and some titles that should help your students to express themselves.

- BFA EDUCATIONAL MEDIA
  2211 Michigan Avenue
  Santa Monica, CA 90404;
    Regional offices located across the country.

All in the Morning Early: A Scottish Folktale. 10 min., color, sound. Elementary. An effective rendition of Sorche Nic Leodhas's book of the same title. The repetitive lines of the story can serve as a model for students who are trying to write their own stories in which lines repeat.

The Boy Who Saw the Wind. 7 min., color, sound. Primary. A daydream view of the world without wind. Young viewers can concoct their own daydream views of the world without light, water, waves, the moon, and so forth.

Celebration of Life: Trees. 11 min, color, sound. Elementary. An adventure into the texture, color, shape of trees, the changing seasons, animals, and sounds of the forest. The film is a source of sights and sounds that student viewers can describe in word pictures.

Magic Words. 9 min., color, sound. Primary. An introduction to the way words work, alliteration, rhyme, and sounds. Student viewers can supply their own examples, modeled after language projected in the film.

Rock in the Road. 6 min., color, no narration. Elementary and secondary. One of the best nonverbal films to trigger talk about people's responsibility to one another. It can show young writers how a story can be told without words.

The Wave: A Japanese Folktale. 9 min., color, sound. Elementary. An effective telling of a Japanese folktale in which a village is saved by Ojiisan's burning of a rice field. Use this film in conjunction with the four Japanese folktale books composed of pop-up pages and movable parts and accompanied with a story tape, available from Educational Progress Corporation (8538 East 41st Street, Tulsa, OK 74145). The pop-up books, called the Paper Play series, are great for students to use in developing their own storytelling techniques.

What's in a Story. 14 min., color, sound. Elementary. An introduction to plot and message relationships in stories, using as examples the fable of *The Milkmaid and Her Pail* and Thurber's *The Unicorn in the Garden.* Use as a springboard to class story creating as youngsters together build messages into their stories.

• STEPHEN BOSUSTOW PRODUCTIONS
1649 Eleventh Street
Santa Monica, CA 90404

The Beginning: A Wigglemen Tale. 4.5 min., color, sound. The creative person who is ridiculed at first but then proves the skeptics wrong. Use this short, cogent film in conjunction with portions of Richard Bach's *Jonathan Livingston Seagull* (Macmillan, 1970). Follow with discussion of being different. Upper elementary through high school.

Birds of a Feather. 6 min., color, animated, no narration. The adventures of a bird who dares to be different. Use this with the preceding film. *The Beginning,* and perhaps with the popular recording *Free to Be, You and Me* with Marlo Thomas. Encourage young people to write their own stories about nonconforming. Elementary and up.

Good Goodies. 4.5 min., color, no narration. A look at the use of superlatives in advertising. Student viewers can write their own superlative-laden ads. Elementary and up.

Legend of John Henry and *Legend of Paul Bunyan*. Each about twelve minutes, color, sound. A good retelling of these tall tales. Student viewers can identify the elements of tall tales and try to write some of their own. Upper-elementary grades.

- INTERNATIONAL FILM BUREAU
  332 S. Michigan Avenue
  Chicago, IL 60604

The Ball That Wanted to Play. 10 min., color, sound. The story of a big orange ball in search of a playmate. A great film for getting young children to invent their own stories that follow the adventures of inanimate objects. Primary.

The Fish. 7 min., color, no narration. The anecdote about the fisherman who catches an immense fish and takes it home with him. Student viewers can write their own fish stories after brainstorming possible plot motifs together. Elementary.

I Know an Old Lady Who Swallowed a Fly. 6 min., color, sound. A Burl Ives rendition of the well-known folktale done in animation. Can introduce the repetitive tale to students as a format for their own writing of stories. Produced by the National Filmboard of Canada. Elementary.

- LEARNING CORPORATION OF AMERICA
  711 Fifth Avenue
  New York, NY 10022

The Little Airplane That Grew. 9 min., color, no narration. A fantasy ride in a paper airplane high above fields and towns. Students can devise their own fantasy rides in response to this imaginative trip. Primary.

The Thunderstorm. 9 min., color, sound. The effects of storm on a boy, dog, plants, and animals. Children can brainstorm thunderstorm words. Elementary.

Wind. 9 min., color, sound. The sights and sounds of the wind as it carries a boy into the world of clouds, swirling leaves, and flying kites. This one is ideal for brainstorming wind words and for writing poems in which wind is perceived as a person. Produced by the National Film Board of Canada. Elementary.

- MILLER-BRODY PRODUCTIONS, INC.
  342 Madison Avenue
  New York, NY 10017

The Dingo Dog and the Kangaroo. 8 min., color, sound. An original fable about a guitar-playing dingo dog, a Tasmanian wolf, a kind kangaroo, and a lamb—all in Australia. A fine film for motivating children to write their own fables in which unexpected animals interact. Elementary.

The Sly Little Rabbit and How He Got Long Ears. 8 min., color, sound. The Aztec legend about Quetzalcoatl and the rabbit who wished to be strong and big. Student viewers then write their own tales about how particular animals came to be the way they are, i.e., How the Frog Got Its Bull Horn, How the Firefly Got Its Light, How the Mosquito Learned to Sting, and so forth. Elementary.

Tale of the Lazy People. 16 min., color, sound. A fine retelling of the Newbery Award book. Stop this one in the middle to see if students can provide their own endings orally in three-person teams. After each team has shared its version, flip on the film to see the actual ending. Upper elementary.

• NATIONAL EDUCATIONAL FILM CENTER
Route Two
Finksburg, MD 21048

The Dot and the Line. 9 min., color, sound. The tale of a Line in love with a Dot, who is in love with a Squiggle. This one is great for showing how stories can be built around inanimate objects. Upper elementary.

Paddle-to-the-Sea. 28 min., color, sound. Holling C. Holling's story of a boat's progress through the Great Lakes and down the St. Lawrence. Students can project where the boat will travel from there. Produced by the National Film Board of Canada. Elementary.

Seashore. 8 min., color, sound. The beauties of the ocean and the life found in and around it. Can be used as content for writing descriptions of things observed. Elementary.

• WESTON WOODS
Weston, CT 06880

Changes, Changes. 6 min., color, animated, sound. The changes that happen to wooden building blocks and dolls. Student viewers can brainstorm change words. Primary.

Mime over Matter. 12 min., color, sound, live-action. A talented mime artist and his company portraying humorous scenes as well as sad ones. Students who view this want to jump right in and try their hand at mime. Elementary and adult.

Patrick. 7 min., color animated, sound. Quentin Blake's story of the boy with a fiddle who carries music into the countryside. This story can easily be converted into a story map by student viewers. Primary.

Peter's Chair. 6 min., color, iconographic, sound. Ezra Jack Keats's story of the boy who is unhappy at the arrival of a baby sister. Younger children can be encouraged to talk about unhappinesses that are similar to Peter's. Primary.

A Story, A Story. 10 min., color, animated, sound. Gail Haley's story of Ananse, the spider man, who spun a web up in the sky. Young people can listen a second time to this film to identify particularly effective ways that language is manipulated. They can make word webs as described in chapter 6 of this book. Elementary.

Tikki Tikki Tembo. 9 min., color, sound, iconographic. Arlene Mosel's story based on an old Chinese fairy tale, which tells why Chinese parents give their children short names. A fine introduction to the whole idea of how things are named. Primary.

GAMES

A number of companies market games that involve young people in language. Here is a listing of game sources with some examples of specific games that can form the content of group learning stations.

· EDUCATIONAL AIDS
General Learning Corporation
Morristown, NJ 07960

Word Decoding Games (V114901). Six games: Turkey, which reinforces recognition and pronunciation of sounds; Balloon, which is a bingo-type game that expands vocabulary; Opposites, which reinforces ability to work with antonyms; Homonym and Antonym Casino, which gives practice in creative language expression and making comparisons; Rhyming Word, which develops sound-word relationships; Sound Domino, which stresses auditory discrimination. Grades 2–6.

Language and Logic Games (V114902). Six games: Who Is Your Favorite? which develops observation and questioning skills;

Poly-strip Sentences, which develops skill in combining words and phrases into sentences; Spin-a-word, which stresses grapheme/ phoneme relationships; Are you Listening? which provides practice in word recognition; Base Word Rummy, which provides practice with prefixes, suffixes, and root words; Parts of Speech Rummy, which provides practice with parts of speech. Grades 2–6.

- CREATIVE TEACHING PRESS, INC.
514 Hermosa Vista Avenue
Monterey Park, CA 91754

Game-Maker. A write 'n wipe game field, a write 'n wipe spinner, bean bags, and a book of ideas—things you can use to make your own classroom games. Grades 2–6.

Open End Write 'N Wipe Game Boards. Four colorful game boards for which you and your students can create original language games. Grades 2–6.

- HARCOURT BRACE JOVANOVICH
757 Third Avenue
New York, NY 10017

The Gramma Game. 144 sentence cards and 72 gramma cards for students to match with words on sentence cards, game style. Upper elementary and junior high.

Sentence Games A. 40 noun phrase tiles and 40 verb phrase tiles for students to build into sentences; directions for 12 different games. Primary and upper elementary level.

Sentence Games B. 40 noun phrase tiles, and 40 verbs and form of *be* tiles, and forty tiles containing structures that may follow verbs; directions for twelve different games. Primary and upper elementary.

Wide, Wide World of Grammar. Five games: Accent on Baseball, which focuses on syllables; The Great Grammatical Golf Tournament, which provides practice in sentence building; Basketword, which provides practice in combining roots and prefixes; Goal Word Soccer, which provides practice in combining roots and suffixes; and End Zone Football, which provides practice in combining nouns, verbs, and adjectives with inflected endings. Grades 6–9.

- HARPER AND ROW
10 East 53rd Street
New York, NY 10022

Mulac, Margaret. *Educational Games for Fun,* 1971. A book describing individual and group games, including some word games. Elementary.

· MILTON BRADLEY
Education Division
Dept. I-S
Springfield, MA 01101

Language Category Games. Four decks of 42 cards for games involving nouns, verbs, adjectives, and adverbs; reinforce and develop skill in sentence building and categorizing. Grades 2–6.

Punctuation Patterns. A lotto-type game in which children match punctuation patterns with unpunctuated sentences. Grades 2–7.

· ST. REGIS INSTRUCTIONAL MATERIALS
3300 Pinson Valley Parkway
Birmingham, AL 35217

Action Grammar. Four sets of sentence cards and a dial board that introduce parts of speech. Intermediate grades.

Young Thinkers Word Game. A playing board, cards, and playing pieces that test knowledge in various curriculum areas. Intermediate grades.

MULTIMEDIA LEARNING PACKAGES

Some of the most stimulating material for use in language arts communications programs is the package that contains tapes or records, color filmstrips, a teacher's guide, related books, and/or related visuals. Although this material often comes with a high price tag, it is generally of good quality and it is certainly attention getting.

More and more companies are marketing such packages. The granddaddy of all in the language-literature field is Weston Woods, Weston, CT 06880. Weston Woods has a fine line of sound filmstrips based on picture storybooks, especially Caldecott Award winners. You can purchase a combination of sound filmstrips and accompanying books for use by students independently or in small groups. Because the titles available from Weston Woods are so extensive, the best way to identify materials is to get yourself on the permanent mailing list of this company.

A second company, growing by leaps and bounds, is Miller-Brody Productions, Inc., 342 Madison Avenue, New York, NY 10017.

Miller-Brody began by marketing sound filmstrips with accompanying paperbacks of Newbery Award winners. This series is excellent for use in upper-elementary grades. Again, you must send for a catalog to identify specific titles that fit your program.

Other companies from which you can purchase particular aids are listed below:

• CENTRON EDUCATIONAL FILMS
  1621 West 9th Street
  Lawrence, KS 66044

Language—The Mirror of Man's Growth. Five filmstrips with cassettes or records and a teacher's guide. Titles in the series: Language and Its Mysteries; Languages Are Born . . . Sometimes They Die; How Is It That Englishmen Speaks English?; What Age Has Done to English; The American Language . . . or When the King's English Came to America. Use this set as the content of a language-origins learning station; it will reinforce activities suggested in chapter 7. Grades 5–8.

• EDUCATIONAL DIMENSIONS CORPORATION
  Box 488
  Great Neck, NY 11022

Perception series. Ten sound filmstrips without narration: Birds, The City, The Seasons, The Sea, and The West. In these filmstrips, sound, music, and picture blend together in a total performance that can inspire young people to express feelings and ideas. Elementary.

Synonyms: In Other Words. Four color sound filmstrips. Groups of synonyms presented in imaginative sequences that add meaning to the words. Grades 3 and 4.

A World of Color and *A World of Shapes*. Each title consists of three color sound filmstrips that view color or shapes from a variety of perspectives. Children can write color thoughts and shape thoughts after viewing. Primary.

• FILMSTRIP HOUSE
  6633 West Howard Street
  Niles, IL 60648

Sentence Power. Four sound filmstrips with accompanying script. One title in the Communication Power series; presents subject and verb as key sentence elements and describes how to vary sentence structure to achieve different effects. Other titles in the series include Composition Power and Paragraph Power. Grades 4–8.

· LYCEUM FILMS
Available from Baker and Taylor
Drawer Z
Momence, IL 60954

Haiku: The Mood of Earth. Filmstrip with record or cassette. A multimedia presentation of Ann Atwood's stunning book *The Mood of Earth,* which is included. A related title from Lyceum is *Haiku: The Hidden Glimmering,* also written and photographed by Ann Atwood—a study of the haiku form with selections by Basha, Issa, and Buson. Young people will develop their own word pictures after experiencing this sound filmstrip presentation. Grade 4 and up.

Sea, Sand and Shore. Two filmstrips and records or cassettes with the book *New Moon Cove.* A visual-sound-word experience in which tides etch patterns on the shore, and pelicans and sandpipers leave their signatures in the sand. Written and photographed by Ann Atwood, this is a terrific content from which to brainstorm words, feelings, and ideas. Grade 4 and up.

· MCGRAW-HILL FILMS
1221 Avenue of the Americas
New York, NY 10020

Children's Literature series. Six sets of sound filmstrips, each consisting of six titles: So Much to Experience; The Many Worlds of Literature; Let's Communicate; What Can Words Do?; Express Yourself!; and Learning About Literature. This material uses books to get children to write their own stories, invent dialogue, compose poetry, and role-play. Devised by Dr. Patricia Cianciolo of Michigan State University. Primary.

· MORELAND-LATCHFORD
6633 Howard Street
Niles, IL 60648

Stories for Creative Expression. Five filmstrips with cassettes and teacher's guides. An introduction to plot and structure in story that encourages children to create stories in different ways. Each strip involves the same three characters in three different adventures: Two People and the Topsy Turvy Hat, Two People and the Flying Space Mobile, Two People and the Wacky Old Car, and so forth. Students can go on to invent other two-people tales. Elementary.

• RANDOM HOUSE/Singer School Division
201 East 50th Street
New York, NY 10022

Aware. A large box of materials including booklets, cards, and tapes to involve students in poetry. You can utilize materials from the box to build into your own learning station adventures. Upper elementary.

The Writing Bug. A large collection of materials including film-strips, U-film, activity cards, wall charts, cassette of sounds, spirit master, and teacher's guide. You can pull this collection apart to use in your own writing center activities. Grade 3 and up.

• TEACHING RESOURCES FILMS
Station Plaza
Bedford Hills, NY 10507

Amelia Bedelia; *Come Back, Amelia Bedelia*; *Thank You, Amelia Bedelia*; and *Play Ball, Amelia Bedelia.* Four sound filmstrips of the well-known Peggy Parish books. Problems with colloquialisms encountered by Amelia Bedelia who interprets words and phrases literally. Good to develop understanding of word meanings. Elementary.

Aesop's Fables. Four sound filmstrips: The Man, The Boy and The Donkey; A Camel in the Tent; The Maid and Her Pail of Milk; and A Bundle of Sticks. Fables with well-known morals show how some of these sayings came into the language. Elementary.

• XEROX FILMS
Education Center
P.O. Box 444
Columbus, OH 43216

Big Blue Marble Folktale Kits. Ten folktale kits, each containing a sound filmstrip, 30 student activity booklets, a poster, and teacher guide. Titles: The Bridge of St. Cloud (France); The Priest and the Magic Pea (China); Fire on the Mountain (Ethiopia); Many Wishes of Dag (Sweden); The Humpbacked Horse (Russia);

King John and the Jester (England); The Princess and the Necklace (India); The Runaway Squash (United States); A Better Friendship (Nigeria); and Three-Cornered Hat of Bad Miguel (Puerto Rico). Use the kits to integrate a study of folktales with social studies investigations of these areas of the world.

PRINT AND PICTURE

Today there is a wide range of print and picture materials that are colorful, attractively packaged, and easily adapted for use in learning stations. Some companies and sample materials from each are listed below.

· ARGUS COMMUNICATIONS
Department G
7440 Natchez
Niles, IL 60648

Posters. 14 x 21 inch full color posters each presenting a striking picture accompanied with a forcefully expressed thought in prose or poetry. These posters are excellent devices to motivate young people to search books of poetry to find lines that correlate with pictures they have found or drawn. Grade 3 and up.

Posters without Words. Twelve photo posters, six in color, six in black and white. Students can search for lines of poetry to affix to the posters or can select lines from an accompanying spirit master. Grade 3 and up.

· CITATION PRESS
50 West 44th Street
New York, NY 10036

Brammer, Miriam. *Poster Packet and Teaching Guide for Primary Classrooms.* Ten colorful posters, each with a ditto master, and a teacher's guide. Ideal for stimulating group or independent activities in language arts, science, math, art, music, cooking, and dramatics. Primary.

Miller, Lynne, and Miriam Brammer, compilers. *Poster Packet and Teaching Guide for Elementary Classrooms.* Twelve color posters on a variety of subjects that can trigger verbal expression; includes spirit masters to accompany each poster so that each can be easily converted into a learning station activity. Elementary.

· CREATIVE TEACHING PRESS
514 Hermosa Vista Avenue
Monterey Park, CA 91754

Creating Learning Centers. Stand-up activity cards for language arts, social studies, mathematics, and science. Serviceable material for independent learning station activity. Set 1 is for intermediates, Set 2 for primaries.

Recipes for Creative Writing. 4 x 6 inch recipe cards that suggest topics for writing. Mount the cards on a learning station backdrop. Students take down cards as they write on the suggested topics. Set 1 is general recipes, Set 2 primary.

Story Starters. A collection of cards containing ideas for writing. Use these to start a writing center. Encourage children to make additional story starter cards, and you make some too. Set 1 is for intermediates, Set 2 for primaries.

· EDUCATIONAL ACTIVITIES, INC.
Freeport, Long Island
NY 11520

Learning about Poetry. Six color filmstrips: How to Read a Poem; Rhythm and Meter in Poetry; Imagery and Figurative Language; Poems That Tell a Story; Poems That Express Feelings; and Poetry Sound, Meaning and Idea. These are good for individual viewing with a filmstrip viewer. Grade 6 and up.

Story Settings. Four color filmstrips that present the beginnings of a story and then ask viewers to develop the plot and finish the story. Each strip has two story starters. Elementary.

· EDUCATIONAL INSIGHTS
20435 South Tillman Avenue
Carson, CA 90746

Write On! A recipe-style box of writing project cards to start a writing station in your classroom. Elementary.

Story Sparkers. Suggestions for writing—questions, pictures, and so on. Elementary.

· FRANKLIN WATTS, INC.
845 Third Avenue
New York, NY 10022

City Workers. Sturdy study prints in black and white that depict what people do in cities, plus teacher's guide. Each print can form a learning station activity. Use the questions in the guide to get children to think about the pictures. A related title in the series is *A Trip Through a School,* which you can use in much the same way. Primary.

Man on the Move. Large, striking prints that zero in on living in today's fast-paced world. Students can react to the questions in the teacher's guide. Upper-grade elementary.

Wildsmith's Animal Portfolio. Eight full-color prints of animals. Young children independently can write expressive captions to go along with each print. Use *Grabianski's Portfolio* in the same way. Primary.

· INSTRUCTO CORP.
  Paoli, PA 19301

Instructo Learning Centers. A series of large plastic bags full of colorful visuals, game pieces, spirit masters, posters, puzzle parts, teacher's guide, self-correcting devices, and cards. Titles include: Decoding Everyday Abbreviations; Comparing Opposites; Creative Writing Stimulators; Alphabetical Order; Contractions Magic Show; Punctuation; Sharpening Letter Writing Skills; Learning When to Capitalize; The Caveman Plurals Center; Homonyms; Fun with Capital and Lowercase Letters; Go-Togethers: Classifying and Matching. These pre-packaged learning stations make fine beginnings for teachers setting up independent learning activity for the first time. They can invent additional activities related to each topic. Lower and middle elementary.

· SCHOLASTIC BOOK SERVICES
  904 Sylvan Avenue
  Englewood Cliffs, NJ 07632

Forms of Poetry 1; Forms of Poetry 2. Two sets, each consisting of eight color and black and white posters that depict different forms of poetry: haiku, limerick, blank verse, sonnet, and so on. Use to mount as the backdrop on a learning station where young people go to write poetry. Grade 3 and up.

A History of the English Language. A bulletin-board size poster that traces the history of the English language in a really interesting manner; shows words borrowed from other languages, an example of old English, a portrait of family members, the coming of English to England, and so on. Grade 3 and up.

· TROLL ASSOCIATES
320 Rt. 17
Mahwah, NJ 07430

Building a Word Study Unit. Attractive transparencies through which young children build words upon such bases as *-ail, -ink, -an,* and *-oat.* Use to help young children see how English words are structured. Older children can build words and use those rhyming words to write limericks and humorous, rhyming two-liners. Elementary.

Building a Story Unit. Multi-panel transparencies that visually relate a story that children can translate into words. Good for learning stations; children can independently write a caption for each transparency. Elementary.

Favorite Poems to Read, See, and Hear. Six filmstrips that project poems on themes: The World of Nature; Holidays and Seasons; Animals; Patriotism; Fun and Laughter; and Adventure. Good for independent viewing since the words are printed directly on the strips. Elementary.

Look, Read and Discover Synonyms, Antonyms, Homonyms. Colorful transparencies in which student viewers search for words that relate to others. Possible answers are indicated on the edge of the transparencies. If masks are placed over the edges they become self-correctional for use in independent learning. Students can project the transparencies on the central panel of a study carrel of the type available from Calloway House (see chapter 1 for details). You may want to use this set with Milton Bradley's Synonym, Antonym, and Homonym Poster Cards, available through J. L. Hammett Co., Vaux Hall Road, Union, NJ 07083. Elementary.

AND BOOKS GALORE

There is much to be learned and much pleasure to be derived from the hundreds of fine books about the structure, origins, changes, sounds, complexities, and confusions of long ago. Here are just a few titles selected from many good ones that will add breadth to your classroom or school library.

Adelson, Leone. *Dandelions Don't Bite.* New York: Pantheon, 1972. An up-to-date introduction to the origins of language, language relatives, changes in language, and the origin of specific words; illustrated with snappy cartoons. Upper elementary.

Andrews, F. Emerson. *Knights and Daze.* New York: Putnam, 1966. A stock of puns and word plays that will start young people punning and playing on their own. Upper elementary.

Asimov, Isaac. *Words from History.* Boston: Houghton Mifflin, 1968. The origin of specific words that have their roots in history: limey, mile, waterloo, yankee, and so forth. See also Asimov's *Words on the Map* (1962) that traces the origins of specific words relating in some way to places in the world; *Words from the Myths* (1961) that discusses the contribution of Greek myths to the English language; and *Words of Science and the History Behind Them* (1959) that traces the origins of science-related words such as virus, acid, and alcohol. Sixth grade and up.

Barnhart, Clarence, Sol Steinmetz, and Robert Barnhart. *The Barnhart Dictionary of New English Since 1963.* New York: Harper & Row, 1973. A dictionary that explains words that came into the language between 1963 and 1972. Upper elementary.

Bodecker, N. M. *Let's Marry Said the Cherry and Other Nonsense Poems.* New York: Atheneum, 1974. A collection of thirty-two nonsensical verses that can serve as models for young people who want to toy with the ridiculous. Grade 3 and up.

Brewer, E. Cobham. *Brewer's Dictionary of Phrases and Fable,* rev. ed. New York: Harper & Row, 1971. A dictionary that explains terms, phrases, and names that have their origin in literature; good source for young people trying to write allusions. Upper elementary.

Chase, Stuart. *Danger—Men Talking! A Background Book on Semantics and Communication.* New York: Parents' Magazine Press, 1969. An introduction to general semantics and the importance of language in society. Grade 7 and up.

Cole, William. *Oh, That's Ridiculous.* New York: Viking Press, 1972. A fun collection of nonsense verses. Grades 4–7.

Davidson, Jessica. *What I Tell You Three Times Is True.* New York: McCall, 1970. A comprehensive look at the social meanings behind language, thought control, and propaganda. Grade 5 and up.

Drysdale, Patrick. *Words to Use: A Primary Thesaurus.* New York: William H. Sadlier, Inc., 1974. A really simple thesaurus with many outline pictures. Primary.

Dudeney, Henry E. *Three Hundred Best Word Puzzles.* New York: Scribner, 1972. Lots of word puzzles. Upper elementary.

Epstein, Sam and Beryl. *The First Book of Words: Their Family Histories.* New York: Franklin Watts, 1954. The origins of words with lots of interesting specific examples. Grades 2–6.

Feelings, Muriel. *Swahili Counting Book.* New York: Dial, 1971. An introduction to a few words in Swahili for the storybook crowd. Primary.

Folsom, Franklin. *The Language Book.* New York: Grosset and Dunlap, 1963. A comprehensive treatment of the story of language—its beginnings, changes, and relationships. Upper elementary.

Frasconi, Antonio. *See Again, Say Again.* New York: Harcourt Brace Jovanovich, 1964. A picture book introduction to words written in English, Spanish, French, and Italian; good for young children making simple language comparison studies. Primary.

Funk, Charles E. *Heavens to Betsy.* New York: Warner, 1972. An explanation of the origins of common expressions such as Johnny-come-lately, to knock on wood, and a drop in the bucket. Grade 3 and up. See also Funk's earlier *Heavens to Betsy and Other Curious Sayings (1955), A Hog on Ice and Other Curious Expressions* (1948), and *Thereby Hangs a Tale: Stories of Curious Word Origins* (1950). The latter three Harper & Row books explore the origin of other interesting words in the English language. Upper elementary and up.

Funk, Charles E., and Charles E. Funk, Jr. *Horsefeathers and Other Curious Words.* New York: Harper & Row, 1958. Origin of hundreds of words such as butterscotch, sputnik, and so forth. Upper elementary and up.

Gardner, Martin. *Perplexing Puzzles and Tantalizing Teasers.* New York: Simon and Schuster, 1969. A collection of ridiculous riddles, tricky questions, tantalizing teasers, palindromes (words or sentences that read the same backward or forward), and picture word equations. Upper elementary.

Greet, W. Cabell, William Jenkins, and Andrew Schiller. *In Other Words: A Beginning Thesaurus.* Glenville, Ill.: Scott, Foresman, 1968. A thesaurus for primary grades. See also Greet's *In Other Words: A Junior Thesaurus* (1969). Clusters of related words for use in intermediate grades.

Kraske, Robert. *The Story of the Dictionary.* New York: Harcourt

Brace Jovanovich, 1975. A history of the dictionary with material on how it is made and some discussion of language origins. Grades 5–8.

Laird, Helene and Charlton. *The Tree of Language.* Cleveland and New York: World Publishing, 1957. One of the best explanations of the beginnings of language, the development of English, and stories associated with some words. Grade 4 and up.

Lear, Edward. *Edward Lear's Nonsense Book.* New York: Grosset and Dunlap, 1967. A collection of wonderful nonsense verses for youngsters with funny bones. Grades 2–6.

Ludovici, James. *Origins of Language.* New York: Putnam, 1965. An easily read explanation of the origins and history of the English language, ways words change and appear in language, and the development of the Roman alphabet. Upper elementary.

Mencken, H. L. *The American Language: An Inquiry into the Development of English in the United States,* 4th ed. New York: Knopf, 1963. The classic book on the subject intended for use by adults but a worthwhile reference for students in upper elementary. Strong chapters on proper names in America and slang.

Moore, John. *Your English Words.* Philadelphia: Lippincott, 1962. An entertaining discussion of the origins of words. Junior high and up.

Morrison, Lillian. *Black Within and Red Without.* New York: Crowell, 1953. Riddles that make a point by playing with sound-meaning relationships. Grades 3–6.

Moss, Norman. *What's the Difference? A British-American Dictionary.* New York: Harper & Row, 1973. A comparison of terms in British and American English. Upper elementary and up.

Nurnberg, Maxwell W. *Fun with Words.* Englewood Cliffs, N.J.: Prentice-Hall, 1970. A collection of games, tricks, and puzzles with words. Elementary.

Nurnberg, Maxwell. *Wonders in Words.* Englewood Cliffs, N.J.: Prentice-Hall, 1968. An explanation of words that come "right off the map," that have animals hiding in them, that have superstitions and prejudices embedded in them, and lots more. Upper elementary and up.

Pei, Mario. *Words in Sheep's Clothing.* New York: Hawthorn Books, 1969. Descriptions of such word developments as "bureaucratic gobbledygook," Madison Avenue jargon, governmental talk, and educational jargon. Junior high and up.

Sarnoff, Jane, and Reynold Ruffins. *What? A Riddle Book.* New York: Scribner, 1975. A great collection of riddles for riddle enthusiasts. Grades 5–8.

Shipley, Joseph. *Word Play.* New York: Hawthorn Books, 1972. An invaluable source of word games: riddles, conundrums, anagram twists, homonym plays, palindromes, and acrostics. Grade 5 and up.

Smith, Elsdon. *New Dictionary of American Family Names.* New York: Harper & Row, 1973. A handy reference to the national origins and meanings of American surnames. Grade 5 and up.

Sorel, Nancy C. *Word People.* New York: American Heritage Press, 1970. An explanation of the origin of teddy bear, quisling, ohm, dunce, sideburns, and other words that come from people's names. Upper elementary and up.

Sparke, William. *Story of the English Language.* New York: Abelard-Schuman, 1965. A discussion of language development and change written clearly with an anecdotal flavor. Upper elementary and junior high.

Wiesner, William. *A Pocketful of Riddles.* New York: Dutton, 1966. A pocket-sized book of riddles that will surely delight. Grades 3–6.